SOUTH • WESTERN

COLLEGE
KEYBOARDING

Lessons 1 • 60

Microsoft® Word 2000
Keyboarding & Formatting

Susie H. VanHuss, Ph.D.
University of South Carolina

Charles H. Duncan, Ed.D.
Eastern Michigan University

Connie M. Forde, Ph.D.
Mississippi State University

Donna L. Woo
Cypress College, California

VISIT US ON THE INTERNET
www.swep.com
www.thomson.com

South-Western
EDUCATIONAL PUBLISHING
Thomson Learning™

Cincinnati • Albany, NY • Belmont, CA • Bonn • Boston • Detroit • Johannesburg • London • Madrid
Melbourne • Mexico City • New York • Paris • Singapore • Tokyo • Toronto • Washington

Team Leader: Karen Schmohe
Project Manager—Keyboarding: Jane Phelan
Consulting Editor: Mary Todd, Todd Publishing Services
Editorial Consulting Services: Connie Bracken, CompuText Productions
Production: D&G Limited, LLC
Editor: Carol Spencer
Production Coordinator: Jane Congdon
Marketing Manager: Tim Gleim
Marketing Coordinator: Lisa Barto
Designer: Ann Small, a small design studio
Photo Editor: Michelle Kunkler, Linda Ellis
Design Coordinators: Michelle Kunkler
Cover and Special Page Illustrations by Elvira Regine

Photo Credits:
p. 58 © Digital Stock
p. xi © EyeWire, Inc.
pp. 3, 5, 8, 9, 11, 12, 13, 14, 15, 16, 18, 19, 20, 21, 22, 23, 24, 37, 38, 40, 42, 44, 46, 48, 50, 52, 54, A20, A21, A22, RG12 Greg Grosse
p. 129 Photo by Photonics
pp. xi, vii, 43, 45, 59, 65, 83, 115 © PhotoDisc, Inc.

Copyright © 2000
by SOUTH-WESTERN EDUCATIONAL PUBLISHING
Cincinnati, Ohio

South-Western Educational Publishing is a division of Thomson Learning. The Thomson Learning logo is a registered trademark used herein under license.

You can request permission to use material from this text through the following phone and fax numbers:
Phone: 1-800-730-2214. Fax: 1-800-730-2215, or visit our web site at http://www.thomsonrights.com.

4 5 6 7 8 9 WV 05 04 03 02 01

Printed in the United States of America

Library of Congress Cataloging-in-Publication Data

College keyboarding, Microsoft Word 2000, keyboarding & formatting : lessons 1-60 / Susie H. VanHuss ... [et al.].
    p. cm.
  Includes index.
  ISBN 0-538-72241-X (alk. paper)
  1. Microsoft Word.   2. Word processing.   I. VanHuss, Susie H.

Z52.5.M52 C6364 1999
652.3'0076--dc21
99-29873
                                    CIP

Microsoft® and Windows® are registered trademarks of Microsoft Corporation.

The names of commercially available software mentioned herein are used for identification purposes only and may be trademarks or registered trademarks of their respective owners. South-Western Educational Publishing disclaims any affiliation, association, connection with, sponsorship, or endorsement by such owners.

preface

COLLEGE KEYBOARDING, MICROSOFT® WORD 2000 is a learning package designed for the new millennium. This exceedingly successful learning package combines *Windows 98,* state-of-the-art operating system; *Microsoft Word 2000,* the leading word processing software; *Keyboarding Pro,* a very effective all-in-one keyboarding instruction program and well-written text materials presented in a concise, easy-to-learn format. This winning combination ensures that you will develop the skills needed for success in the automated office.

Keyboarding is a skill needed for success in virtually every career! Students, administrative employees, managers, attorneys, physicians, scientists, engineers, musicians, and factory workers use their keyboards to compose e-mails and memos, access databases, manipulate numbers, and communicate with coworkers. The keyboard provides access to critical information—and information is power.

Industry integrates and requires employees to use tools that facilitate communication, such as keyboarding, *Microsoft Word,* the Internet, and the entire *Office 2000* suite of application software. To function effectively in their jobs, most employees need basic skills using all applications in the suite and in-depth skills in one or more applications. Combining the learning of keyboarding, word processing, Internet usage, and other software applications minimizes learning time and effort. *College Keyboarding* is designed to help you develop the skills needed in today's workplace.

Keyboarding is a skill. As with any skill, you will be successful if you apply proper techniques and meaningful practice in each session. And, your keyboarding practice won't be dull! *Keyboarding Pro,* an all-in-one keyboarding instruction program, will teach you the alphabetic, numeric, and symbol keys and the keypad. When you're ready, *Skill Builder* is on your desktop to boost your speed and accuracy with 20 lessons that can be completed in either speed or accuracy mode. Challenging games, along with progress graphs, colored photos, sound effects, and a full-featured word processor will keep you motivated.

In the new millennium, the skills needed for success in virtually every career include keyboarding skills, skills using the Internet, basic skills in all applications in software suites, such as Office 2000, and in-depth skills in one or more applications in the suite.

Organization and Learning Goals

College Keyboarding, Lessons 1–60, is organized into two carefully planned and written levels.

In Level 1, Lessons 1–30, you will:

- Learn to key the alphabetic and numeric keys "by touch" using appropriate techniques.
- Build basic keyboarding skill.
- Use *Keyboarding Pro*, a software designed exclusively for building and extending your keyboarding skills.

In Level 2, Lessons 31–60, you will:

- Continue to build keyboarding skill—improving both your speed and accuracy in keying.
- Learn basic *Microsoft Word* functions for creating, edit-ing, and formatting documents.
- Learn to use e-mail and the Internet.
- Learn to format letters, memos, simple reports, and tables.

Design Features to Enhance Learning

COLLEGE KEYBOARDING, *MICROSOFT*® *WORD 2000* incorporates numerous design features that simplify learning and ensure mastery of keyboarding, word processing, and document formatting.

Skillbuilding. In both Levels 1 and 2, skillbuilding activities are an integral part of most lessons, and three Skillbuilding Workshops provide extra practice. Additionally, the Skill Builder module of *Keyboarding Pro* can be utilized on an ongoing basis once the alphabetic keys have been learned.

Formatting. In Level 2, you will learn to format basic business documents. Major emphasis is placed on applying principles of good design and utilizing software defaults whenever possible to maximize productivity.

***Microsoft Word* functions.** Colorful graphics and extensive screen captures supplement the step-by-step procedures for each new function. Preapplication drills apply the function before you encounter it in a document. Function reviews highlight commands recently learned.

Optional e-mail and Internet activities. You will embark on the superhighway of communication—the Internet. Optional Internet activities are integrated throughout Level 2. Optional Internet activities are integrated after each module, beginning in Level 2. Activities begin with the basics of opening a Web site, using the browser toolbar, setting up an E-mail account and advance to using a simple search engine.

News and views. These segments highlight topics of current interest that will broaden your knowledge of workforce trends and issues.

Illustrations and models. Full-page models introduce all new document formats and help you apply good design principles. Additional practice follows on unformatted documents and prerecorded documents on disk so that you will learn to make appropriate decisions without guidance.

Checkpoints. In Level 2, each module concludes with both objective and performance assessment to help you gauge whether you have mastered the skills and knowl-edge presented in the module.

Workshops and special features. Skillbuilding, com-munication, file management, editing, and numeric key-pad workshops supplement the lessons.

Software Support

Software for learning to keyboard, to build skill, and to check assignments accompanies *College Keyboarding.*

Keyboarding Pro is an all-in-one *Windows* alphabetic, numeric, skillbuilding, and keypad program. A timed-writing option is available in all review lessons. A *Windows* word processor with a timer adds flexibility. *Keyboarding Pro Multimedia* is a CD-ROM version with enhanced graphics, 3-D viewer and video clips. See p. xii for more information. *Keyboarding Pro Multimedia* is also equipped for the Internet, with an easy-to-use Send option for sending files to your instructor.

MicroPace Pro is skill-development and timed-writing software. The program includes the program disk template disk for checking the timed writings in the textbook (*MicroPace Pro for Windows*) plus the *College Keyboarding* textbook.

Formatting Template assists in the completion of textbook exercises. This free template contains prestored documents (files for Lessons 31–120).

Distance Education/Web Enhanced Support

Web-based learning tools such as flashcards, on-line quizzes, interactive exercises, and downloadable lesson slides and enrichment materials are options that are available for this course.

table of contents

summary
of functions

welcome
to Windows 98

Exploring Windows

Windows 98 is the operating system software you are using to control the operation of your computer and the peripherals such as the mouse and printer. Software applications that run under *Windows 98* have many common features. They all use similar icons and consistent menus. A typical *Windows* desktop is shown below. Your *Windows* desktop will have most of the icons shown, and you may have additional icons. Note in particular three icons:

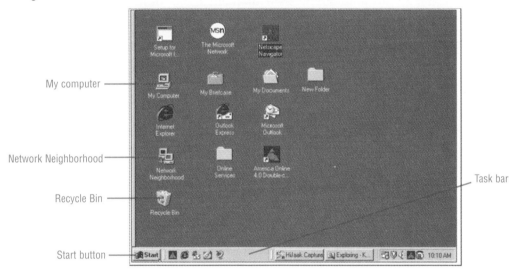

My Computer displays the disk drives, CD-ROM, and printers that are attached to your computer.

Network Neighborhood allows you to view the available resources if your computer is connected to a network environment.

Recycle Bin stores documents that have been deleted from the hard drive. Documents in the Recycle Bin may be restored and returned to their folders. When the Recycle Bin is emptied, the documents are deleted and cannot be restored.

Windows enables you to choose the classic desktop shown or an active desktop that resembles an Internet Web page. You will learn about using the active desktop in a later module. The gray bar at the bottom of the desktop is the **taskbar**. The taskbar contains the **Start button** on the left and the system clock on the right. The Start button is always visible when *Windows* is running. The Start button is used to run the *Windows* application software that you will use such as *Windows Explorer* or *Microsoft Word*. The taskbar may have shortcut buttons near the Start button as shown in the figure above, and it may also have buttons for software applications such as *Windows Explorer* that may be running.

In the next few pages, you will learn the basics of *Windows 98*. These basic concepts can be used with all *Windows 98* application software. If you have access to the CD-ROM disk containing your *Windows 98* software, you should view the *Windows 98* overview and work through the brief tutorial.

Using the mouse

Windows 98 software requires the use of a mouse or other pointing device. The pointing device may be separate or may be built into your keyboard. Note that the mouse contains both a left button and a right button. The left button is used to select, open, or drag objects. The right mouse is used to display a shortcut or context menu. In *Windows 98*, you can also drag objects with the right mouse button. If you have used previous versions of *Windows* software, you will note that the right mouse button is used more extensively in *Windows 98* than in previous versions.

Mouse pointer

The mouse pointer changes in appearance depending on its location on the desktop and the task that it is doing.

I   The I-beam indicates that the mouse pointer is located in the text area. When you pause, it blinks.

↖   The arrow selects items. It displays when the mouse is located outside the text area. You can position or hover this arrow over a toolbar icon to display the function of that icon.

⧖   The hourglass indicates that *Windows* is processing your command. You must wait until *Windows* finishes what it is doing before keying text or entering another command.

↔   A double-headed arrow appears when the pointer is at the border of a window or object and is used to change its size.

The pointer is moved by moving the mouse on a padded, flat surface usually called a mouse pad. The pointer can be repositioned by picking up the mouse and placing it in another spot on the mouse pad. If you have a touch pad on your keyboard, the pointer is moved by moving your finger on the touch pad. The mouse performs four basic actions:

Point: Move the pointer so that it touches an icon or text. Positioning the pointer on some items such as those on the Start menu will display the options available.

Click: Point to a desired item, then press the mouse button once and release. Pressing the left mouse button selects the item; pressing the right mouse button provides quick access to menus or commands.

Double-click: Point to a desired item; then quickly press and release the left mouse button twice. This action opens an object or issues a command.

Drag: Point to the desired item; hold down the mouse button and drag the item to a new location on the desktop; then release the button.

Working with Windows 98

To run an application, click the Start button on the opening *Windows 98* screen. Notice that the Start menu appears. The Start menu is divided into three sections:

The *top* portion of the menu contains applications that you may add such as *America Online* or *WordPerfect*.

The *center* portion of the menu contains a list of options such as Help, Documents, or Programs. Note that the Programs option is highlighted.

The *lower* portion of the menu contains basic commands such as Log On and Shut Down.

The right triangular arrows indicate that a cascading or submenu is available for that option. When you point to one of the triangular arrows, a list of options appears at the right side of the Start menu.

To open an application that appears in the list, move the pointer to the application and click it. Note that *Windows Explorer* is highlighted. *Windows Explorer* is an application used to manage files and folders. If you click *Windows Explorer*, the following **window** will display.

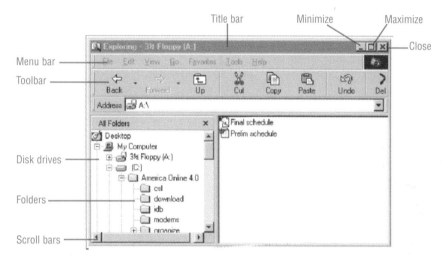

Window: A work area on the desktop that can be resized or moved. To resize a window, point at the border. When the pointer changes to a double arrowhead, drag the window to the desired size. To move a window, point to the title bar and drag it to the new position. Release the mouse button when the window has been moved to the desired position.

Title bar: Displays the name of the application that is currently open. Provides other information such as folder or filename.

Minimize button: Minimizes window. By clicking the minimize button, the window disappears and becomes a button on the taskbar. It can be restored by clicking the button.

Maximize button: Maximizes window. By clicking the maximize button, the window enlarges to full-screen size.

Close button: Closes the application.

Scroll bars: Allow you to see information that requires more space than available on one screen. Click the up or down arrow to view additional information.

Shutting Down

To exit *Windows*, use the Shut Down option on the Start menu. Click Start; then Shut Down to display the Shut Down dialog box. Then click OK. Never just turn your computer off. *Windows* may notify you when the computer can be turned off or it may automatically shut down once you click OK. This will vary depending upon how your computer has been set up. Many people leave their computers turned on most of the time.

Help

Online help is provided with *Windows* software. Help is also available with each software application that you use. Generally, you will use the Help feature provided with the software application. To access **Help**, click the Start menu and then click Help.

The **Contents tab** is illustrated in the illustration at the left. To get help using the Contents tab, browse through the topics to find the appropriate one, then select it and click. The information will display in the right pane.

Clicking the Index tab causes the list of specific topics included in Help to display in alphabetical order. As you key the characters of the topic in the entry box, the pointer moves to items beginning with the letters keyed. When the desired topic is displayed, select it and choose Display.

To search for a topic using the Search tab, key the topic in the entry box and press ENTER to see a display of Help pages that contain the topic. Select the topic and click Display to present the information.

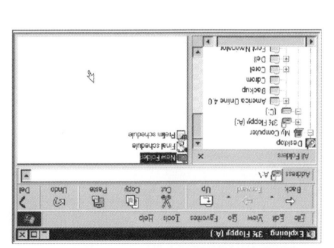

Commands

Commands may be selected by clicking the toolbar or by clicking the Menu bar to display a pull-down menu. Select Drive C and click File on the Menu bar. From the drop-down menu, click New and then Folder to create a New Folder, as shown in the following screen. Key **Keyboarding** and press ENTER to name the folder appropriately for your keyboarding class.

Folders are extremely important in managing files. For example, you could use the same procedure to set up folders for each of your classes. Documents you prepare for each class could then be saved as a file in the folder for the appropriate class. Files that are not in an appropriate folder can be organized by dragging them to the desired folder. File management is discussed in more detail in the File Management section on page A2.

know your computer

Computers consist of these essential parts:

1. **Central processing unit:** The internal operating unit, including the processing unit, memory chips, disk drives, etc.

2. **Disk drive:** A unit that reads and writes onto disks.

3. **Monitor:** A screen that displays information as it is keyed and messages from the computer called *prompts*.

4. **Mouse:** Input device. *Windows* software is designed to be used with a mouse.

5. **Keyboard:** Input device for entering alphabetic, numeric, and symbols as well as special keys for entering commands.

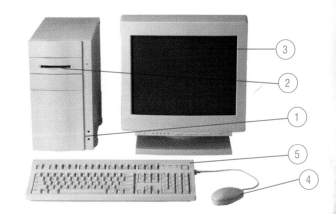

Keyboard Arrangement

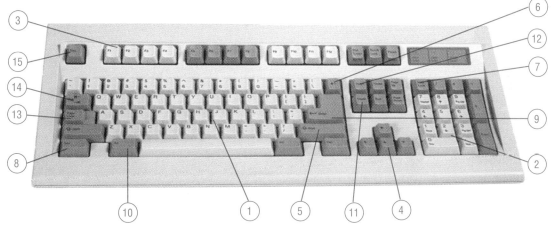

1. **Alphanumeric keys:** Center portion of the keyboard.

2. **Numeric keypad:** Calculator type keys used for entering statistical data. To turn on the keypad, press the NUMLOCK key.

3. **Function keys:** Perform a software function; used by themselves or with other keys.

4. **Arrow keys:** Move the insertion point.

5. **SHIFT key:** Makes lowercase letters uppercase.

6. **BACKSPACE:** Deletes the character to the left of the insertion point.

7. **NUMLOCK:** Switches the numeric keypad between numeric and editing.

8. **CTRL (Control):** Expands the use of function keys.

9. **ENTER:** Advances the insertion point to the next line. ENTER is often used to execute a command.

10. **ALT (Alternate) key:** Used with another key to execute a function.

11. **DELETE key:** Erases text to the right of the insertion point.

12. **Insert key:** Toggles the software between insert mode and typeover/overstrike mode.

13. **CAPS LOCK:** Capitalizes all alphabetic characters.

14. **TAB:** Moves the cursor to a preset position.

15. **ESC (Escape):** Exits a menu or dialog box in word processing software.

Welcome

to Keyboarding Pro

With the full-featured *Keyboarding Pro* software, you can use the power of your computer to learn alphabetic and numeric keyboarding and the keypad. The 30 alphabetic and numeric software lessons correlate with the first 30 lessons in the *College Keyboarding* textbook. After you complete Lesson 13, you can use Skill Builder to boost your speed and accuracy.

Your computer should be turned on, and either *Windows 3.1* or *Windows 98* or *Windows 95* should be displayed.

1. Open *Keyboarding Pro.*

   Windows 98 or Windows 95:

   - Click the **Start** button.
   - Point to the Programs menu; a submenu displays to the right listing all the programs.
   - Click **Keyboarding Pro** in the programs submenu.

   Windows 3.1:

   - Locate the South-Western Keyboarding program group and double-click the icon to open it.
   - Double-click the **Keyboarding Pro** icon to start the program.

2. Click anywhere in the opening screen to remove it and bring up the Log In dialog box.

3. Select the appropriate name from the list that appears in the Log In dialog box. Then, enter the correct password to continue. Click the **Guest** button only if instructed. (See Figure 1.)

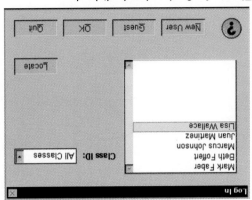

Figure 1: Student Log In dialog box

When using the program for the first time, you click the **New User** button and complete the New Student Registration dialog box (as described on the next page).

4. After you log in, the program will either display the Main menu or prompt you to continue where you left off. If the Main menu appears, choose the appropriate lesson. A check mark appears next to each lesson that you have completed unless you used the Guest option to log in. Check marks also appear on the Notebook tabs to show which exercises have been completed.

New student registration

The first time you use *Keyboarding Pro*, you must enter the following information: name, class ID, and password. You must also identify where to store the data.

1. Click the **New User** button shown in the Log In dialog box. The New Student dialog box appears. (See Figure 2.)

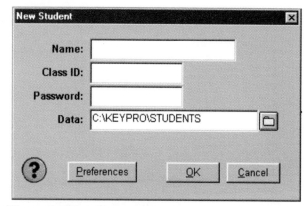

Figure 2: New Student dialog box

2. Enter user name (first name, last name).

3. Record the class ID.

4. Enter a password. Write the password on a piece of paper and store it in a safe place.

5. Specify the data location if necessary. For example, the path may already be set to **c:\keypro\students.** If you have your own subdirectory, which was created previously, you must set the path accordingly (e.g., **c:\keypro\students\lopez**). You can click on the **Folder** icon to browse through the directories to locate the folder.

6. If necessary, click the **Preferences** button and update the required information.

7. Click the **OK** button to complete the registration process.

Main menu

Click any of the four keyboarding buttons shown in the center of the Main menu to proceed directly to the corresponding *Keyboarding Pro* module. (See Figure 3.)

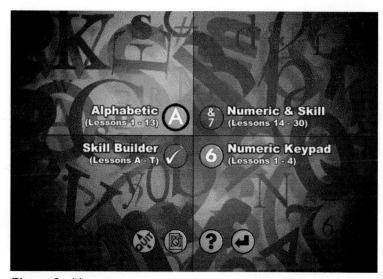

Figure 3: Main menu

Alphabetic: You will learn the alphabetic keys in this module.

Numeric & Skill: Activities focus on building skill as well as learning the top-row and symbol keys. Diagnostic Writings are available to analyze your progress.

Skill Builder: After you know the alphabetic keys, use these 20 lessons to boost your keyboarding speed and control. Each lesson can focus on either speed or accuracy, so you really have 40 lessons.

Numeric Keypad: You will learn the numeric keypad operation by completing four lessons in this module. See Appendix C for additional practice.

Module activities

Alphabetic/numeric and skill

A variety of exercises are included in each lesson. In *Textbook keying*, the software directs you to key an exercise from the textbook. Space is available to key 20 lines. If you complete the exercise more than once, only the most recent exercise is stored and displayed in the Lesson report. Click the **Print** button to print the current exercise before repeating the exercise.

Timed writing: This exercise occurs in each review lesson. Indicate the length of your timing in the Timed Writing dialog box (see Figure 4). You will key from the textbook. The software highlights the errors along with providing the gross words a minute (*gwam*). If you complete the exercise more than once, only the most recent writing is stored and displayed in the Lesson Report. Click the **Print** button at the bottom of the screen to print the current timed writing before repeating the timing.

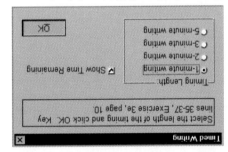

Figure 4: Timed Writing dialog box

Additional features

Game: The Commander Key game challenges you to meet a speed goal as you key drill lines from the screen. A score area shows your progress.

Lesson Report: After the last exercise in a lesson, a Lesson Report appears showing which lessons and lesson parts were completed and, if applicable, your speed scores and keying lines for *Build skill*, *Textbook keying*, and *Timed writing*.

Open Screen: The Open Screen is a word processor that includes many formatting options, a spell checker, and a built-in timer. You can practice your keyboarding skills, key letters and reports, and take a speed timed writing. These features can be accessed from the menu bar, and many of them are available on the toolbar. When you take a timed writing in the Open Screen, click the Timer button and save each timing with its own name. For example, 8e-t1 (exercise 8e, timing 1) and 8e-t2 (exercise 8e, timing 2).

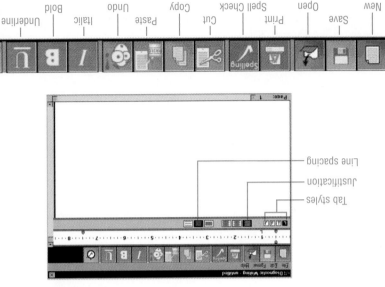

Diagnostic writings: Timed writings can also be taken using the Diagnostic Writings option, which provides extensive error analysis. The Diagnostic Writings feature measures both speed and accuracy. Writings are keyed from the textbook. You may do a 1', 3', or 5' writing. Diagnostic Writings are available from the lesson menus of Numeric & Skill and Skill Builder.

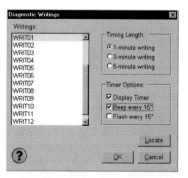

Diagnostic Writing Selection

Quick review: This feature of the Skill Builder module presents drill lines for you to practice various keys.

Games: Each of the keyboarding modules (Alphabetic, Numeric & Skill, Skill Builder, and Numeric Keypad) incorporates a game into various lessons. These games are a fun way to focus on improving your keyboarding skills. Top-ten lists that show student performance will challenge you to improve your speed and accuracy.

Student reports

The *Keyboarding Pro* software provides numerous reports: Lesson Report, Summary Report, Keypad Data Sets, Top-Ten Lists, Certificate of Completion, and Performance Graphs. All of these reports, except the Lesson Report, are accessed by using the Reports menu.

The Lesson Report shows your performance data for each lesson. Performance Graphs are accessed by clicking the *Graph* button on Lesson Report. The Alphabetic keyboarding module performance graph represents your average/fastest speed for Build Skill sections. The Numeric & Skill keyboarding module also has a performance graph for the Commander Key game.

Quitting *Keyboarding Pro*

To quit *Keyboarding Pro:*

1. Click the **Quit** button on the Main menu.
2. Or, choose *Exit* from the File menu.

Quitting *Windows*

After you quit *Keyboarding Pro*, your instructor may want you to leave the computer running, or you may be instructed to shut down the computer. You need to shut down *Windows* before you turn off or restart your computer. To avoid damaging files, always shut down *Windows* before turning off your computer.

1. Click the **Start** button on the taskbar.
2. Click **Shut Down** from the drop-down list.
3. From the Shut Down dialog box, click **Yes**. A screen message lets you know when you can safely turn off your computer.

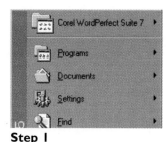

Step 1

Step 2

Keyboarding Pro Multimedia

Keyboarding Pro Multimedia is the CD-ROM version of *Keyboarding Pro*. The new features are highlighted in the Main menu shown below. *Keyboarding Pro Multimedia* also gives classes the option of using one or two spaces after a period and audio instruction is available for using the exercises. The other features of *Keyboarding Pro Multimedia* are exactly the same as *Keyboarding Pro*. Refer to the discussion of *Keyboarding Pro* (pages xii–xv) for information on starting the software, the Open Screen, student reports, and more.

Main menu

Click any of the four keyboarding titles to proceed directly to the corresponding module. The buttons on the Main Menu help you to access various features quickly and manipulate the software easily.

Games: The four games provide fun ways for improving your skills.

Movies: The movies discuss keyboarding issues and demonstrate correct techniques.

3-D Animations: See precisely and clearly a view of the correct body posture and the proper slant of your arms, curvature of your fingers, and position of your wrists and fingers. You can manipulate the scenes and view the scenes from any angle.

Open screen: *Windows* word processor with a timer button.

Help: Help is also available from nearly every screen throughout the program.

Exit: Click the **Exit** button to exit the program.

Send file: Send the electronic file containing your lesson report to your instructor using the *Send File* button. *Send File* can also be accessed from the Lesson Report screen.

Quick review: Use it to practice alphabetic keys, numeric keys or specific reaches.

Back: Returns you to the previous menu.

Level

1

LEARNING TO OPERATE THE KEYBOARD

OBJECTIVES

Keyboarding

To key the alphabetic and number keys by touch.
To key approximately 25 *wam* with good accuracy.

Communication Skills

To apply proofreaders' marks and revise text.

Document 10 SC
**Table with
hypertext links**

1. Key the table at the right. *Word* will convert the Web address to a hyperlink when you strike the Space Bar at the end of each address.
2. Bold headings.
3. Apply 15% shading to Row 1.
4. Save as **Nelson**.

NELSON, CANADA

Web Site Information

Subject	Name of Site	Web Site Address
Nelson and surrounding area	Nelson Area Communities Connect	http://www.kics.bc.ca
Schools	School District 81 Fort Nelson	http://www.schdist81.bc.ca
City of Nelson	City of Nelson	http://www.city.nelson.bc.ca
Library	Nelson Municipal Library	http://www.kics.bc.ca/~library
Newspaper	Nelson Daily News	http://www.sterlingnews.com/Nelson/home.html
Sports	Nelson World Mid-Summer Curling Bonspiel	http://www.midsummerbonspiel.nelson.bc.ca

Document 11
**E-mail with
hypertext link and
attachment**

1. Click on the E-mail button to display e-mail screen.
2. Send the memo to **All Selkirk Employees.**
3. Subject: **Consider Relocating to Nelson**
4. Key the memo at right.
5. After keying **Nelson and Area Communities Connect**, click on the Insert Hyperlink button.
6. Under Link to, click **Existing File** or **Web Page**.
7. Key **http://www.kics.bc.ca** in the file or Web page name box.
8. When finished with the memo, click the **Attachment** button.
9. Click *Look in.* Select *3.5 Floppy (A:).*
10. Select *Nelson.*
11. Select *Attach. Nelson.doc* now appears in the Attach box.
12. Save as **m8-d11**.

As you are all aware, the Board of Directors voted at the November 27, 1999 meeting to move the corporate headquarters of Selkirk Communications from Portland, OR to Nelson, BC.

Nelson is surrounded by the Selkirk Mountains and sits on the shores of Kootenay Lake. Its heritage, charm, and stunning scenery create the quintessential small-town setting. The city, with a population of 9,500, has a unique mix of urban sophistication and rural ambiance.

We would like you to consider relocating with us to Nelson. To help acquaint you with the area, please take the time to view Nelson and Area Communities Connect. (Double-clicking on the underlined text will take you to this Web site.) Additional information on Nelson can be found in the Web sites in the attachment to this memo.

xxx

Attachment

ALPHABETIC KEYREACHES

OBJECTIVES

1. Key the alphabetic keys by touch.

2. Key using proper techniques.

3. Key at a rate of 14 *gwam* or more.

Home Row, Space Bar, ENTER, I

1a ●

GETTING started

Open *Keyboarding Pro* software

As you learn and practice the alphabetic keys, you will use *Keyboarding Pro* software. Many lessons introduce new keys, while others review what you have learned. Some lessons contain a challenging keyboarding game. You will key from the screen and from your textbook. The software tracks your performance and provides feedback. The first time you use *Keyboarding Pro* you must complete the registration process. Turn to p. 7.

From the Main menu, you can click any of the four buttons to go directly to the corresponding *Keyboarding Pro* lessons. The Main menu also includes the following buttons that appear at the bottom of the screen—Quit, Open Screen, Help, and Back.

 Click Quit to exit *Keyboarding Pro*. The Quit button appears only on the Main menu.

 Click the Open Screen button to access the built-in word processor, to practice your keyboarding skills, or to take a timed writing.

 Click the Help button to display help for the feature you are currently using. The context-sensitive Help button appears on almost every screen throughout the program.

 From the Main menu, clicking Back returns you to the Log In dialog box. On other screens, Back takes you to the previous menu. Click the large A button to go directly to *Alphabetic*, which you will use in Lessons 1-13.

DS

After the first breakout sessions, participants will join | 462
for lunch in the H. L. Calvert Union Building. The Steering | 474
Committee recommends that Mayor Alton johnson address the | 486
topic of meeting educational challenges of the next century. *p.m.* | 498
¶ A repeat of the morning breakout sessions will begin at 1:30. | 512
This repeat will allow participants to contirube to antoher | 524
topic. ~~In~~ the closing session, breakout facilitators will | 536
present the goals and plans to the audience. | 546
During

Sponsors | 547

The Steerting Committee has discussed the sponsorhsip of | 559

a goals conference with a number of partners in the Nelson | 570

area. The following organizations have agreed to serve as | 582

sponsors: Nelson Economic Development Foundation, Bank of | 594

Canada, Northeast Bottling Company, ~~and~~ Bank of Nelson, and | 605

Farthington's Clothiers. | 610

Summary | 612

The Steering Committee strongly recommends this goals | 623

conference. The committee will be avilable at the C*h*amber | 635

of commerce meeting to answer any questions. | 644

Document 9
Agenda

1. Prepare a sheet that will precede the agenda. Use 1.5" top margin; center-align APPENDIX in 14 point; DS and center the title of the agenda. Number this page in sequence.

2. Format the agenda using the Table feature; do not include lines. Add a row between items so the agenda appears DS.

SC

Goals Conference Agenda | 5

9:30 a.m.-9:45 a.m.	Welcome	11
9:45 a.m.-10:15 a.m.	Opening Remarks	19
	Overview of Community Quality	25
	Initiative	27
SS	Purpose of Goals Conference	33
	Process	34
	Introduction of Community Leaders	41
	and Chamber Officers	45
10:15 a.m.-10:35 a.m.	Refreshment Break	54
10:35 a.m.-12 noon	Breakout Sessions: *List the 5 sessions SS*	62
12 noon-1:00 p.m.	Lunch	79
SS	Speaker on Educational Challenges	86
	of the 21st Century	90
1:00 p.m.-2:30 p.m.	~~Goals Setting Workshops~~ *Breakout Sessions*	98
2:30 p.m.-2:45 p.m.	Refreshment Break	106
2:45 p.m.-4:00 p.m.	Presentation of Goals	115

DS between items

To select a lesson from *Alphabetic*, click the number next to the desired lesson with the left mouse button. Any time you want to practice your keyboarding skills, you can simply click the Open Screen button to access the built-in word processor.

Once you select a lesson, the first activity is displayed. In the illustration below, *Learn home row* is in yellow because this activity is active. You can move to a selected exercise by clicking one of the tabs. Follow the directions on screen and press ENTER. Key directly from the screen unless directed otherwise by the software or your instructor.

Alphabetic Keyboarding button

Lesson buttons

Open Screen

Help

Back

Figure 1-1 Alphabetic Keyboarding Lesson Menu

Lesson tabs

Activity tabs

Figure 1-2 Alphabetic Keyboarding (Lesson 1: Learn Home Row and i)

Ib ●

Locate home keys

Examine the naming/numbering system for finger positions in the illustration at the right. Then, practice several times the steps below for placing fingers in home row position and for reaching to ENTER and the Space Bar.

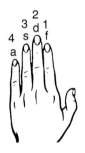

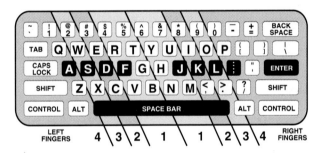

Drop hands to the side; allow fingers to curve naturally.
Lightly place the left fingertips over **a s d f**.
Lightly place right fingertips over **j k l** ; . Repeat.

ENTER: Reach with the 4th (little) finger of the right hand to ENTER and press it. Quickly return the finger to its home position (over ;).

Space Bar: Strike the Space Bar with a down-and-in motion of the right thumb.

contribute to ~~the~~ the achievement of these goals. A Publicity com-   170

mittee will be resonsible for informing the community.   181

Goals Conference Format   186

    The Steering Committee recommends that the confence be   197

held at Marion Hall, Canadian International College (CIC), on ~~March~~ May 18,   211

200-, from 9:30 a.m. to 4:00 p.m. Facilities can be   222

reserved by calling Patzy Frazier at (606) 555-3789.   233

    The conference would begin with an opening session and   244

should inlcude introductions of key leaders in the community   256

as well as Chamber of Commerce officers. The keynote   267

speaker should be a prominent state leader who has vision for   279

quality communities.   284

    Following the opening sessions, participants will   294

choose from one of the following five breakout groups: edu-   306

cation, youth services, ~~education~~ recreation, economic development,   317

~~youth services, recreation~~ and crime. Breakout sessions   323

will be directed by facilitators trained in working with   335

diverse groups. Groups will brainstorm and then set ~~Lunch will follow and be served in the~~   345

goals and prepare plans for achieving the specific ~~Banquet Room of the college. The afternoon sessions will be~~   355

goals of the conference. The sessions will run for ~~a repeat of the workshops so that participants may attend~~   366

one hour. ~~different sessions.~~   368

Recommended facilitators include: team leaders and the following   381

Team	Team Leaders	Facilitators	
			387
Education	Dale Coppage, Nelson BC	Ellen Obert, Spokane, WA	399
Youth Services	Lawrence Riveria, Portland, OR	Jack Jones, Vancouver BC	413
Recreation	Bradley Greger, Nelson BC	Carlos Pena, Calgary AB	425
Economic Development	Jon Guyton, Nelson BC	Harvey Lewis, Nelson BC	439
Crime	Monica Brigham, Toronto ON	Shawn McNullan, NC "	450

Ic

Learn home row keys

Select *Learn Home Row* from Lesson I menu. Follow on-screen instructions.

Optional:

In Open Screen, key each line once single spaced (SS); press ENTER twice to double-space (DS) between 2-line groups. Do not key the numbers.

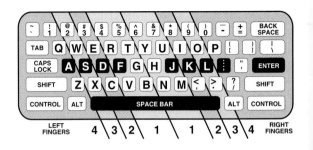

LEFT FINGERS 4 3 2 1 1 2 3 4 RIGHT FINGERS

Press Space Bar once.

```
1  fff  jjj  fjf  fff  jjj  fjf  fjf  jfj  jfj  fjf
2  ddd  kkk  dkd  ddd  kkk  dkd  dkd  kdk  kdk  dkd
```
Press ENTER twice to **DS**.
```
3  sss  lll  sls  sss  lll  sls  sls  lsl  lsl  sls
4  aaa  ;;;  a;a  aaa  ;;;  a;s  a;a  ;a;  ;a;  a;a
```
DS
```
5  ff  jj  ff  jj  fj  fj  fj  dd  kk  dd  kk  dk  dk  dk
6  ss  ll  ss  ll  sl  sl  sl  aa  ;;  aa  ;;  a;  a;  a;
```
```
7  fj  fj  dk  dk  sl  sl  a;  a;  fjdksla;  jfkdls;a
8  fj  fj  dk  dk  sl  sl  a;  a;  fjdksla;  jfkdls;a
```

Id

Learn ENTER

Key each line once; double-space (DS) between lines.

```
9  f  j  d  k  s  l  a  ;
```
DS
```
10  ff  jj  dd  kk  ss  ll  aa  ;;
```
```
11  fff  jjj  ddd  kkk  sss  lll  aaa
```
```
12  ff  jj  dd  kk  ss  ll  aa  ;;  fjdksla;  fjdksla;
```

Ie

Practice reaches

each line once; repeat if time permits

```
13  a  a;  al  ak  aj  s  s;  sl  sk  sj  d  d;  dl  dk  dj
```
DS
```
14  j  ja  js  jd  jf  k  ka  ks  kd  kf  l  la  ls  ld  lf
15  a;  sl  a;sl  dkfj  a;sl  dkfj  a;sldkfj  asdf  jk
16  a;  sl  a;sl  dk  fj  dkfj  a;sl  dkfj  fkds;a;  fj
17  f  ff  j  jj  d  dd  k  kk  s  ss  l  ll  a  aa  ;  ;;  fj
18  afj;  a  s  d  f  j  k  l  ;  asdf  jkl;  fdsa  jkl;  f
```

Document 7
Standard memo with table

After keying table, sort items in alphabetical order. Format the table attractively.

		words
TO:	All Staff, Spokane Branch	6
FROM:	Marilyn Josephson, Office Manager	14
DATE:	Current	19
SUBJECT:	American versus Canadian Spelling	28

All correspondence addressed to our Canadian office should now include 42
Canadian spelling. Some of the differences are shown in the following 56
table. We'll need to get a list of other words that differ as well. 70

U.S. Spelling	Canadian Spelling	
		77
counseling	counselling	81
honor	honour	84
endeavor	endeavour	88
defense	defence	91
center	centre	94
check (meaning money)	cheque	99
color	colour	102
marvelous	marvellous	106
z	"zed"	107

Document 8
Multiple-page report with table and appendix

1. Format the report as a DS unbound report. Proofread carefully; not all errors are marked.
2. Use the Table feature to format the table.
3. Use full alignment.
4. Include the agenda as an appendix in the report. (See the directions, p. 185.)
5. Prepare a title page. Assume that the report was prepared for **Nelson Chamber of Commerce by Richard R. Holmes, President**. Date the report **March 15**.

PROPOSAL FOR COMMUNITY GOALS CONFERENCE   8

The Steering Committee for the chamber of commerce com-   19
munity enhancement proposes the sponsorship of a goals con-   31
ference for all citizens of Nelson. This recommendation is   43
based on research data compiled from conferences sponsored   55
in other cities similar to Nelson. Also, the recommendation   66
is supported by the committee's combined experience in work-   79
ing with varied groups of citizens and commitment to   90
progress. The reports presents a proposed outline for a   101
goals conference.   105

Purpose of Conference   109

The purposes of this conference are (1) to improve educa-   121
tion, economic development, youth services, and recreation and   133
(2) to reduce crime in the Nelson and district. All members   145
of the community will be invited to attend this conference and   157

If

Learn i

1. Find i on the illustrated keyboard; find it on your keyboard.
2. Reach up with the *right second* finger.
3. Watch your finger make the reach to i and back to k a few times without striking the keys. Keep fingers curved and wrists low.
4. Try to keep your eyes on the copy as you key.

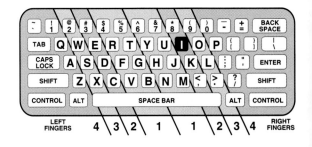

i Reach up with *right second* finger.

```
19  i ik ik ik is is id id if if ill i ail did kid lid
20  i ik aid ail did kid lid lids kids ill aid did ilk

21  id aid aids laid said ids lid skids kiss disk dial
22  id aid ail fail sail jail ails slid dill sill fill
```

Ig

Review

each line once; DS between 2-line groups; repeat as time permits

```
23  as as ask ask ad ad lad lad all all fall fall asks
24  as asks did disk ail fail sail ails jail sill silk
                                                    DS
25  ask dad; dads said; is disk; kiss a lad; salad lid
26  fill a sail; aid a lad; is silk; if a dial; a jail

27  is a disk; dads said; did fall ill; if a lass did;
28  aid lads; if a kid is; a salad lid; kiss a sad dad

29  as ad all ask jak lad fad said ill kill fall disks
30  is all sad lass a lid; is silk; silk disk; dad is;
```

Ih •

End the lesson

1. Review and print your Lesson Report.
2. To exit the software:
   - From the Lesson menu, click the **Back** button.
   - Click the **Quit** button on the Main menu.
   - Remove your storage disk. Store materials as directed.

The figure below shows the Lesson Report for Lesson 1. A check mark opposite an exercise indicates that the exercise has been completed. At the bottom of the screen are various buttons. Click the **Print** button to print your Lesson Report. Click the **Graph** button to view the Performance Graph. To get help concerning the Lesson Report, click the **Help** button. If you click the **Back** button here, you return to the Lesson menu.

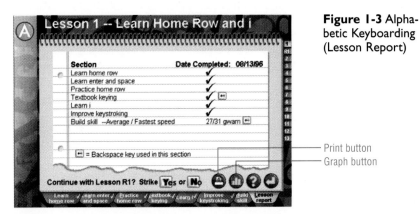

Figure 1-3 Alphabetic Keyboarding (Lesson Report)

Print button
Graph button

Note: Word counts for missing parts have been added to appropriate lines.

Document 4
Table

1. Format the purchase order as a 4-column table.
2. Merge the cells in Row 1. Key the main heading and subheading in Row 1.
3. Center, shade, and bold the column headings.
4. Calculate the total price for each item.
5. Shade the last row; join the cells in the first three columns (A9, B9, and C9).
6. Calculate the total; center table.

Document 5
Block letter

1. Insert Document 4 table in this order letter using Copy and Paste.
2. Use the current date.
3. Add an appropriate salutation.
4. Format the company name in closing lines in ALL CAPS.
5. Make adjustments in vertical space that allow the letter to print on a letterhead.

Document 6
Table

This table will be used by the president in one of his workshops.

1. Keep the type size large. Select an attractive format for the table or shade Row 1 20% and the remainder of Column A 10%.
2. Add at least 2 words that you frequently misspell.
3. Supply the correct spelling in Column B.

				words
PURCHASE ORDER				3
(Current date)				7
Quantity	**Description**	**Unit Price**	**Total Price**	15
2	Ergonomic Comfort computer chairs	$455.00		26
2	Slide-out keyboard shelf	54.00		33
36	3 1/2" high-density/double-sided formatted disks	1.99		46
1	10-ream carton laser printer paper (20 lb.)	54.25		57
3	HP LaserJet Series 4 toner cartridge #92298A	145.89		69
2	Address labels 1" x 2 5/8", white, #5160	24.95		80
	Total			83

West Coast Office Supplies — 9
3245 Granville St. — 12
Vancouver BC V6B 5J8 — 17

Please ship the following items, which are listed in — 32
your current office supplies catalog. — 39

Insert the table here (Document 4)

Please bill this to our account number 4056278. This — 50
order is urgent; therefore, ship it overnight by Loomis. — 62

Yours truly — 64
Selkirk Communications — 69

Allan Burgess, Purchasing Agent — 75

Frequently Misspelled Words — 6

Misspelled / Correct Spelling — 11

recieve — 14
accomodate — 19
convience — 23
similiar — 27
to (meaning also) — 31
congradulations — 38
envelop — 41
inclosure — 45

1Ra ●

GETTING started

Review home row

1. Open *Keyboarding Pro* software.
2. Click the ↓ next to *Class ID* and select your section. Click your name.
3. Key your password and click **OK**.
4. Click **A** for *Alphabetic* and then select *Lesson R1*.

Key each line once; DS between groups. Repeat if time permits.

Fingers curved and upright

LEFT FINGERS 4 3 2 1   1 2 3 4 RIGHT FINGERS

```
1  f j fjf jj fj fj jf dd kk dd kk dk dk dk
2  s ; s;s ;; s; s; s; aa ;; aa ;; a; a; a;
                                          DS
3  fj dk sl a; fjdksla; jfkdls;a ;a ;s kd j
4  f j fjf d k dkd s l sls a ; fj dk sl a;a
5  a; al ak aj s s; sl sk sj d d; dl dk djd
6  ja js jd jf k ka ks kd kf l la ls ld lfl
7  f fa fad s sa sad f fa fall fall l la lad s sa sad
8  a as ask a ad add j ja jak f fa fall; ask; add jak
```

1Rb ●

Review i

each line once; repeat as time permits

```
9   ik ki ki ik is if id il ij ia ij ik is if ji id ia
10  is il ill sill dill fill sid lid ail lid slid jail
11  if is il kid kids ill kid if kids; if a kid is ill
12  is id if ai aid jaks lid sid sis did ail; if lids;
```

1Rc ●

Review all reaches

each line once; DS between groups; repeat

```
13  a lass; ask dad; lads ask dad; a fall; fall salads
14  as a fad; ask a lad; a lass; all add; a kid; skids
15  as asks did disk ail fail sail ails jail sill silk
16  ask dad; dads said; is disk; kiss a lad; salad lid
17  aid a lad; if a kid is; a salad lid; kiss sad dads
18  as ad all ask jak lad fad kids ill kill fall disks
```

**Document 2
Block letter**

This letter includes the company name. Key it a DS below the complimentary closing in ALL CAPS. QS to the writer's name.

February 8, 200- | Chamber of Commerce | 225 Hall St. | Nelson BC V1L   13
5X4 | CANADA   15

Selkirk Communications will be relocating its headquarters from   32
Spokane, Washington, to downtown Nelson on April 1. We are an inter-   46
national communications company, offering the following services: 59

1. Written and oral communications refresher workshops   70
2. Customized training on-site or in our training center   82
3. Mail-order newsletters   87
4. Computer training on popular business software   97
5. Individualized or group training sessions   106

I would like to attend the Nelson Chamber of Commerce meeting in   119
March to share some of the exciting ways we can help Chamber members   133
meet their training needs. Is there time available for us on your March   147
agenda? Please contact Anthony Baker, public relations coordinator, at   162
our Nelson office at (604) 555-1093.   169

Selkirk Communications will be holding an open house during the month   183
of April, and we will be inviting you and the Nelson community to attend.   198
We look forward to becoming actively involved with the business com-   212
munity of Nelson.   216

Yours truly | SELKIRK COMMUNICATIONS | Richard R. Holmes, President   229

Tip:

To format a numbered list, key the items without the numbers. Select the items and click the **Numbering** button.

**Document 3
Memorandum**

TO: Marilyn Smith, Public Relations Media Assistant | **FROM:** Anthony   14
Baker, Public Relations Coordinator | **DATE:** February 16, 200- | 26
SUBJECT: Electronic Presentation   33

Richard Holmes has been invited to introduce our company at the March   47
15 meeting of the Nelson Chamber of Commerce. Please prepare a 20-   60
minute electronic presentation for this meeting by extracting the key   74
points from Richard's speech, which is attached.   84

As you prepare the presentation, remember these key points: 96

- Write phrases, not sentences, so that listeners focus on the key points.   111
- Use parallel structure and limit wraparound lines of text.   124
- Create *builds* to keep the audience alert.   133
- Add transitions between slides (suggest fade in and out).   145
- Add graphics and humor--we want them to remember us.   156

Please have the presentation ready for Richard to review by February 24.   171
After he has made his revisions and the presentation is final, print the   186
presentation as a handout. | xx | Attachment   194

Tip:

To add bullets, key the items, select them, and click the **Bullets** button.

E and N

2a
GETTING started

1. Open *Keyboarding Pro* software.
2. Insert your student data disk into Drive A.
3. From the Log In dialog box, select your section and then your name.
4. Key your password and click **OK**.
5. Click **A** for *Alphabetic* and then select *Lesson 2*.

SKILLBUILDING WARMUP

Home position

1 ff dd ss aa ff dd ss aa jj kk ll ;; fj dk sl a; a;

2 fj dk sl a; fjdksla; a;sldkfj fj dk sl a; fjdksla;

3 aa ss dd ff jj kk ll ;; aa ss dd ff jj kk ll ;; a;

4 ki ik ki ik di si li ia is if ji id ia il ik li id

2b

Review home keys and i
each line once; DS between groups

5 ff ss kk dd fs ks ds sk lf as fa ll kk ff lk fl kl

6 as as ad ad fad fad al all fall fall lass jak jaks

7 a lass; ask dad; all lads; add all; all fall; dads

8 a lad; a lad asks; lads ask dad; adds all; ask all

9 as as ask ask ad ad add dad a ja jak jak ad ad add

10 ki ik ki ik di si li ia is if ji id ia il ik li id

11 as is; if ad; aid jak lid fad sad jak ail if a lad

12 aid laid said did jak flak is id if dial disk jaks

13 if a lad; a jail; is silk; is ill; a dais; did aid

14 aid jak lid fad sad jak ail if a lad; as if; if ad

SELKIRK COMMUNICATIONS

OBJECTIVES

1. Apply your keyboarding, formatting, and word processing skills.

2. Work with few *specific* directions.

Selkirk Communications, Project

Selkirk Communications is a training company that is relocating its office from Spokane, Washington, to Nelson, Canada. As an administrative assistant, you will prepare a number of documents using many of the formatting and word processing skills you have learned throughout Lessons 31-60. Selkirk Communications uses the block letter format and unbound report style.

Document 1 **S C**
Invitation

Format this document attractively. Use a different font for the main heading and callouts (PLACE, TIME, etc.). Vary font size. DS between listed items; position the document attractively on the page. Save as **m8-d1**.

		words
	OPEN HOUSE	2
PLACE:	Selkirk Communications	8
	1003 Baker St.	11
	Nelson BC V1L 5N7	15
TIME:	1:00-4:00 p.m.	20
DATE:	Saturday and Sunday, April 27 and 28	29

Selkirk Communications is excited to open its tenth international communications office in downtown Nelson. Please plan to attend the Open House. | | 43 / 57 / 58

Come in and meet our friendly staff. Learn how we can help meet your training needs. | | 72 / 76

Selkirk Communications specializes in: | | 84
* Instructor-Led Training in Our Classroom or Your Facility | | 96
* Newsletters Designed to Meet Your Needs | | 104
* Authorized Training Center for *Microsoft Office* and *Corel WordPerfect* | | 118
* Oral and Written Communication Refresher Courses | | 128

2c ●

Learn e and n

Read carefully the "Standard procedures for learning new keyreaches" at the right. Use them to learn new keyreaches in this lesson and in lessons that follow.

Standard procedures for learning new keyreaches

1. Find the new key on the illustrated keyboard; then find it on your keyboard.
2. Study the illustrated keyreach.
3. Watch your finger make the reach to the new key a few times. Keep other fingers curved in home position. For an upward reach, straighten the finger slightly; for a downward reach, curve it a bit more.
4. Key each line twice (slowly, then faster).
5. Repeat if time permits. Work to eliminate pauses.

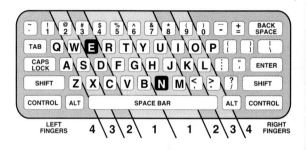

e Reach *up* with *left second* finger.

n Reach *down* with *right first* finger.

2d ●

Improve keystroking
each line once; repeat the drill

End the lesson

1. Print the Lesson Report.
2. Exit *Alphabetic*; remove the disk and store.
3. Follow these procedures for the remaining lessons.

e

15 e ed ed led led lea lea ale ale elf elf eke eke ed
16 e el el eel els elk elk lea leak ale kale led jell
17 e ale kale lea leak fee feel lea lead elf self eke

n

18 n nj nj an an and and fan fan and kin din fin land
19 n an fan in fin and land sand din fans sank an sin
20 n in ink sink inn kin skin an and land in din dink

all reaches learned

21 den end fen ken dean dens ales fend fens keen knee
22 if in need; feel ill; as an end; a lad and a lass;
23 and sand; a keen idea; as a sail sank; is in jail;

24 de de ed ed led fed ade lea lead ale fale eke deal
25 de jell sake lake led self sea fled sled jell feel
26 jn jn nj nj in fan fin an; ink sin and inn an skin
27 jn din sand land nail sank and dank skin sans sink
28 if fin in end is den fen as ink lee fed an jak and
29 in nine inns; if an end; need an idea; seek a fee;
30 add a line; and safe; asks a lass; sail in a lake;
31 dine in an inn; fake jade; lend fans; as sand sank

LESSON 2   E AND N   **8**

Activity twelve

Map a trip

Determining the route to your destination city is most important in ensuring a pleasant journey. The printed atlas is a valuable tool for mapping a trip; however, with today's technology, we can map our trips electronically using the Maps hyperlinks provided by several search engines. This invaluable site will search for the specific route you specify and provide you an overview map and turn-by-turn maps with text.

Practice

1. Click the **Search** button in your Web browser. Browse the search engines to locate the hyperlinks for *Maps*; click to open.

2. Your destination city is Asheville, North Carolina. Enter your city and state as the starting point. Search for a turn-by-turn map with text. Print the directions.
   What is the total distance? _____ What is the estimated time? _____

3. You are having a party and need to give several guests directions to your home. Using the Excite search engine, go to *Maps* and choose *Map a U.S. Address* to search for directions to your home. Enter your street address, city, state, and ZIP. Print and trim the map to fit in your party invitation.

4. Use *Maps* from the AltaVista search engine to create a map of your city. Use the *Fancy Features* and enter your phone number. Print the map.

Activity thirteen

Use a comprehensive search engine

Using a comprehensive search engine can be very helpful in locating various information quickly. The All-in-One Web site (http://www.AllOneSearch.com) is a compilation of various search tools found on the Internet. Search tools include various categories, such as People, News/Weather, Desk Reference, and Other Interesting Searches/Services.

Practice

1. Open the All-in-One Web site (http://www.AllOneSearch.com). Browse the various categories and the many search tools within the categories.

2. From the *People* category:
   a. Use BigFoot to find the email address for (*provide a name*).
   b. Use Ahoy! to find the home page for (*provide a name*).

3. From the *News/Weather* category:
   a. Use Pathfinder Weather Now to find your current weather.
   b. Use one of the news searches to find news articles about (*provide current event*).

4. From the *Desk Reference* category:
   a. Find the area code for Jackson, Mississippi _____; Cincinnati, Ohio
      _____.
   b. Find a quotation from Bartlett's Quotations about (*provide the topic*).

5. From the *Other Interesting Searches/Services* category:
   a. Convert the U.S. Dollar to Canadian dollar. _____
   b. Locate a recipe for red velvet cake (*or your recipe choice*).

6. Choose a category and determine a search. List category, question, and answer.

Review

3a

GETTING started

Follow the steps on p. 7 to open *Keyboarding Pro*.

Key each line at a slow, steady pace; strike and release each key quickly. Key each line again at a faster pace.

home 1 ad ads lad fad dad as ask fa la lass jak jaks alas

n 2 an fan and land fan flan sans sand sank flank dank

i 3 is id ill dill if aid ail fail did kid ski lid ilk

all 4 ade alas nine else fife ken; jell ink jak inns if;

3b

Master keys learned
key the lines once SS; DS between groups

Technique goals
- fingers curved
- wrists low, but not resting
- eyes on copy

Eyes on copy; feet flat on floor

LEFT FINGERS 4 3 2 1 1 2 3 4 RIGHT FINGERS

home 5 a s d f j k l ; as df jk l; asdf jkl; a; sl dk fj;

6 a as ask ad add fad dad all fall jaks lass sad sak

i 7 i ik ik ik is is id id il il if if ail kid did lid

8 i ik aid did lid kids aid ail sill fill ails fails

e 9 e ed ed el el led led els els elk elk lea lea leak

10 e ale lea fee lea elf eke lead feel leaf deal kale

n 11 jn jn nj nj in fan fin an; din ink sin and inn an;

12 n de den end fen an an and and ken keen fens deans

3c

Review stroking techniques
each 2-line group twice SS

home row: fingers curved and upright

13 jak lad as lass dad sad lads fad fall la ask ad as

14 asks add jaks dads a lass ads flak adds sad as lad

upward reaches: straighten fingers slightly; return quickly to home position

15 fed die led ail kea lei did ale fife silk leak lie

16 sea lid deal sine desk lie ale like life idea jail

double letters: don't hurry when stroking double letters

17 fee jell less add inn seek fall alee lass keel all

18 dill dell see fell eel less all add kiss seen sell

Activity

ten

Update table with data extracted from the Internet

Data used in tables can change frequently and become outdated quickly. The World Wide Web is a great source of updated information for updating data in tables.

Practice

1. Open *54d-d2*. Delete the date in the secondary heading. Save the document as **Activity10**.
2. Log on the Internet. Click in the Location, Address, or Netsite box. (*Terms will vary according to browser.*) Key **msn.com** and strike ENTER. The *Microsoft* Home page displays.
3. Scroll down the page to find the stock quotes. Copy the numbers under Last, Chg, and % Chg on a piece of paper. Exit the Internet.
4. Use *Word* to open *Activity10*. Use the Overtype feature to replace the numbers in the table with the current ones.
5. Save and print.

Activity

eleven

Update table with data extracted from the Internet

Changing currency rates is another area in which the Web can be used in order to update tables in a *Word* document.

Practice

1. Open *54d-d5*. Delete the date in the secondary heading. Save the document as **Activity11**.
2. Log on the Internet. Key **x-rates.com** and strike ENTER. The Exchange Rates Home page displays.
3. Click the Exchange rates drop-list arrow. A list of international currency displays.
4. Select *United States Dollar*.
5. Click the **Table** button.
6. Click the **Submit** button.
7. Copy the data from Columns B and C for each currency listed in 54d-d5. Exit the Internet.
8. Use *Word* to open *Activity11*. Use the Overtype feature to replace the numbers in the table with the current ones.
9. Save and print.

3d

Practice easy words and phrases

Key each line at an easy speed; do not key the vertical rules separating phrases.

easy words

19 if is as an ad el and did die eel fin fan elf lens

20 as ask id lid kid and ade aid el eel feel ilk skis

21 ail fail aid did ken ale led an flan inn inns alas

22 le le led led ad ad fad fad al al all all fall ale

23 as as ask ask ad ad lad lad id id lid lid kid kids

24 and and land land el el elf elf self self ail nail

easy phrases

25 ask a lass;|as a dad|a fall fad|as all ask;|sad ad

26 as a jak;|as a lass|ask dad|as a lad;|as a fall ad

27 is as if;|is a disk|aid all kids|did ski|is a silk

28 skis skid|is a kid|aid did fail|if a dial|laid lid

29 as kale|sees a lake|elf fled|as a deal|sell a sled

30 sell a lead|seal a deal|feel a leaf|as a jade sale

3e

Practice common reaches

each line once
The reach is identified in the first two letters of each line.

31 ea sea lea seas deal leaf leak lead leas flea keas

32 as ask lass ease as asks ask ask sass as alas seas

33 sa sad sane sake sail sale sans safe sad said sand

34 le sled lead flee fled ale flea lei dale kale leaf

35 el eel eld elf sell self el dell fell elk els jell

36 in fin inn inks dine sink fine fins kind kine lain

37 an and fan dean elan flan land lane lean sand sane

Using copied software. Using software for which a license has not been   481
issued has become a common violation of the copyright law. While some   495
software is labeled public domain, other software is copyrighted and a   509
license is required. Make a policy never to pirate software. Be sure all   524
software being used at home or at the office has been officially licensed   539
and is legal.   542

Photocopying copyrighted materials. Copying a textbook in part or in its   557
entirety is a violation most people do without considering it as an infringe-   572
ment. Consequently, public copiers often have displayed the text of the   587
copyright law in an effort to warn offenders. Again, by allowing entire text-   603
books or parts of books to be photocopied, the offender is depriving the   617
authors and publishing companies of income. Consider the effect on   631
today's and future originators if the copyright law did not prohibit copying   646
in this manner.   650

Using copyrighted materials without permission. When using graphics in   664
presentation handouts and/or electronic presentations, students and   678
teachers are often using cartoons and other graphics without seeking per-   692
mission from the owner.   Presenters need to know that many graphics in   706
printed and in electronic media are copyrighted.   Permission to use these   721
copyrighted materials is possible by submitting a request to the owner.   A   736
fee for a one-time use may be assessed.   Using a cartoon without permis-   751
sion becomes more complicated when the violator receives remuneration   765
for the presentation or submits the manuscript for publication.   778

Conclusion   780

Because technology has broadened the areas of copyright infringement, it   794
is very important for students and teachers to be knowledgeable of possi-   809
ble copyright violations. Be sure to give credit to authors or creators for   824
their copyrighted work. If you want to reproduce or reprint portions or   839
perhaps use a cartoon in a presentation, always write to the appropriate   853
individual for written permission.   860

REFERENCES   863

Document 2
Leftbound report
Rekey Document 1, format-
ting as a leftbound report.

Bayless, Marsha L., Debbie D. DuFrene, and Florence E. Elliott-Howard.   877
    "Sound and Sight: Legal Dimensions of Multimedia." *1995 South-*   890
    west Administrative Services Association Proceedings.   Phoenix,   903
    December 1995.   906

Ricks, Betty R., Ann J. Swafford, and Kay E. Gow. *Information and Image*   920
    Management. 3d ed. Cincinnati: South-Western Publishing Co.,   933
    1992.   934

U.S. Constitution, art. 1, sec. 8, cl. 8.   942

LESSON 4

Left Shift, H, T, Period

4a

GETTING started

each line twice SS; keep eyes on copy

home row   1   al as ads lad dad fad jak fall lass asks fads all;

e/i/n   2   ed ik jn in knee end nine line sine lien dies leis

all reaches   3   see a ski; add ink; fed a jak; is an inn; as a lad

easy   4   an dial id is an la lake did el ale fake is land a

4b

Learn left SHIFT and h

each line twice SS

Follow the "Standard procedures for learning new keyreaches" on p. 8 for all remaining reaches.

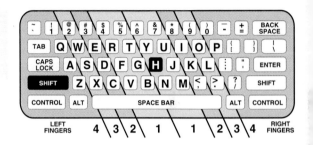

left shift Reach *down* with *left fourth* (little) finger; shift, strike, release.

h Reach to *left* with *right first* finger.

left shift

5   J Ja Ja Jan Jan Jane Jana Ken Kass Lee Len Nan Ned

6   and Ken and Lena and Jake and Lida and Nan and Ida

7   Ina Kale; Jill Lask; Nels Insa; Ken Jalk; Lin Nial

h

8   h hj hj he he she she hen aha ash had has hid shed

9   h hj ha hie his half hand hike dash head sash shad

10   aha hi hash heal hill hind lash hash hake dish ash

all reaches learned

11   Nels Kane and Jake Jenn; she asked Hi and Ina Linn

12   Lend Lana and Jed a dish; I fed Lane and Jess Kane

13   I see Jake Kish and Lash Hess; Isla and Helen hike

4c

Practice ENTER

Key the drill once; DS and repeat. Use fluid, unhurried movements.

enter: return without looking up

14   Nan had a sale;

15   He did see Hal;

16   Lee has a desk;

17   Ina hid a dish;

words

COPYRIGHT LAW: IMPLICATIONS FOR STUDENTS AND TEACHERS   11

Assess reports
Time schedule:

Assemble materials . . . . . 2'

Timed production . . . . . . 25'

 (Key problems in order;
 proofread and correct errors
 as you work.)

Final check . . . . 6'

 (Proofread and circle any
 remaining errors. Calculate
 g-pram—total words keyed
 divided by 25'.)

Document I
Unbound report

Format and key the unbound
report at the right.

• DS the report.

• Format main, side, and
 paragraph headings appropriately. Divide main heading into two lines.

• Indent direct quotation;
 bold and italicize as shown.

The subject of copyright law is an area of much attention today. The   25
technological advancements in the areas of software, CD-ROMs with   38
sight and sound clips, videotaping, and electronic publishing are only   52
the beginning of questions being raised. There is also a need to   66
understand the Copyright Act of 1976. Groups will continue to work   79
toward change of copyright laws to broaden the use of these new   92
media. This report will present information about the Copyright Act of   106
1976 and identify implications of the copyright law related specifically   121
to students and teachers.   126

Copyright Act of 1976   131

The Copyright Act of 1976 states that things to be copyrighted include   145
"original works of authorship fixed in any tangible medium of   157
expression." Hard copy is only one form of many types of media.   171
Other media include software stored on floppy disk or hard drive,   184
sound recordings, movie productions, still photographs stored on CD-   197
ROM, and the list grows as the technology advances. Publishers have   211
interpreted this copyright law as they print the following statement on   225
copyrighted materials: 230

> **ALL RIGHTS RESERVED.** *The text of this publication, or*   241
> *any part thereof, may not be reproduced or transmitted in any*   254
> *form or by any means, electronic or mechanical, including*   265
> *photocopying, recording, storage in an information retrieval*   277
> *system, or otherwise, without the prior written permission of*   290
> *the publisher.*   293

Implications for Students and Teachers   301

Students and teachers are two groups often facing decisions regarding   315
copyright infringements. For this reason, these groups should be   328
aware of the following situations where the copyright law is prevalently   343
violated.   345

Plagiarizing. Using the work of another without citation is a major   359
offense. Manuscript style manuals clearly delineate the proper manner   373
to cite work borrowed from another. Student term papers as well as   386
faculty manuscripts submitted for publication in journals should   399
include appropriate documentation.   407

Copying music. The composers of the music and the lyrics are pro-   420
tected by copyright law. The copyright protects these individuals' abil-   434
ities to earn profit by disallowing copying of music. For that reason,   449
music directors are required to purchase the needed number of origi-   462
nals for the group.   467

4d ●

Learn t and . (period)
each line twice SS

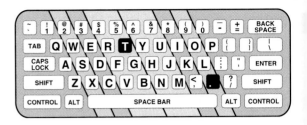

Period: Space once after a period that follows an initial or an abbreviation. To increase readability, space twice after a period that ends a sentence.

t Reach *up* with *left first* finger.

. (period) Reach *down* with *right third* finger.

t

18	t tf tf aft aft left fit fat fete tiff tie the tin
19	tf at at aft lit hit tide tilt tint sits skit this
20	hat kit let lit ate sit flat tilt thin tale tan at

. (period)

21	.l .l l.l fl. fl. L. L. Neal and J. N. List hiked.
22	Hand J. H. Kass a fan. Jess did. I need an idea.
23	Jane said she has a tan dish; Jae and Lee need it.

all reaches learned

24	I did tell J. K. that Lt. Li had left. He is ill.
25	Lee and Ken left at ten; the jet had left at nine.
26	I see Lila and Ilene at tea. Jae Kane ate at ten.

4e ●

Practice new reaches
each line once; DS between 2-line groups

reach review	27	tf .l hj ft ki de jh tf ik ed hj de ft ki l. tf ik
	28	elf eel left is sis fit till dens ink has delt ink
		DS
	29	it if id fit sit let hat at tie let lit hit id lid
i/t	30	if it|if it|it has|it has|if it is|if it is|it has
	31	he he she she held held shed shed ash ash has hash
h/e	32	she had; held sale; has jade; had jade; he had ash
	33	Hal and Nel; Jade dishes; Kale has half; Jed hides
shift	34	Hi Ken; Helen and Jen hike; Jan has a jade; Ken is
	35	Ina lies in the sand at ten; she needs a fast tan.
all	36	Jan asks if I had all the tea that Len said I had.

60 Assessment

LESSON

GETTING started

each line 3 times SS; DS
between 3-line groups

SKILLBUILDING WARMUP

alphabet 1 Jack Voxall was amazed by the quiet response of the big audience.
fig/sym   2 Our #3865 clocks will cost K & B $12.97 each (less 40% discount).
shift   3 In May, Lynn, Sonia, and Jason left for Italy, Spain, and Turkey.
easy   4 It is the duty of a civic auditor to aid a city to make a profit.

| 1 | 2 | 3 | 4 | 5 | 6 | 7 | 8 | 9 | 10 | 11 | 12 | 13 |

60b • 11'

SKILLBUILDING

Assess statistical-copy skill

Key a 3' and a 5' writing; circle errors; determine *gwam*.

  all letters/figures

gwam 3' | 5'

Now and then the operation of some company deserves a closer	4	2	41

Now and then the operation of some company deserves a closer 4 | 2 | 41
look by investors. For example, Zerotech Limited, the food, oil, 8 | 5 | 44
and chemical company, says in its monthly letter that it will be 13 | 8 | 46
raising its second-quarter dividend to 85 cents a share, up from 17 | 10 | 49
79 3/4 cents a share, and that a dividend will be paid July 12. 21 | 13 | 51

This fine old area firm is erecting an enviable history of 25 | 15 | 54
dividend payment, but its last hike in outlays came back in 1987, 30 | 18 | 56
when it said a share could go above 65 cents. Zerotech has, how- 34 | 21 | 59
ever, never failed to pay a dividend since it was founded in 38 | 23 | 61
1937. The recent increase extends the annual amount paid to 42 | 25 | 64
$5.40 a share. 43 | 26 | 65

In this monthly letter, the firm also cited its earnings for 47 | 28 | 67
the second quarter and for the first half of this year. The net 52 | 31 | 70
revenue for the second quarter was a record $1.9 billion, up 24.2 56 | 34 | 72
percent from a typical period just a year ago. Zerotech has its 61 | 36 | 75
main company offices at 9987 Nicholas Drive in Albany. 64 | 38 | 77

3' | 1 | 2 | 3 | 4 |
5' | 1 | 2 | 3 |

R, Right Shift, C, O

5a •

GETTING started

each line twice SS; keep eyes on copy

5b •

Learn r and right SHIFT

each line twice SS

r Reach *up* with *left first* finger.

right shift Reach *down* with *right fourth* finger; shift, strike, release.

5c •

Practice techniques

each line once, striving for the goals listed below:

Lines 14-15: smoothly, without pauses

Lines 16-17: without looking at hands or keyboard

Lines 18-20: without pausing or looking up from the copy

home keys 1	a; ad add al all lad fad jak ask lass fall jak lad
t/h/i/n 2	the hit tin nit then this kith dint tine hint thin
left shift/. 3	I need ink. Li has an idea. Hit it. I see Kate.
all reaches 4	Jeff ate at ten; he left a salad dish in the sink.

r

5 r rf rf riff riff fir fir rid ire jar air sir lair

6 rf rid ark ran rat are hare art rant tire dirt jar

7 rare dirk ajar lark rain kirk share hart rail tart

right shift

8 D D Dan Dan Dale Ti Sal Ted Ann Ed Alf Ada Sid Fan

9 and Sid and Dina and Allen and Eli and Dean and Ed

10 Ed Dana; Dee Falk; Tina Finn; Sal Alan; Anna Deeds

all reaches learned

11 Jake and Ann hiked in the sand; Asa set the tents.

12 Fred Derr and Rae Tira dined at the Tree Art Fair.

13 Alan asked Dina if Neil and Reed had left at nine.

14 Kent said that half the field is idle in the fall.

15 Lana said she did sail her skiff in the dark lake.

16 All is still as Sarah and I fish here in the rain.

17 I still see a red ash tree that fell in the field.

18 I had a kale salad;

19 Elia ate his steak;

20 and Dina drank tea.

Document 3
3-column table

Merge cells in Rows 1 and 2 for titles. Adjust column widths. Shade Row 1. Add FedWorld in alphabetical order. Center table vertically and horizontally.

Technology review

Key the Internet address as shown. Do not insert spaces in the address. Strike the Space Bar after the last letter in the address. *Word* will automatically make this a hypertext link. Double-clicking on the hypertext link will automatically take you to the Web site if your terminal is connected to the Internet.

words

EMPLOYMENT RESOURCES			
April 200-			
Title	**Address**	**Description**	
American Employment Weekly	http://branch.com/aew/aew.html	Employment tabloid with ads from the Sunday edition of 50 leading newspapers	
Datamain	http://www.datamain.com	Allows applicants to fill out a structured resume or search an online job center	
Help Wanted	http://helpwanted.com	Searchable index of openings compiled from companies that have paid to be listed	
Job Center	http://www.jobcenter.com	Employment service for professionals with database searching	
Job Trak	http://www.jobtrak.com	Largest online job listing service in the United States	
Job Web	http://www.jobweb.org	Employment information, job listings, tips, and more	
Online Career Center	http://www.occ.com	Career center and employment databank	
FedWorld	*http://www.fedworld.gov*	*Bulletin board of job listings from the federal government*	

Words column:
4
6
12
23, 29, 35, 39
49, 53, 57, 61
89, 93, 97, 102
114, 118, 121
132, 136, 139
147, 151, 156
166, 171
72, 76, 78

Document 4
Interoffice memo

TO: Rosa Garcia | FROM: John David Schoenholtz | DATE: Current | 13
SUBJECT: Internships Available 20

Two internships are still open for senior business technology majors 34
for the fall semester. Companies requesting student interns are 47
Fountain Insurance Agency and Heights-McDonnell Telecommuni- 59
cation Ltd. Both companies have agreed to pay the interns minimum 72
wage for 90 hours. 76

Please post the enclosed flyer that announces the positions with con- 90
tact names and phone numbers. I would also appreciate your taking 103
a few minutes in your first class meeting to announce these openings 117
and to share the benefits of completing an internship during the senior 131
year. Please note that students must have a 3.0 GPA to enroll in the 145
internship course. 149

xx | Enclosure 152

Learn c and o
each line twice SS

c Reach *down* with *left second* finger.

o Reach *up* with right *third* finger.

c

21 c c cd cd cad cad can can tic ice sac cake cat sic
22 clad chic cite cheek clef sick lick kick dice rice
23 call acid hack jack lack lick cask crack clan cane

o

24 o ol ol old old of off odd ode or ore oar soar one
25 ol sol sold told dole do doe lo doll sol solo odor
26 onto door toil lotto soak fort hods foal roan load

all reaches learned

27 Carlo Rand can call Rocco; Cole can call Doc Cost.
28 Trina can ask Dina if Nick Corl has left; Joe did.
29 Case sent Carole a nice skirt; it fits Lorna Rich.

Practice new reaches
each line once SS; key at a steady pace

o/r
30 or or for for nor nor ore ore oar oar roe roe sore
31 a rose|her or|he or|he rode|or for|a door|her doll

i/t
32 is is tis tis it it fit fit tie tie this this lits
33 it is|it is|it is this|it is this|it sits|tie fits

e/n
34 en en end end ne ne need need ken ken kneel kneels
35 lend the|lend the|at the end|at the end|need their

c/o
36 ch ch check check ck ck hack lack jack co co cones
37 the cot|the cot|a dock|a dock|a jack|a jack|a cone

all reaches
38 Jack and Rona did frost nine of the cakes at last.
39 Jo can ice her drink if Tess can find her a flask.
40 Ask Jean to call Fisk at noon; he needs her notes.

Assess document skills
Time schedule:
Assemble materials . . . . 2'

Timed production . . . . . 25'
  (Key problems in order; proofread and correct errors as you work.)

Final check . . . . 5'
  (Proofread and circle any remaining errors. Calculate *g-pram*—total words keyed divided by 25'.)

Document I
Editing exercise
Use the following format:

DS

TM: 1.5"

LM: 1.5"

RM: 1"

Make the revisions marked in the document.

No More Waiting (14 pt)

3

(12 pt) How often do you sit by the phone waiting for a call?   14

You cant make calls because you might miss your call.   25

Adding to your frustration a friend calls to talk for only   37

ital one minute.   Of course, that one minute is when your other   49

caller choses to dial your number.   Unfortunately, you have   61

no way of knowign that you have missed the long-awaited   73

call.   You return to your waiting and still anticipateing the   84

call.   Put an end to missing calls with **Call Waiting.**   You   96

can enjoy the pleasure of using your phone at anytime.   107

When another call comes in, you can answer the second call   119

without hanging up on the first one.   What are you waiting   131

for?   Dial 555-2379 and start enjoying no more waiting.   142

Document 2
Letter in block format
Key this average-length letter in block format.

January 28, 200- | Mr. Patrick Horton | 1873 Lindsey Ave. | Fair Haven, NJ   14
07704-3821 | Dear Patrick   19

Thank you for visiting with me and the other faculty from Helmings   32
Community College who attended Career Day at your high school   45
on January 20, 200-.   We are very pleased that you are interested in a   60
degree in business technology.   66

The faculty and I commend you for your thorough search of academic   79
programs by browsing colleges' home pages on the Internet.   Currently,   94
our home page has been visited by over two thousand prospective stu-   107
dents.   We are very happy to count you among our new students.   120

Since our visit last week, I have forwarded your name and address to the   135
following offices: admissions, financial aid and scholarships, recruiting,   150
honors programs, and extracurricular programs.   You will be receiving   164
information from these groups in the next few weeks.   Be sure to read   178
the materials carefully, watching specifically for application deadlines.   193

Please call me at 555-0039 for an appointment to schedule your fall   206
classes.   208

Sincerely | Lahitia Graeter | Business Instructor | xx   218

6
W, Comma, B, P

6a ● 8'

GETTING started

each line twice; avoid pauses

Note suggested minutes for practices shown in headings.

6b ● 12'

Learn w and , (comma)
each line twice

w Reach *up* with *left third* finger.

, (comma) Reach *down* with *right second* finger.

home row 1 a ad as lad las fad sad; jak flask fall jaks salad
n/i/t 2 in tin nit nil its tan din tie ten tine fins stein
c/h/r/o 3 code herd rode cold hock hark roll rock ache chore
all reaches 4 Holt can see Dane at ten; Jill sees Frank at nine.

Comma: Space once after a comma.

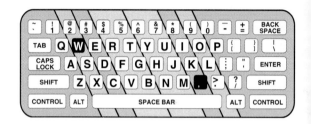

w

5 w ws ws was was wan wit low win jaw wilt wink wolf
6 ow wow how owl howl owe owed row cow cowl new knew
7 wide sown wild town went jowl wait white down walk

, (comma)

8 k, k, k, irk, ilk, ask, oak, ark, lark, jak, rock,
9 skis, a dock, a fork, a lock, a fee, a tie, a fan,
10 Jan, Lee, Ed, and Dan saw Nan, Kate, Len, and Ted.

all reaches learned

11 Win, Lew, Drew, and Walt will walk to West Willow.
12 Ask Ho, Al, and Jared to read the code; it is new.
13 The window, we think, was closed; we felt no wind.

6c ● 5'

Improve techniques
each line once; DS between groups; repeat

shift keys: shift; strike key; release both quickly

14 Fiji, Don, Cara, and Ron will see East Creek soon.
15 Kane Losh and Janet Hart will join Nan in Rio Ono.

double letters

16 Renee took a class at noon; call her at Lann Hall.
17 Ed and Anne saw three deer flee across Wood Creek.

Assessment

GETTING started

each line 3 times SS; DS
between 3-line groups

SKILLBUILDING WARMUP

alphabet	1	Jayne promised to bring the portable vacuum for next week's quiz.
figures	2	Our main store is at 6304 Grand; others, at 725 Mayo and 198 Rio.
1st finger	3	After lunch, Brent taught us to try to put the gun by the target.
easy	4	He may make a profit on corn, yams, and hay if he works the land.

| 1 | 2 | 3 | 4 | 5 | 6 | 7 | 8 | 9 | 10 | 11 | 12 | 13 |

SKILLBUILDING

Assess straight-copy skill

Key a 3' and a 5' writing; proofread and circle errors; determine *gwam* for both writings.

 all letters

gwam   3'   5'

	3'	5'
At a recent June graduation ceremony, several graduates were	4	2	43
heard discussing the fact that they had spent what they thought	8	5	46
was a major part of their lives in school classrooms. They esti-	13	8	48
mated the amount of time they had been in elementary school, in	17	10	51
high school, in college, and in graduate school had to be about	21	13	54
nineteen or twenty years.	23	14	55
Indeed, two decades is a significant span of time. Even if	27	16	57
little additional effort is used seeking education, about a	31	19	59
quarter of a person's life will have been spent on learning ac-	35	21	62
tivities. Graduation is a time for looking at the past and the	39	24	65
present and analyzing how they can be merged to form a future.	44	26	67
And thus begins The Search.	45	27	68
The Search begins with introspection--attempting to sort out	50	30	71
and pinpoint all that has gone before, to identify purpose behind	54	32	73
the years of effort and expense, to focus it all on some goal.	58	35	76
If encouraged to name the goal, we call it, probably for lack of	63	38	78
a more definitive name, Success. We desire to be successful.	67	40	81
But what is "success"?	68	41	82

3' | 1 | 2 | 3 | 4 |
5' | 1 | 2 | 3 |

Learn b and p
each line twice

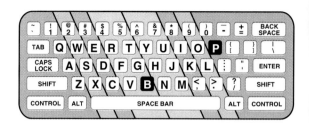

b Reach *down* with *left first* finger.

p Reach *up* with *right fourth* (little) finger.

Build technique
each line once; keep hand movement to a minimum

b

18 b bf bf biff boff bit bid bib bird boa ban bon bow
19 be rib fib sob dob cob bob crib lab slab fobs blob
20 born oboe blab bribe able bode belt bath bide both

p

21 p p; p; pa pa; pal pal pan pad par pen pep pap per
22 pa pa; lap lap; nap nap; hep ape spa asp leap clap
23 span park paper pelt tips soap pane pops rope ripe

all reaches learned

24 Barb and Bob wrapped a pepper in paper and ribbon.
25 Rip, Joann, and Dick were all closer to the flash.
26 Bo will be pleased to see Japan; he works in Oslo.

all reaches
27 ws ws ,k ,k bf bf p; p; ol ol cd cd rf rf nj nj ed
28 ah was kid fab fab pal for tic poll cod row jak to

s/w
29 ws ws lows now we shown win cow wow wire jowl when
30 Wes saw an owl in the willow tree in the old lane.

b/p
31 bf bf fib rob bid ;p p; pal pen pot nap hop cap bp
32 Rob has both pans in a bin at the back of the pen.

33 Dick owns a dock at this lake; he paid Ken for it.
34 Jane also kept a pair of owls, a hen, and a snake.

all reaches
35 Blair soaks a bit of the corn, as he did in Japan.
36 I blend the cocoa in the bowl when I work for Leo.

37 Albert, Lisa Planke, and I saw a few hidden flaws.
38 Karla has the first slot; she wants to win for Jo.

Objective Assessment

Answer the questions below to see if you have mastered the content of this module.

1. A vertical list of information is called a _____ ; whereas a horizontal array of information is called a _____ .

2. To move to a previous cell of keyed information in a table, press _____ .

3. _____ above and below the tables within documents.

4. To recenter a table after column widths have been adjusted, choose _____ from the Table menu.

5. To align text at the decimal, select the _____ and set a _____ on the Horizontal Ruler.

6. Whole numbers are generally aligned at the _____ ; whereas text in tables is generally aligned at the _____ .

7. The Shading feature can be accessed by clicking on the Format menu, then _____ and _____ .

8. The Center Page command is accessed on the _____ menu.

9. To join the cells of Row 1 of a two-column table, select Cells _____ and _____ ; choose _____ from the Table menu.

10. The vertical line spacing of tables should be changed to _____ to make the table more readable.

Performance Assessment

1. Create a 2-column, 9-row table.
2. Merge Cells A1 and B1.
3. Split Cells B2-B9 into two columns.
4. Center, bold, and shade all headings 10%.
5. Align as marked.
6. Change line spacing to 1.5; adjust column width; center table horizontally and vertically.
7. Save as **ckpt7-d1** and print.
8. Delete Communications row.
9. Add a row for the Management Department that has 1,298 majors and an 8.45% growth rate. Position in alphabetical order. Save as **ckpt7-d2**.

COLLEGE OF BUSINESS ADMINISTRATION		
Department	**Majors**	**Growth Rate**
Accounting	945	3.65%
Banking, Finance, and Insurance	1,021	2.17%
Communications	326	-2.5%
Economics	453	1.4%
International Business	620	14.74%
Management Science	1,235	11.8%
Marketing	1,357	10.38%

↑ Left-align   ↑ Right-align   ↑ Decimal tab

Review

GETTING started

each line twice; begin new lines promptly

SKILLBUILDING WARMUP

home row	1	fa la la; a sad lad; jaks fall; a lass had a salad
1st row	2	Ann Bascan and Cabal Naban nabbed a cab in Canada.
3d row	3	Rip went to a water show with either Pippa or Pia.
all letters	4	Dick will see Job at nine if Rach sees Pat at one.

Review new reaches

each line once; keep hands quiet

5 ws ws was was wan wan wit wit pew paw nap pop bawl
6 bf bf fb fb fob fob rib rib be be job job bat back
7 p; p; asp asp pan pan ap ap ca cap pa nap pop prow

8 Barb and Bret took an old black robe and the boot.
9 Walt saw a wisp of white water renew ripe peppers.
10 Pat picked a black pepper for the picnic at Parks.

Build speed

1. Key each line once; DS between groups.
2. Key a 1' writing on each of lines 17-19.

Think, say, and *key* words and phrases.

concentrate on words

11 a an pan so sot la lap ah aha do doe el elf to tot
12 bow bowl pin pint for fork forks hen hens jak jaks
13 chap chaps flak flake flakes prow prowl work works

concentrate on phrases

14 is in a|as it is|or if|as a|is on a|to do it|is so
15 is for|did it|is the|we did a|and so|to see|or not
16 as for the|as for the|and to the|to see it|and did

concentrate on words and phrases

17 Jess ate all of the peas in the salad in the bowl.
18 I hid the ace in a jar as a joke; I do not see it.
19 As far as I know, he did not read all of the book.

| 1 | 2 | 3 | 4 | 5 | 6 | 7 | 8 | 9 | 10 |

Document I

INTERVIEW SCHEDULE — 4

Conference Room 1 — 7

10:00-10:50 a.m.	Alice Salva, Marketing Manager	17
11:00-11:50 a.m.	Roger Eason, Advertising Director	28
12:15-1:45 p.m.	Catered Lunch with Sales Team	38
2:00-3:30 p.m.	Ginger Fogler, Vice President of Marketing	49

Document 2
1. Right-align Columns B, C, and D.
2. Shade the Total row 20%.

ESTIMATES ON KITCHEN CABINETRY — 6

Kitchen Component	VSP Kitchens	Designs by Pat	Euro Image	
Cabinetry	$34,475	$22,100	$38,350	24
Granite countertops	8,150	7,950	10,275	32
Halogen lighting	1,450	1,600	1,800	39
Appliances (allowance)	12,000	12,000	12,000	48
Total	$56,075	$43,650	$62,425	54

(18 — header row)

Document 3
1. Create a 3-column, 9-row table.
2. Merge the cells in Row I for the title.
3. Split Cells B3-B9 into two columns.
4. Split Cells C3-C9 into two columns.
5. Shade Row I 20%.
6. Alignment:
   Column A, left
   Columns B & D, right
   Columns C & E, decimal

INTERNATIONAL EXPORTS					
Exports	1999		2000		
Goods and Services	$ Millions	% of Total	$ Millions	% of Total	
Agriculture	3,798	8.8	4,783	9.5	27
Mining	23,587	54.6	25,261	50.4	33
Manufacturing	11,582	26.8	15,438	30.8	41
Other Goods	410	1.0	518	1.0	46
Services	3,791	8.8	4,155	8.3	52
Total	43,168	100.0	50,155	100.0	58

(INTERNATIONAL EXPORTS — 4; Exports/1999/2000 — 8; header — 21)

Document 4

Retrieve Document I and add the information at the right as Row I and Row 6 to keep the time in correct order (total words, 65).

9:00-9:50 a.m.	Mark Baker, Project Manager
3:45-4:30 p.m.	Jan Mason, Human Resources Manager

7d ● 13'

Check spacing/shifting technique

each set of lines once SS; DS between 3-line groups

▼ Space once after a period following an abbreviation.

spacing: space *immediately* after each word

20 ad la as in if it lo no of oh he or so ok pi be we
21 an ace ads ale aha a fit oil a jak nor a bit a pew
22 ice ades born is fake to jail than it and the cows

spacing/shifting　　　▼　　　　　　　　　▼

23 Ask Jed.　Dr. Han left at ten; Dr. Crowe, at nine.
24 I asked Jin if she had ice in a bowl; it can help.
25 Freda, not Jack, went to Spain.　Joan likes Spain.

Enter: reach for ENTER without looking up

26 Blake owns a pen for the foal.
27 Jan lent the bowl to the pros.
28 He fit the panel to the shelf.
29 This rock is half of the pair.
30 I held the title for the land.

7e ● 6'

Build skill

Key each line twice, trying to increase your speed the second time.

31 Jake held a bit of cocoa and an apricot for Diane.
32 Jan is to chant in the still air in an idle field.
33 Dick and I fish for cod on the docks at Fish Lake.
34 Kent still held the dish and the cork in his hand.
　| 1 | 2 | 3 | 4 | 5 | 6 | 7 | 8 | 9 | 10 |

7f ● 5'

Check speed

Take two 1' writings.
Determine *gwam*.

Goal: 12 *gwam*

　　　　　　　•　　　　　4　　　•　　　　8　　　•
It is hard to fake a confident spirit.　We will do
　　　　　12　　　•　　　16　　　•
better work if we approach and finish a job and
20　　　•　　　24　　　•　　　28　　　•
know that we will do the best work we can and then
　　　32
not fret.
　| 1 | 2 | 3 | 4 | 5 | 6 | 7 | 8 | 9 | 10 |

Assessment

GETTING
started

each line 3 times SS; DS
between 3-line groups

SKILLBUILDING WARMUP

alphabet	1	Jacob Kazlowski and five experienced rugby players quit the team.
figures	2	E-mail account #82-4 is the account for telephone (714) 555-6039.
double letters	3	Anne will meet with the committee at noon to discuss a new issue.
easy	4	The men may pay my neighbor for the work he did in the cornfield.

| 1 | 2 | 3 | 4 | 5 | 6 | 7 | 8 | 9 | 10 | 11 | 12 | 13 |

58b ● 10'

SKILLBUILDING

Assess straight-copy skill
Take one 3' and one 5' writing; determine *gwam*; proofread and circle errors.

all letters

	gwam	3'	5'

	3'	5'
Whether any company can succeed depends on how well it fits	4	2 44
into the economic system. Success rests on certain key factors	8	5 47
that are put in line by a management team that has set goals for	13	8 49
the company and has enough good judgment to recognize how best to	17	10 52
reach those goals. Because of competition, only the best orga-	21	13 55
nized companies get to the top.	23	14 56
A commercial enterprise is formed for a specific purpose;	27	16 58
that purpose is usually to equip others, or consumers, with	31	19 61
whatever they cannot equip themselves. Unless there is only one	36	21 63
provider, a consumer will search for a company that returns the	40	24 66
most value in terms of price; and a relationship with such a com-	44	27 68
pany, once set up, can endure for many years.	47	28 70
Thus our system assures that the businesses that manage to	51	31 73
survive are those that have been able to combine successfully an	56	33 75
excellent product with a low price and the best service--all in a	60	36 78
place that is convenient for the buyers. With no intrusion from	64	39 80
outside forces, the buyer and the seller benefit both themselves	69	41 83
and each other.	70	42 84

3' | 1 | 2 | 3 | 4 |
5' | 1 | 2 | 3 |

58c ● 33'

Assessment: Tables

Time schedule

Planning time	3'
Timed production	25'
Final check; proofread; determine *g-pram*	5'

Center each table horizontally and vertically. After each table has been keyed, change line spacing to 1.5. Adjust column width. Key for 25'.

$$g\text{-}pram = \frac{total\ words\ keyed}{25'}$$

G, Question Mark, X, U

8a ● 8'

GETTING started

each line twice SS; eyes on copy

8b ● 12'

Learn g and ?

each line twice SS; DS between 2-line groups; eyes on copy

g Reach to *right* with *left first* finger.

? Left SHIFT; reach *down* with *right fourth* finger.

8c ● 5'

Practice new reaches

each line once; DS between groups

concentrate on correct reaches; repeat

SKILLBUILDING WARMUP

all letters	1	We often can take the older jet to Paris and back.
w/b	2	As the wind blew, Bob Webber saw the window break.
p/,	3	Pat, Pippa, or Cap has prepared the proper papers.
all reaches	4	Bo, Jose, and Will fed Lin; Jack had not paid her.

Question mark: The question mark is usually followed by two spaces.

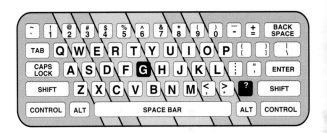

g

5 g g gf gaff gag grog fog frog drag cog dig fig gig
6 gf go gall flag gels slag gala gale glad glee gals
7 golf flog gorge glen high logs gore ogle page grow

?

8 ? ?; ?; ? ? Who? When? Where? Who is? Who was?
9 Who is here? Was it he? Was it she? Did she go?
10 Did Geena? Did he? What is that? Was Jose here?

all reaches learned

11 Has Ginger lost her job? Was her April bill here?
12 Phil did not want the boats to get here this soon.
13 Loris Shin has been ill; Frank, a doctor, saw her.

14 gf nj ng gin gin rig ring go gone no nog sign hang
15 to go|to go|go on|go in|go in|to go in|in the sign
16 I said to enter Ga. for Georgia and Id. for Idaho.

17 ?; ?;? who? when? where? how? what? who? Is it I?
18 Did Reno jog to the new sign at the lake? Did Jo?
19 Did Ti look for a sharp thorn, a cobweb, or a saw?

57d, *continued*

Document 2
Edit table

Retrieve Document 1; add Rows 4 and 8 (shown in italic) and delete Row 6 as shown.

SAFETY AWARDS			words
			3
Award Winner	**Department**	**Amount**	9
Josephine C. Schlictman	Engineering	$2,500	18
Robert R. Bauerschmidt	*Maintenance*	*2,250*	26
Christopher J. Westmoreland	Marketing	2,000	35
~~Marjorie T. Stankiewiez~~	~~Purchasing~~	~~1,500~~	
Frederico P. Hernandez	Research	1,000	43
Franklin T. Cousins	*Security*	*500*	49

Document 3
Challenge document

Create the table shown at the right.

CANADA GEOGRAPHICAL INFORMATION						words
						6
Key Islands		**Key Mountains**		**Key Lakes**		14
Island	**Sq. Miles**	**Mountain**	**Height**	**Lake**	**Sq. Miles**	23
Baffin	195,928	Logan	19,524	Superior	31,700	32
Victoria	83,897	St. Elias	18,008	Huron	23,000	41
Ellesmere	75,767	Lucania	17,147	Great Bear	12,095	51
Newfoundland	42,031	Fairweather	15,300	Great Slave	11,030	63
Banks	27,038	Waddington	13,104	Erie	9,910	71
Devon	21,331	Robson	12,972	Winnipeg	9,416	80
Melville	16,274	Columbia	12,294	Ontario	7,540	89

57e ● 3'

S E L F ✔ **check**

Answer the True/False questions at the right to see whether you have mastered the material presented in this lesson.

T F

1. To divide cells into two columns, use the Split command on the Table menu.

2. To add a row within the body of a table, position the insertion point in the last column of the row and press TAB.

3. Rows can be inserted above or below the insertion point.

4. Cells must be selected in order to merge the cells or to split the cells.

5. The Delete rows command deletes the row containing the insertion point.

Learn x and u
each line twice SS

x Reach *down* with *left third* finger.

u Reach *up* with *right first* finger.

Check speed
Take a 1' writing on each paragraph (¶). Follow the directions at the right.

x
20 x x xs xs ox ox lox sox fox box ex hex lax hex fax
21 sx six sax sox ax fix cox wax hex box pox sex text
22 flax next flex axel pixel exit oxen taxi axis next

u
23 u uj uj jug jut just dust dud due sue use due duel
24 uj us cud but bun out sun nut gun hut hue put fuel
25 dual laud dusk suds fuss full tuna tutus duds full

all reaches learned
26 Paige Power liked the book; Josh can read it next.
27 Next we picked a bag for Jan; then she, Jan, left.
28 Is her June account due? Has Lou ruined her unit?

Timed writing in the Open Screen
1. From the Lesson menu, click the **Open Screen** button.
2. Click the **Timer** button on the toolbar. In the Timer dialog box, check **Count-Down Timer** and time; click **OK.**
3. Key until the Timer reaches zero.
4. In the File menu, save the timing, using the exercise and number of the timing as the filename.
   Example: **8e-t1** (exercise 8e, timing 1)
5. Click the **Timer** button to start a new timing.
6. Each new timing must be saved with its own name, such as **8e-t2** (8e, timing 2).

```
                    •           4            •           8            •
How a finished job will look often depends on how
              12          •           16           •           20
we feel about our work as we do it.  Attitude has
              •          24           •           28           •
a definite effect on the end result of work we do.


                    •           4            •           8            •
When we are eager to begin a job, we relax and do
              12          •           16           •           20
better work than if we start the job with an idea
              •          24           •           28           •
that there is just nothing we can do to escape it.
```

57c, *continued*

Insert and delete rows within a table

To insert or delete rows in a table, the insertion point must be positioned at the appropriate location in the table.

To insert a row:

- Click where the new row will be inserted.
- Select *Table, Insert,* and then *Rows Above* or *Rows Below.*

To delete a row:

- Click on the row to be deleted.
- Select *Table, Delete,* and then *Rows.*

Drill 2

1. Follow Instructions 1-3 of Drill 1 to create the following table.
2. Key the table shown below.
3. Position the insertion point in the last cell (C4) and press TAB to add a row.
4. Add the row: **Presentation software 4,367,650 8,986,317**
5. Position the insertion point in Row 3. From the Table menu, select *Insert*, then *Rows Above.*
6. Add the row: **Word processing software 85,974,216 91,574,319**
7. Position the insertion point in Row 5 (Graphics software) to delete the row.
8. From the Table menu, select *Delete*; then select *Rows.*

SOFTWARE APPLICATION SALES		
Product Line	**1999**	**2000**
Spreadsheet software	$63,829,000	$71,385,210
Graphics software	12,847,927	10,274,287

57d • 23'

FORMATTING

Key the tables; adjust column widths; shade the heading row 20%; center tables vertically and horizontally.

Document 1

1. Create a 2-column, 6-row table.
2. Merge the cells (A1 and B1) in Row 1.
3. Split the cells B2-B6 into two columns.
4. Key the table and save.

SAFETY AWARDS			words
			3
Award Winner	**Department**	**Amount**	9
Josephine C. Schlictman	Engineering	$2,500	18
Christopher J. Westmoreland	Marketing	2,000	26
Marjorie T. Stankiewicz	Purchasing	1,500	35
Frederico P. Hernandez	Research	1,000	42

LESSON 9

Q, M, V, Apostrophe

9a ● 8'

GETTING started

each line twice SS

all letters 1 Lex gripes about cold weather; Fred is not joking.

space bar 2 Is it Di, Jo, or Al? Ask Lt. Coe, Bill; he knows.

easy 3 I did rush a bushel of cut corn to the sick ducks.

easy 4 He is to go to the Tudor Isle of England on a bus.

9b ● 12'

Learn q and m

each line twice SS

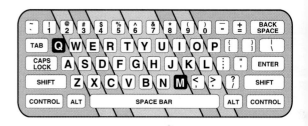

q Reach *up* with *left fourth* finger.

m Reach *down* with *right first* finger.

q

5 q qa qa quad quad quaff quant queen quo quit quick

6 qa qu qa quo quit quod quid quip quads quote quiet

7 quite quilts quart quill quakes quail quack quaint

m

8 m mj mj jam man malt mar max maw me mew men hem me

9 m mj ma am make male mane melt meat mist amen lame

10 malt meld hemp mimic tomb foam rams mama mire mind

all reaches learned

11 Quin had some quiet qualms about taming a macaque.

12 Jake Coxe had questions about a new floor program.

13 Max was quick to join the big reception for Lidia.

9c ● 8'

Practice reaches

each pair of lines once; repeat

eyes on copy; arms and hands quiet; finger-action keystroke ■

g 14 fg gn gun gun dig dig nag snag snag sign grab grab

n 15 Georgia hung a sign in front of the union for Gib.

u 16 ju uj cu cue cut cut cute cute tuck tucks cuts

c 17 Chuck and Jo can check accurate accident accounts.

n 18 nj nj nu nun mint mint mend mend man union minimum

m 19 Emma Max expressed an aim to make a mammoth model.

Merge/Split Cells

GETTING started

Key each pair of lines 3 times at a controlled rate. DS between 6-line groups.

SKILLBUILDING WARMUP

direct reaches
1 June and my brother, Bradly, received advice from junior umpires.
2 My bright brother received minimum reward for serving many years.

adjacent reaches
3 Clio and Trey were sad that very few voters were there last week.
4 Western attire was very popular at the massive auction last week.

double letters
5 Tommie Bennett will go to a meeting in Dallas tomorrow afternoon.
6 Lee will meet Joanne at the swimming pool after accounting class.

| 1 | 2 | 3 | 4 | 5 | 6 | 7 | 8 | 9 | 10 | 11 | 12 | 13 |

57b ● 8'

SKILLBUILDING

Improve accuracy
Key a 2' writing; count errors. Key two more 2' writings. Try to reduce errors with each writing.

A all letters   *gwam*   2'

Little things do contribute a lot to success in keying.   6 | 53
Take our work attitude, for example.   It's a little thing; yet,   12 | 59
it can make quite a lot of difference.   Demonstrating patience   18 | 66
with a job or a problem, rather than pressing much too hard for a   25 | 72
desired payoff, often brings better results than we expected.   31 | 79
Other "little things," such as wrist and finger position, how we   38 | 85
sit, size and location of copy, and lights, have meaning for   44 | 91
any person who wants to key well.   47 | 94

| 1 | 2 | 3 | 4 | 5 | 6 |

57c ● 10'

NEW FUNCTION

Merge/split cells

Cells can be joined or divided by selecting the cells and using the Merge or the Split command on the Table menu. Merge joins cells horizontally.

Drill 1

1. Create a 2-column, 4-row table.
2. Select Cells A1 and B1. From the Table menu, choose *Merge Cells*.
3. Select Cells B2, B3, and B4. From the Table menu, choose *Split Cells* and *Number of Columns: 2*.
4. Key the table as shown below.
5. Position the insertion point in the last cell (C4) and press TAB to add a row.
6. Add: **Service and supplies sales   82,385,023   91,404,573**

PRODUCT LINE SALES COMPARISON		
Product Line	**1999**	**2000**
Hardware sales	$180,485,284	$195,210,357
Software sales	136,947,201	128,794,203

9d ● 17'

Learn v and ' (apostrophe)
each line twice SS (slowly, then faster)

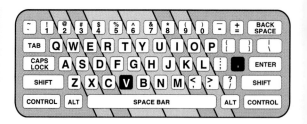

Apostrophe: The apostrophe shows (1) omission (as Rob't for Robert or it's for it is) or (2) possession when used with nouns (as Joe's hat).

v Reach *down* with *left first finger.*

' Reach to ' with *right fourth finger.*

v

20 v vf vf vie vie via via vim vat vow vile vale vote
21 vf vf ave vet ova eve vie dive five live have lave
22 cove dove over aver vivas hive volt five java jive

' (apostrophe)

23 '; '; it's it's Rod's; it's Bo's hat; we'll do it.
24 We don't know if it's Lee's pen or Norma's pencil.
25 It's ten o'clock; I won't tell him that he's late.

all reaches learned

26 It's Viv's turn to drive Iva's van to Ava's house.
27 Qua, not Vi, took the jet; so did Cal. Didn't he?
28 Wasn't Fae Baxter a judge at the post garden show?

29 I'd wear gloves to pack those boxes of quince jam.
30 Jacques Poll might fix the seven wrecked tugboats.
31 Two judges found ropes and fixed the broken limbs.

32 Quade quit squirting Quarla after quite a quarrel.
33 Most of them jammed the museum to see the mummies.
34 We walked to the window to watch as the wind blew.

9e ● 5'

Build skill
Key ¶ at an easy pace.
Repeat; try to increase speed.

```
                 •              4              •              8
We must be able to express our thoughts with ease
          12            •            16            •            20
if we desire to find success in the business world.
        •          24            •            28
It is there that sound ideas earn cash.
|  1  |  2  |  3  |  4  |  5  |  6  |  7  |  8  |  9  |  10  |
```

56c, *continued*

Document 3

1. Format as a table.
2. Right-align Column C.
3. Select the table and change line spacing to 1.5; adjust column width.
4. Shade the heading row 10%.
5. Center the table horizontally and vertically.

CANADIAN PROVINCES

Province	Capital	Population	
			4
			9
Alberta	Edmonton	2,375,300	15
British Columbia	Victoria	2,889,200	22
Manitoba	Winnipeg	1,071,250	28
New Brunswick	Fredericton	710,450	34
Newfoundland	St. John's	568,350	41
Northwest Territories	Yellowknife	52,250	49
Nova Scotia	Halifax	873,200	55
Ontario	Toronto	9,113,500	60
Prince Edward Island	Charlottetown	126,650	68
Quebec	Quebec	6,540,300	73
Saskatchewan	Regina	1,010,200	79
Yukon	Whitehorse	23,500	84

Document 4

1. Format as a table.
2. Select table; change spacing to 1.5 lines.
3. Adjust column width.
4. Center table vertically and horizontally.
5. Decimal-align Columns B and C.
6. Shade total row 10%.

March Expenses

Date	Hotel Charges	Other Expenses	
			3
			10
March 2-4	$ 350.97	$46.82	15
March 15-20	1,859.58	268.73	21
Total	$2,210.55	$315.55	25

56d ● 5'

S E L F ✔

c h e c k

Answer the True/False questions at the right to see if you have mastered the material presented in this lesson.

T F

1. To apply shading to cells, the cells to be shaded must be selected.

2. To align text at the decimal, select the column and set a decimal tab by clicking at the appropriate position on the Horizontal Ruler.

3. To center a table vertically on a page, position the insertion point on the page and use the options on the Format menu to center the page.

4. The Vertical Alignment box is located on the Margins tab of the Page Setup box.

5. The Shading feature can be accessed through Borders and Shading in the Format menu.

LESSON Z, Y, Quotation Mark, Tab

10a • 8'

GETTING started

each line twice SS

10b • 12'

Learn z and y
each line twice SS

z Reach *down* with *left fourth* finger.

y Reach *up* with *right first* finger.

10c • 10'

Practice specific keyreaches
each line twice SS; repeat troublesome lines

SKILLBUILDING WARMUP

all letters 1 Quill owed those back taxes after moving to Japan.

spacing 2 Didn't Vi, Sue, and Paul go?   Someone did; I know.

q/v/m 3 Marv was quite quick to remove that mauve lacquer.

easy 4 Lana is a neighbor; she owns a lake and an island.

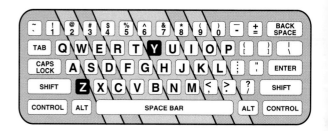

z

5 za za zap zap zing zig zag zoo zed zip zap zig zed

6 doze zeal zero haze jazz zone zinc zing size ozone

7 ooze maze doze zoom zarf zebus daze gaze faze adze

y

8 y yj yj jay jay hay hay lay nay say days eyes ayes

9 yj ye yet yen yes cry dry you rye sty your fry wry

10 ye yen bye yea coy yew dye yaw lye yap yak yon any

all reaches learned

11 Did you say Liz saw any yaks or zebus at your zoo?

12 Relax; Jake wouldn't acquire any favorable rights.

13 Has Mazie departed?   Tex, Lu, and I will go alone.

g 14 Is Gregg urging Gage to ship eggs to Ragged Gorge?

x 15 Dixi expects Bix to fix her tax bill on the sixth.

u 16 It is unusual to house unused units in the bunker.

b 17 Barb Robbes is the barber who bobbed her own hair.

p 18 Pepe prepared a pepper salad for a special supper.

FORMATTING

Document 1

1. Change the line spacing to 1.5 after keying the table. Adjust column width.
2. Shade the heading row 10%, center, and bold.
3. Center the table horizontally and vertically.
4. Set a decimal tab at approximate center of Columns B and C.

The dollar sign is included with the first figure of a column and with totals. To align the dollar sign, blank spaces may need to be inserted between the figure and the $ sign.

Use Center Page to center the table vertically. Choose *File*, *Page Setup*, *Layout* tab, *Vertical alignment*, *Center*. ■

FALL DRY CLEANING SPECIALS — 5

Garment	Regular Price	Special Price	
Wool sweater	$ 6.00	$ 4.75	18
Men's two-piece suit	6.00	4.75	24
Men's three-piece suit	7.25	5.50	31
Women's two-piece suit	5.50	4.25	37
Leather jacket	12.50	10.00	43
Slacks	2.25	1.75	46
Skirt	2.00	1.50	49
Blazer	3.50	2.00	53
Silk blouse	4.75	4.25	57

(heading row words: 13)

Document 2

1. After keying the table, select it and change the line spacing to 1.5; adjust column width.
2. Shade the Total row 10%.
3. Center the table horizontally and vertically.
4. Set a decimal tab at approximate center of Column C.

MILE-HIGH PASTRIES, INC. — 5

Item	Quantity	Price	
Blueberry muffins	3 dozen	$18.75	16
Dinner rolls	2 dozen	8.00	21
Whole wheat breadsticks	2 dozen	10.50	28
Brownies	1 dozen	7.50	33
Pastries	2 dozen	9.75	37
Total		$54.50	40

(heading row words: 9)

Learn " (quotation mark) and TAB
each line once

" Shift; then reach to " with *right fourth* finger.

TAB Reach up with *left fourth* finger.

" (quotation mark)

19 "; "; " " "lingo" "bugs" "tennies" I like "malts."
20 "I am not," she said, "going." I just said, "Oh?"

tab key

21   The tab key is used for indenting paragraphs and aligning columns.
22   Tabs that are set by the software are called default tabs, which are usually a half inch.

all reaches learned

23   The expression "I give you my word," or put
24 another way, "Take my word for it," is just a way I
25 can say, "I prize my name; it clearly stands in back
26 of my words." I offer "honor" as collateral.

Check speed
Take two 1' writings on ¶ 1.
Suggested goal: 15 *gwam*

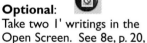

Optional:
Take two 1' writings in the Open Screen. See 8e, p. 20, for instructions if necessary.

    All of us work for progress, but it is not
always easy to analyze "progress." We work hard
for it; but, in spite of some really good efforts,
we may fail to receive just exactly the response we
want.

    When this happens, as it does to all of us,
it is time to cease whatever we are doing, have
a quiet talk with ourselves, and face up to the
questions about our limited progress. How can we
do better?

LESSON 56

Tables with Shading

56a • 6'

GETTING
started

each line 3 times SS; DS
between 3-line groups

SKILLBUILDING WARMUP

alphabet 1 Frank expected to solve a jigsaw puzzle more quickly than before.

figures 2 I moved from 1892 Oak Street, Apt. 3, to 7065 Oak Street, Apt. 4.

adjacent reaches 3 Pop walked to the hilltop when we were here last autumn with Guy.

easy 4 If I burn the signs, the odor of enamel may make a toxic problem.

| 1 | 2 | 3 | 4 | 5 | 6 | 7 | 8 | 9 | 10 | 11 | 12 | 13 |

56b • 10'

Shading
Read the information at the right; then format the table in the drill as shown.

To access the Help feature, click the **Office Assistant,** type your question, and then select *Search.* ■

Shading cells

For emphasis, shading can be applied to cells. Normally, shading is applied to emphasize headings, totals, or divisions or sections of a table.

To shade cells:

1. Select the cells to be shaded.

2. Click on **Borders and Shading** in the Format menu. The Borders and Shading dialog box displays.

3. Click on the Shading tab.

4. Click on the down arrow to change *Clear* to *20%* in the Style box.

5. Click **OK.**

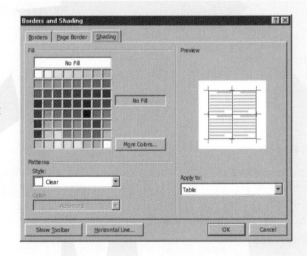

Drill
Key table as illustrated at the right.

Committee Member	Telephone Number
Christopher H. McMaster	(803) 555-3928
Eric W. Blankenship	(604) 555-1749

Keyboarding Mastery

GETTING started

each line twice SS
(slowly, then faster)

Improve keying techniques
each line once

Practice new reaches
each line once; repeat if you do not key the lines fluently

Work for smoothness, not for speed. ■

SKILLBUILDING WARMUP

alphabet 1 Max Jewel picked up five history quizzes to begin.
" (quote) 2 Can you spell "chaos," "bias," "bye," and "their"?
y 3 Ty Clay may envy you for any zany plays you write.
easy 4 She kept the fox, owls, and fowl down by the lake.
| 1 | 2 | 3 | 4 | 5 | 6 | 7 | 8 | 9 | 10 |

first row: keep hand movement to a minimum; pull fingers under

5 Can my cook, Mrs. Zackman, carve the big ox roast?
6 Did Cam, the cabby, have extra puzzles? Yes, one.

home row: use fingertips; keep fingers curved

7 Jack was sad; he had just lost his gold golf ball.
8 Sal was glad she had a flashlight; Al was as glad.

third row: straighten fingers slightly; do not move hands forward

9 Did Troy write to Terry Reppe? Did he quote Ruth?
10 Powers quit their outfit to try out for our troop.

11 za za zap az az maze zoo zip razz zed zax zoa zone
12 Liz Zahl saw Zoe feed the zebra in an Arizona zoo.

13 yj yj jy jy joy lay yaw say yes any yet my try you
14 Why do you say that today, Thursday, is my payday?

15 xs xs sax ox box fix hex ax lax fox taxi lox sixes
16 Roxy, you may ask Jay to fix any tax sets for you.

17 qa qa aqua quail quit quake quid equal quiet quart
18 Did Enrique quietly but quickly quell the quarrel?

19 fv fv five lives vow ova van eve avid vex vim void
20 Have Vivi, Vada, or Eva visited Vista Valley Farm?

55d, *continued*

Document 3
Key the table; adjust column widths as needed. Center the table horizontally.

OFFICIAL BIRDS AND FLOWERS
For Selected States

State	Official Bird	Official Flower	
Alaska	willow ptarmigan	forget-me-not	24
Arkansas	mockingbird	apple blossom	31
California	California valley quail	golden poppy	41
Connecticut	American robin	mountain laurel	49
Delaware	blue hen chicken	peach blossom	57
Georgia	brown thrasher	Cherokee rose	65
Idaho	mountain bluebird	syringa	71
Illinois	cardinal	native violet	78
Louisiana	eastern brown pelican	magnolia	88
Maryland	Baltimore oriole	black-eyed Susan	94
Massachusetts	chickadee	mayflower	101
Nebraska	western meadowlark	goldenrod	109
New Jersey	eastern goldfinch	purple violet	117
New Mexico	roadrunner	yucca	123
North Carolina	cardinal	dogwood	129

Header word counts: OFFICIAL BIRDS AND FLOWERS — 5; For Selected States — 9; State / Official Bird / Official Flower — 17.

VIEWS

on… **Dress**

Appropriate dress plays an important role in the impression an employee creates with clients, customers, and other employees. To help employees judge what is *appropriate*, many companies define (in written or unwritten fashion) attire for business and for special events or days. Often companies classify attire as *business*, *business casual*, or *casual attire*.

Business attire is the traditional, conservative clothing worn by professional employees. For men, business attire refers to a suit or a sport coat with coordinated slacks, a tie, and dress shoes. For women, business attire refers to a suit or tailored dress with dress shoes. Often a coordinated pants suit is acceptable.

Business casual connotes a more relaxed and less formal attire. For men, business casual refers to slacks, a shirt with a collar, and shoes with socks. Jeans, shorts, T-shirts, and sandals are not appropriate. For women, business casual usually refers to a comfortable dress, skirt and blouse, or a slacks set. "City shorts" (longer length with hose) are considered acceptable in most cases. Jeans, shorts, and T-shirts are not.

Casual attire refers to slacks, jeans, shorts, and other comfortable apparel worn to picnics and similar events. Good taste and a conservative approach are recommended, however.

Control service keys
each line once; DS between groups

enter: key smoothly without looking at fingers

21 Make the return snappily
22 and with assurance; keep
23 your eyes on your source
24 data; maintain a smooth,
25 constant pace as you key.

space bar: use down-and-in motion

26 us me it of he an by do go to us if or so am ah el
27 Have you a pen? If so, print "Free to any guest."

shift keys: use smooth shift-key-release motions

28 Juan Colon will see Lyle Branch in Oak Creek Park.
29 Mo, Lucy, and Sky left for New Orleans, Louisiana.

Check speed
Take two 1' writings.

Goal: 16 *gwam*

Optional:

1. Click the **Open Screen** button.
2. Key all ¶s once SS using wordwrap. Work for smooth, continuous stroking (not speed).
3. Save as **11e**.
4. Take a 1' timing on each ¶. Note your *gwam*.
5. **Optional:** Take a 2' writing on all ¶s. (To set the Timer, click **Variable** and enter **2** in the Minutes box.)

Copy difficulty

What factors determine whether copy is difficult or easy? Research shows that difficulty is influenced by syllables per word, characters per word, and percent of familiar words. Carefully controlling these three factors ensures that speed and accuracy scores are reliable—that is, increased scores reflect increased skill.

In Level 1, all timings are easy. Note "E" inside the triangle above the timing. Easy timings contain an average of 1.2 syllables per word, 5.1 characters per word, and 90 percent familiar words. Easy copy is suitable for the beginner who is mastering the keyboard.

E all letters   *gwam* 2'

```
              •             4          •             8
    Have  we  thought  of  communication  as  a  kind         4  31
    •              12          •             16
of war that we wage through each day?                         8  35

              •             4          •             8
    When  we  think  of  it  that  way,  good  language       12  39
    •              12          •             16          •
would  seem  to  become  our  major  line  of  attack.        17  44

              •             4          •             8
    Words  become  muscle;  in  a  normal  exchange  or  in   22  49
    •              12          •             16          •           20
a  quarrel,  we  do  well  to  realize  the  power  of  words. 27  54
```

FORMATTING

Adjust column widths and center table

1.5" top margins

Document 1

1. Key the table.
2. Select table; change line spacing to 1.5.
3. Select column heads in Row 1 and click **Bold** and **Center Align** buttons.
4. Using the mouse, adjust column widths to have about .5" of space between the text and border. (Your screen will look similar to the screen at right.)
5. Center the table horizontally.

COLLEGE SPORTS PROGRAM   5

Fall Events	Winter Events	Spring Events	
Football	Basketball	Golf	18
Soccer	Gymnastics	Baseball	23
Volleyball	Swimming	Softball	29

(13 — row 1)

Document 2

1. Format the table.
2. Bold and center headings.
3. Change line spacing to 1.5.
4. Adjust column widths to have equal space between the text and border.
5. Right-align Column C.
6. Center the table horizontally.

MAJOR METROPOLITAN AREAS OF CANADA   7

City	Province	Population	
Toronto	Ontario	3,427,250	17
Montreal	Quebec	2,921,375	22
Vancouver	British Columbia	1,380,750	30
Ottawa	Ontario	819,275	34
Winnipeg	Manitoba	625,325	40
Quebec	Quebec	603,275	44
Hamilton	Ontario	557,250	49

(12 — header row)

Review

12a ● 8'

GETTING
started

each line twice SS
(slowly, then faster)

alphabet 1 Which big market for quality jazz has Vi expanded?

q 2 Quin Racq quickly and quietly quelled the quarrel.

z 3 Zaret zipped along sizzling, zigzag Arizona roads.

easy 4 Can they handle the auditory problems of the city?
| 1 | 2 | 3 | 4 | 5 | 6 | 7 | 8 | 9 | 10 |

12b ● 12'

Practice new reaches

each line once; DS between
groups; work for smoothness,
not for speed

b/f 5 bf bf fab fab ball bib rf rf rib rib fibs bums bee

6 Did Buffy remember that he is a brass band member?

z/y 7 za za zag zig zip yj yj jay eye day lazy hazy zest

8 Liz amazed us with the zesty pizza on a lazy trip.

q/u 9 qa qa quo qt. quit quay quam quarm que uj jug quay

10 Where is Quito? Qatar? Boqueirao? Quebec? Quilmes?

v/m 11 vf vf valve five value mj mj ham mad mull mass vim

12 Vito, enter the words vim, vivace, and avar; save.

all 13 I faced defeat; only reserves saved my best crews.

14 In my opinion, I need to rest in my reserved seat.

all 15 Holly created a red poppy and deserves art awards.

16 My pump averages a faster rate; we get better oil.

12c ● 7'

Control service keys

each line once

enter: do not pause or look up to return

17 Successful keying is not just

18 a matter of speed; rather, it

19 is a combination of rapid and

20 slow, but constant, movements.

space bar: use correct spacing after each punctuation mark

21 Was it there? I saw it; Jan saw it, too. We did.

shift keys: depress shift key firmly; avoid pauses

22 Pam was in Spain in May; Bo Roy met her in Madrid.

Column width

You can also adjust column width by pointing to the column markers on the Horizontal Ruler and moving the markers to the right or left. ■

Adjust column widths

The columns of tables extend the full width of the margins. Often tables would be more attractive if the columns were narrower or if the table were centered horizontally on the page.

Column widths can be changed manually using the mouse or automatically using AutoFit. In this lesson, we'll use the mouse. Using the mouse allows you to adjust the width just as you like it. Before adjusting the width of a column, change the line spacing to 1.5. Once you change the overall width of the table, it will no longer be centered between margins. You must therefore center the table horizontally.

To adjust column width using the mouse:

1. Point to the column border between the first and second column in the table.

2. When the pointer changes to ←‖→, drag the border to the left to make the column narrower.

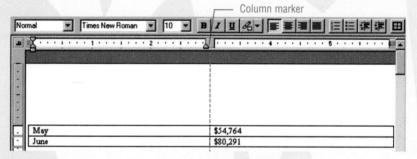

3. Adjust the column widths attractively to leave approximately the same amount of space between the text and the border in each column.

4. Adjust the width of the second column by dragging the right border to the left to leave about an inch between the text and the border.

To center a table horizontally:

1. With the insertion point in the table, choose *Table Properties* from the Table menu.

2. Click the **Table** tab, if necessary.

3. Choose the *Center* option in the Alignment box and click **OK**.

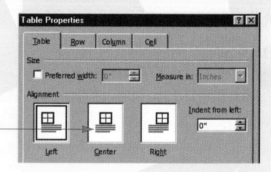

Drill

1. Create a 2-column, 2-row table.

2. Adjust column width; center table horizontally.

3. Change line spacing to 1.5. Save as **55c**.

| May | $54,764 |
| June | $80,291 |

Improve keystroking

each line once; work for smooth, unhurried keying

```
        23 ed fed led deed dell dead deal sled desk need seed
  de/ed
        24 Dell dealt with the deed before the dire deadline.

        25 old tolls doll solo look sole lost love cold stole
  ol/lo
        26 Old Ole looked for the long lost olive oil lotion.

        27 as say sad ask pass lass case said vase past salsa
  as/sa
        28 Ask the lass to pass the glass, saucers, and vase.

        29 pop top post rope pout port stop opal opera report
  op/po
        30 Stop to read the top opera opinion report to Opal.

        31 we few wet were went wears weather skews stew blew
  we/ew
        32 Working women wear sweaters when weather dictates.
```

Check speed

Take two 1' writings on ¶ 1.

Goal: 16 *gwam*

Optional:

1. Click the **Open Screen** button.
2. Key ¶s once SS using word-wrap. Work for smooth, continuous stroking (not speed).
3. Save as **12e**.
4. Take a 1' timing on ¶ 1. Save as **12e-t1**.
5. Take a 1' timing on ¶ 2. Save as **12e-t2**. Print the better 1' writing.
6. Set the Timer for 2'. Take a 2' writing on both ¶s. Print.

To determine gross-words-a-minute (*gwam*) rate for 2'

Follow these steps if you are *not* using the Timer in the Open Screen.

1. Note the figure at the end of the last line completed.
2. For a partial line, note the figure on the scale directly below the point at which you stopped keying.
3. Add these two figures to determine the total gross words a minute (*gwam*) you keyed.

 all letters   *gwam*   2'

```
              •                 4           •           8
     There should be no questions, no doubt, about       5 | 35
      •          12            •           16        •
the value of being able to key; it's just a matter      10 | 40
     20         •           24          •          28        •
of common sense that today a pencil is much too slow.   15 | 45

              •                 4           •           8
     Let me explain.  Work is done on a keyboard         19 | 49
      •          12            •           16        •
three to six times faster than other writing and       24 | 54
     20         •           24          •          28
with a product that is a prize to read.  Don't you      29 | 59
      •
agree?                                                   30 | 60
```
```
2' |      1      |      2      |      3      |      4      |      5      |
```

Adjusting Column Width

55a ● 6'

GETTING started

Key each pair of lines 3 times at a controlled rate SS. DS between 4-line groups.

2d finger
1 Dick Cen said he did kick Ike, but he did not intend to kick him.
2 Kami, Cedric, and Dick decided to check Dudley's new cedar cabin.

3d/4th fingers
3 Paul saw six-year-old Polly swallow a pepper plant last Saturday.
4 Zam said that Wallace will wash and wax all his old autos weekly.

| 1 | 2 | 3 | 4 | 5 | 6 | 7 | 8 | 9 | 10 | 11 | 12 | 13 |

55b ● 12'

SKILLBUILDING

Key one 3' and one 5' writing.
Goal: maintain good control

all letters

gwam 3' | 5'

	3'	5'
Something that you can never escape is your attitude.	4	2	44
It will be with you forever. However, you decide whether your	8	5	47
attitude is an asset or a liability for you. Your attitude	12	7	49
reflects the way you feel about the world you abide in and	16	9	52
everything that is a part of that world. It reflects the way you	20	12	54
feel about yourself, about your environment, and about other peo-	25	15	57
ple who are a part of your environment. Oftentimes, people with	29	17	59
a positive attitude are people who are extremely successful.	33	20	62
At times we all have experiences that cause us to be	36	22	64
negative. The difference between a positive and a negative per-	41	24	66
son is that the positive person rebounds very quickly from a bad	45	27	69
experience; the negative person does not. The positive person is	49	30	72
a person who usually looks on the bright side of things and	53	32	74
recognizes the world as a place of promise, hope, joy, excite-	58	35	77
ment, and purpose. A negative person generally has just the	62	37	79
opposite view of the world. Remember, others want to be around	66	40	82
those who are positive but tend to avoid those who are negative.	70	42	84

3' | 1 | 2 | 3 | 4 |
5' | 1 | 2 | 3 |

Review

Getting started

each line twice SS
(slowly, then faster)

SKILLBUILDING WARMUP

alphabet	1	Bev quickly hid two Japanese frogs in Mitzi's box.
shift	2	Jay Nadler, a Rotary Club member, wrote Mr. Coles.
, (comma)	3	Jay, Ed, and I paid for plates, knives, and forks.
easy	4	Did the amendment name a city auditor to the firm?

| 1 | 2 | 3 | 4 | 5 | 6 | 7 | 8 | 9 | 10 |

13b ● 10'

Practice response patterns

each line once SS

word-level response: key short, familiar words as units

5 is to for do an may work so it but an with them am
6 Did they mend the torn right half of their ensign?
7 Hand me the ivory tusk on the mantle by the bugle.

letter-level response: key more difficult words letter by letter

8 only state jolly zest oil verve join rate mop card
9 After defeat, look up; gaze in joy at a few stars.
10 We gazed at a plump beaver as it waded in my pool.

combination response: use variable speed; your fingers will let you feel the difference

11 it up so at for you may was but him work were they
12 It is up to you to get the best rate; do it right.
13 This is Lyn's only date to visit their great city.

| 1 | 2 | 3 | 4 | 5 | 6 | 7 | 8 | 9 | 10 |

13c ● 8'

Practice keyreaches

each line once; fingers well curved, wrists low; avoid punching keys with 3d and 4th fingers

p	14	Pat appears happy to pay for any supper I prepare.
x	15	Knox can relax; Alex gets a box of flax next week.
v	16	Vi, Ava, and Viv move ivy vines, leaves, or stems.
'	17	It's a question of whether they can't or won't go.
?	18	Did Jan go? Did she see Ray? Who paid? Did she?
.	19	Ms. E. K. Nu and Lt. B. A. Walz had the a.m. duty.
"	20	"Who are you?" he asked. "I am," I said, "Marie."
;	21	Find a car; try it; like it; work a price; buy it.

| 1 | 2 | 3 | 4 | 5 | 6 | 7 | 8 | 9 | 10 |

54d, *continued*

Document 4
Challenge
1. Open *54d-d3*.
2. Delete the memo heading.
3. Send the body of the memo as an e-mail to your instructor.

Document 5
1. 1.5" top margin; center and bold headings.
2. Use a decimal tab to align the numbers.
3. Save and print.

UNITED STATES DOLLAR TABLE

Rates from January 27, 1999

Foreign Currency	To United States Dollar	In United States Dollar	words
			6
			11
			16
			25
Australian Dollars	1.5941	0.6273	31
Austrian Schillings	11.9853	0.834	38
Belgian Francs	35.1362	0.0285	44
British Pounds	0.6066	1.6485	50
Greek Drachmas	280.0000	0.0036	56
Italian Lira	1686.4994	0.0006	62
Japanese Yen	115.6200	0.0086	68
Malaysian Ringgit	3.8000	0.2632	74
Portuguese Escudo	174.6207	0.0057	81
Singapore Dollars	1.6890	0.5921	87
South Korean Won	1176.0000	0.0009	94
Taiwan Dollars	32.3600	0.0309	100

13d ● 12'

Practice troublesome pairs

each line once; repeat if time permits

Keep hands and arms still as you reach up to the third row and down to the first row. ■

t 22 at fat hat sat to tip the that they fast last slat

r 23 or red try ran run air era fair rid ride trip trap

t/r 24 A trainer sprained an arm trying to tame the bear.

m 25 am me my mine jam man more most dome month minimum

n 26 no an now nine once net knee name ninth know never

m/n 27 Many men and women are important company managers.

o 28 on or to not now one oil toil over only solo today

i 29 it is in tie did fix his sit like with insist will

o/i 30 Joni will consider obtaining options to buy coins.

a 31 at an as art has and any case data haze tart smart

s 32 us as so say sat slap lass class just sassy simple

a/s 33 Disaster was averted as the steamer sailed to sea.

e 34 we he ear the key her hear chef desire where there

i 35 it is in tie did fix his sit like with insist will

e/i 36 An expression of gratitude for service is desired.

| 1 | 2 | 3 | 4 | 5 | 6 | 7 | 8 | 9 | 10 |

13e ● 12'

Check speed

Take two 1' writings on ¶ 1.

Goal: 16 gwam

Optional:
1. In the Open Screen, key the ¶s once SS.
2. Save as **13e**.
3. Take a 1' timing on ¶ 1. Save as **13e-t1**.
4. Take a 1' timing on ¶ 2. Save as **13e-t2**.
5. Print the better 1' writing.
6. Take a 2' writing on both ¶s. Start over if time permits.

all letters   gwam 2"

    •   4   •   8

The questions of time use are vital ones; we   5

  •   12   •   16

miss so much just because we don't plan.   9

         •   4   •   8

When we organize our days, we save time for   13

  •   12   •   16

those extra premium things we long to do.   17

2' | 1 | 2 | 3 | 4 | 5 |

SALES OF BOOKS BY LEE RICE

words

Document 1

1. Key the table with alignment and formatting as
shown.
2. Set decimal tab in Columns
C and D to cause the fig-
ures to appear centered
under the column heading.

Book Title	Publication	Amount of Sale	Unit Price	
Horrel Hill Adventures	1995	$138,769.00	$16.25	15
Tales of Tom's Creek	1998	92,761.00	8.95	25
Pommery Springs	1999	561,039.00	14.50	33

Book Title ... 5

Left-align   Center-align   Decimal-align   41

Document 2

1. Center and bold headings.
2. Use a decimal tab to align
the numbers.

MICROSOFT INVESTOR

4

Quotes for Current Date

9

Symbol	Name	Last	Chg	%Chg	
$INDU	Dow Jones Industrials Index	9,200.23	-124.35	-1.33%	26
XAX	Amex Composite Index	702.19	+0.83	+0.12%	34
COMP	Combined Composite Index	2,407.14	-26.27	-1.08%	44
SPX	S&P 500 Index	1,243.19	-9.12	-0.73%	52

Symbol ... 14

Source: Microsoft Network Home Page (msn.com)   61

Document 3
Memo with table

1. Key memo in proper
format.
2. Center and bold column
heads in table.
3. Center Columns A and C.

TO:	Eugene Fernando	4
FROM:	Lori Smith	8
DATE:	Current	12
SUBJECT:	Purchase Order 1522	18

The items that you requested on Purchase Order 1522 will be shipped to 32
you today. However, item #702 is currently backordered and is not expected 48
to be available for shipping for another six weeks. 58

We have the following similar cabinets currently in stock. Please let us know 74
if one of these cabinets would be a suitable replacement. We will ship the 88
cabinet to you the same day we receive your order. 98

Item Number	Description	Unit Price	
329	Lordusky locking cabinet	212.00	112
331	Anchorage heavy-duty locking cabinet	265.00	122
387	Lordusky locking cabinet (unassembled)	175.00	132

Item Number ... 105

xx   133

SKILLBUILDING WORKSHOP

Use the Open Screen for Workshop 1. Save each drill as a separate file.

Drill 1

Goal: reinforce key locations

Key each line at a comfortable, constant rate; check lines that need more practice; repeat those lines.

Keep
- your eyes on source copy
- your fingers curved, upright
- your wrists low, but not touching
- your elbows hanging loosely
- your feet flat on the floor

A We saw that Alan had an alabaster vase in Alabama.
B My rubber boat bobbed about in the bubbling brook.
C Ceci gave cups of cold cocoa to Rebecca and Rocco.
D Don's dad added a second deck to his old building.
E Even as Ellen edited her document, she ate dinner.
F Our firm in Buffalo has a staff of forty or fifty.
G Ginger is giving Greg the eggs she got from Helga.
H Hugh has eighty high, harsh lights he might flash.
I Irik's lack of initiative is irritating his coach.
J Judge J. J. Jore rejected Jeane and Jack's jargon.
K As a lark, Kirk kicked back a rock at Kim's kayak.
L Lucille is silly; she still likes lemon lollipops.
M Milt Mumm hammered a homer in the Miami home game.
N Ken Linn has gone hunting; Stan can begin canning.
O Jon Soto rode off to Otsego in an old Morgan auto.
P Philip helped pay the prize as my puppy hopped up.
Q Quiet Raquel quit quoting at an exquisite marquee.
R As Mrs. Kerr's motor roared, her red horse reared.
S Sissie lives in Mississippi; Lissa lives in Tulsa.
T Nat told Betty not to tattle on her little sister.
U Ula has a unique but prudish idea on unused units.
V Eva visited every vivid event for twelve evenings.
W We watched as wayworn wasps swarmed by the willow.
X Tex Cox waxed the next box for Xenia and Rex Knox.
Y Ty says you may stay with Fay for only sixty days.
Z Hazel is puzzled about the azure haze; Zack dozes.
alphabet Jacky and Max quickly fought over a sizable prawn.
alphabet Just by maximizing liquids, Chick Prew avoids flu.
| 1 | 2 | 3 | 4 | 5 | 6 | 7 | 8 | 9 | 10 |

54c, *continued*

To select a column, click the top border or grid-line. ■

To decimal-align text in a table:

1. Display the Horizontal Ruler (choose *Ruler* from the View menu).
2. Select column to be aligned.
3. Click the **Tab marker** at the far left of the Horizontal Ruler to change the type of tab to a decimal tab.
4. Click on the Horizontal Ruler to set a decimal tab at the desired point.

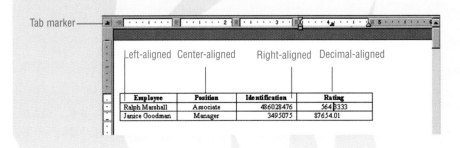

Tab marker

Left-aligned   Center-aligned   Right-aligned   Decimal-aligned

Drill 2

Just below the table you created in Drill 1, create a three-row, four-column table. Format the table as shown at the right.

Employee	Position	Identification	Rating
Ralph Marshall	Associate	486028476	564.3333
Janice Goodman	Manager	3495075	87654.01

Left-align   Center-align   Right-align   Decimal-tab

54d ● 25'

FORMATTING

Format tables

Review the guidelines for formatting tables. Then complete Documents 1-4 on pp. 157-158. Use 1.5" top margins.

Table format guides

Effective use of character formats and appropriate alignment improves the readability and appearance of tables. Character formats (e.g., bold) provide emphasis. Alignment positions the text within a cell for easy reading.

Main heading: Center; ALL CAPS; bold.

Secondary heading: Center; bold; DS below main heading; capitalize main words.

Column headings: Bold; capitalize main words; shade row (optional). Alignment: Generally center; however, headings may be left-, right-, or center-aligned.

Vertical placement: Use a top margin of 1.5" or center vertically on the page.

General: Use italic for publication titles. Use underlining only in tables without borders. Right-align whole numbers. Align decimal numbers at the decimal.

Tables within documents: DS above and below.

Drill 2

Goal: strengthen up and down reaches

Keep hands and wrists quiet; fingers well curved in home position; stretch fingers up from home or pull them palmward as needed.

home position

1 Hall left for Dallas; he is glad Jake fed his dog.
2 Ada had a glass flask; Jake had a sad jello salad.
3 Lana Hask had a sale; Gala shall add half a glass.

down reaches

4 Did my banker, Mr. Mavann, analyze my tax account?
5 Do they, Mr. Zack, expect a number of brave women?
6 Zach, check the menu; next, beckon the lazy valet.

up reaches

7 Prue truly lost the quote we wrote for our report.
8 Teresa quietly put her whole heart into her words.
9 There were two hilarious jokes in your quiet talk.

Drill 3

Goal: strengthen individual finger reaches

Rekey troublesome lines.

first finger

1 Bob Mugho hunted for five minutes for your number.
2 Juan hit the bright green turf with his five iron.
3 The frigates and gunboats fought mightily in Java.

second finger

4 Dick said the ice on the creek had surely cracked.
5 Even as we picnicked, I decided we needed to diet.
6 Kim, not Mickey, had rice with chicken for dinner.

third/fourth finger

7 Pam saw Roz wax an aqua auto as Lex sipped a cola.
8 Wally will quickly spell Zeus, Apollo, and Xerxes.
9 Who saw Polly? Zoe Pax saw her; she is quiet now.

Drill 4

Goal: strengthen special reaches

Emphasize smooth stroking. Avoid pauses, but do not reach for speed.

adjacent reaches

1 Falk knew well that her opinions of art were good.
2 Theresa answered her question; order was restored.
3 We join there and walk north to the western point.

direct reaches

4 Barb Nunn must hunt for my checks; she is in debt.
5 In June and December, Irvin hunts in Bryce Canyon.
6 We decided to carve a number of funny human faces.

double letters

7 Anne stopped off at school to see Bill Wiggs cook.
8 Edd has planned a small cookout for all the troop.
9 Keep adding to my assets all fees that will apply.

| 1 | 2 | 3 | 4 | 5 | 6 | 7 | 8 | 9 | 10 |

Format Tables

54a • 5'

GETTING started

Key entire drill working at a controlled rate. Repeat.

adjacent key
1 her err ire are cash said riot lion soil join went wean news
2 art try pew sort tree post upon copy opera maker waste three
3 sat coil riot were renew forth trade power grope owner score

one hand
4 him bear joy age kiln casts noun loop facet moon deter edges
5 ad null bar poll car upon deed jump ever look feed hill noon
6 get hilly are imply save phony taste union versa yummy wedge

balanced hand
7 aid go bid dish elan glen fury idle half jamb lend make name
8 oak pay hen quay rush such urus vial works yamen amble blame
9 cot duty goal envy focus handy ivory lapel oriel prowl queue

| 1 | 2 | 3 | 4 | 5 | 6 | 7 | 8 | 9 | 10 | 11 | 12 |

54b • 10'

SKILLBUILDING

1. Key three 1' guided writings; determine *gwam*.
2. Key two 2' writings; try to maintain your best 1' rate.

A all letters

gwam 1' 2'

	1'	2'
Good plans typically are required to execute most tasks	11	6 50
successfully. If a task is worth doing, it is worth investing	24	12 56
the time that is necessary to plan it effectively. Many people	37	18 62
are anxious to get started on a task and just begin before they	49	25 69
have thought about the best way to organize it. In the long run,	63	31 75
they frequently end up wasting time that could be spent more	75	37 81
profitably on important projects that they might prefer to tackle.	88	44 88

1' | 1 | 2 | 3 | 4 | 5 | 6 | 7 | 8 | 9 | 10 | 11 | 12 | 13 |
2' | 1 | 2 | 3 | 4 | 5 | 6 |

54c • 10'

Format cells

Read about formatting cells. Complete Drills 1 and 2 and save both as **54c**.

Drill 1

1. Create a 3-column, 3-row table.
2. Bold headings and align columns as shown.
3. Change line spacing to 1.5.

To format cells:

1. Select the cell or cells (columns or rows) to be formatted.
2. Click the appropriate button (**Bold, Italic, Underline, Center Align,** or **Right Align**) on the Formatting toolbar.

Employee	Position	Identification
Ralph Marshall	Associate	486028476
Janice Goodman	Manager	3495075

↑ Left-align   ↑ Center   ↑ Right-align

Drill 5

Goal: improve troublesome pairs

Use a controlled rate without pauses.

1 ad add did does dish down body dear dread dabs bad
d/k 2 kid ok kiss tuck wick risk rocks kayaks corks buck
3 Dirk asked Dick to kid Drake about the baked duck.

4 deed deal den led heed made needs delay he she her
e/i 5 kit kiss kiln kiwi kick kilt kind six ribs kill it
6 Abie had neither ice cream nor fried rice in Erie.

7 fib fob fab rib beg bug rob bad bar bed born table
b/v 8 vat vet gave five ever envy never visit weave ever
9 Did Harv key jibe or jive, TV or TB, robe or rove?

10 aft after lift gift sit tot the them tax tutu tyro
t/r 11 for far ere era risk rich rock rosy work were roof
12 In Toronto, Ruth told the truth about her artwork.

13 jug just jury judge juice unit hunt bonus quiz bug
u/y 14 jay joy lay you your only envy quay oily whey body
15 Willy usually does not buy your Yukon art in July.

Drill 6

Goal: build speed

Set the Timer for 1'.
Key each sentence for 1'. Try to complete each sentence twice (20 *gwam* or more). Ignore errors for now.

1 Dian may make cocoa for the girls when they visit.
2 Focus the lens for the right angle; fix the prism.
3 She may suspend work when she signs the torn form.
4 Augment their auto fuel in the keg by the autobus.
5 As usual, their robot did half turns to the right.
6 Pamela laughs as she signals to the big hairy dog.
7 Pay Vivian to fix the island for the eighty ducks.

| 1 | 2 | 3 | 4 | 5 | 6 | 7 | 8 | 9 | 10 |

	words	30"	20"

Drill 7

Goal: build speed

From the columns at the right, choose a *gwam* goal that is 2-3 words higher than your best rate. Set the Timer for **Variable** and then either **20"** or **30"**. Try to reach your goal.

	words	30"	20"
1 Did she make this turkey dish?		12	18
2 Blake and Laurie may go to Dubuque.		14	21
3 Signal for the oak sleigh to turn right.		16	24
4 I blame Susie; did she quench the only flame?		18	27
5 She turns the panel dials to make this robot work.		20	30

| 1 | 2 | 3 | 4 | 5 | 6 | 7 | 8 | 9 | 10 |

Document 3
1. Key the table.
2. Select the table; apply 1.5 spacing.

KEY PROJECT DATES

Architectural plans completed	November 15, 1999	13
Site engineering and preparation	December 12, 1999	23
Foundation and framing completed	January 18, 2000	33
Phase I construction completed	March 15, 2000	43
Phase II construction completed	May 6, 2000	51
Final construction completed	August 30, 2000	60

Document 4
1. Open *Pommery*; save as **53e-d6**.
2. Edit the table as marked.
3. Apply 1.5 spacing.

Position insertion point in last cell and press TAB to add a row.

POMMERY SPRINGS PROJECT STATUS   *Center and Bold*   6

Job	Description	Date Completed	
			12
Road work	Building and grading	February 10, 2000	22
Drain	Adding french drain	February 25, 2000	31
Lot prep *~aration* ^	Clearing and leveling	March 12, 2000	42
Pond	Adding silt fence	March 15, 2000 *(add row)*	49

53f ● 3'

S E L F ✓

c h e c k

Answer the True/False questions at the right to see if you have mastered the material presented in this lesson.

T F

1. Rows are labeled alphabetically from top to bottom.

2. To move to a previous cell in a table, press BACKSPACE.

3. The Insert menu is used to insert a table in a document.

4. Extra spacing can be added between rows by selecting the table and changing line spacing.

5. A cell is an intersection of a row and a column.

Drill 8

Goal: build staying power
1. Key each ¶ as a 1' timing.
2. Key a 2' timing on both ¶s.

all letters

These writings may be used as Diagnostic Writings.

Writing 1: **18 gwam**   gwam 2'

```
      •            4           •            8          •
Why spend weeks with some problem when just a few          5
      12           •           16          •
quiet minutes can help us to resolve it.                   9

      •            4           •            8          •
If we don't take time to think through a problem,          15
      12           •           16          •
it will swiftly begin to expand in size.                   18
```

Writing 2: **20 gwam**

```
      •            4           •            8          •
We push very hard in our quest for growth, and we          5
      12           •           16          •           20
all think that only excellent growth will pay off.         10

      •            4           •            8          •
Believe it or not, one can actually work much too          15
      12           •           16          •           20
hard, be much too zealous, and just miss the mark.         20
```

Writing 3: **22 gwam**

```
      •            4           •            8          •
A business friend once explained to me why he was          5
      12           •           16          •           20
often quite eager to be given some new project to          10
      •
work with.                                                 11

      •            4           •            8          •
My friend said that each new project means he has          16
      12           •           16          •           20
to organize and use the best of his knowledge and          21
      •
his skill.                                                 22
```

Writing 4: **24 gwam**

```
      •            4           •            8          •
Don't let new words get away from you.  Learn how          5
      12           •           16          •           20
to spell and pronounce new words and when and how          10
      •           24
finally to use them.                                       12

      •            4           •            8          •
A new word is a friend, but frequently more.  New          17
      12           •           16          •           20
words must be used lavishly to extend the size of          22
      •           24
your own word power.                                        24
```

```
2' |     1     |     2     |     3     |     4     |     5     |
```

**Adjust line spacing
in tables**

Tables are easier to read when extra spacing is placed between the rows. Change the line spacing on a table after the table is keyed.

1. Key the table.
2. Select the table, then choose *Paragraph* from the Format menu.
3. From the Indents and Spacing tab, select *1.5 Lines* in the Line spacing box and click **OK**.

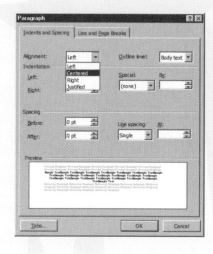

FORMATTING

Create tables
1.5" top margin on each table

Document 1
1. Center and bold the main heading; press ENTER twice. Change alignment to left below the heading.
2. Create a 2-column, 5-row table.
3. Key the table; press TAB to move from cell to cell.
4. Select the table and apply 1.5 spacing.

Document 2
1. Center and bold the main heading; press ENTER twice.
2. Create a 3-column, 6-row table.
3. Key the table.
4. Select the table and apply 1.5 spacing.

words

QUOTATION ON TIMBER PRICES — 5

Pine poles	$50.00 per ton	11
Pine saw timber	$36.50 per ton	17
Pine pulpwood	$8.50 per ton	22
Hardwood saw timber	$20.00 per ton	29
Hardwood pulpwood	$7.00 per ton	36

KEY CONTACTS FOR BUILDING PROJECT — 7

Lara G. Elkins	Architect	(555) 134-5867	15
James C. Weatherwax	Contractor	(555) 156-3190	24
Peggy R. Lancaster	Engineer	(555) 176-2480	33
Joanna B. Breckenridge	Site Supervisor	(555) 183-2164	43
Marshall C. Dinkins	Interior Designer	(555) 156-0937	54
Patrick R. Hinson	Kitchen Consultant	(555) 183-0926	64

Writing 5: **26** *gwam*   *gwam*   2'

We usually get best results when we know where we   5

are going. Just setting a few goals will help us   10

quietly see what we are doing.   13

Goals can help measure whether we are moving at a   18

good rate or dozing along. You can expect a goal   23

to help you find good results.   26

Writing 6: **28** *gwam*

To win whatever prizes we want from life, we must   5

plan to move carefully from this goal to the next   10

to get the maximum result from our work.   14

If we really want to become skilled in keying, we   19

must come to see that this desire will require of   24

us just a little patience and hard work.   28

Writing 7: **30** *gwam*

Am I an individual person? I'm sure I am; still,   5

in a much, much bigger sense, other people have a   10

major voice in thoughts I think and actions I take.   15

Although we are each a unique person, we all work   20

and play in organized groups of people who do not   25

expect us to dismiss their rules of law and order.   30

2' | 1 | 2 | 3 | 4 | 5 |

You can create and format tables automatically using word processing, spreadsheet, or database software. Word processing software offers advantages for creating tables with complex formatting; whereas, spreadsheet software works better for complex calculations. Database software provides powerful sorting and searching capabilities.

53c ● 10'

Create tables

Drill I

Create a 2-column, 5-row table.

Drill 2

Create a 4-column, 4-row table.

To select a table, click the insertion point in one of the cells. From the Table menu, choose *Select* and then *Table*. ▧

Create a table

You can create and format tables using several different methods. In this module, you will learn to create and format basic tables using the Table menu. You can specify the number of columns and rows in the table. *Word* will generate a table with columns of equal width spread across the writing line. (Note the default setting of AutoFit in the dialog box.)

1. From the Table menu, choose *Insert Table*. The Insert Table dialog box displays.
2. Click the spin arrows to change the number of rows and columns.
3. Click **OK** to display the table.

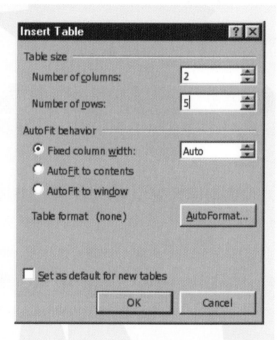

Move within a table

When a table is created, the insertion point is in Cell A1. To move in a table, use the arrow keys, the TAB key, or the mouse. Refer to this table as you learn to enter text in a table:

Press	Movement
TAB	To move to the next cell.
SHIFT + TAB	To move to a previous cell.
ENTER	To increase the height of the row. If you press ENTER by mistake, press BACKSPACE to delete the line.
TAB	To add a row, insertion point must be in the last cell.

FIGURE AND SYMBOL KEYS

OBJECTIVES

1. Key the numeric keys by touch.

2. Master selected symbol keys.

3. Develop a relaxed, confident attitude.

4. Apply correct number expression.

LESSON 14

1 and 8

14a ● 7'

GETTING started

each line twice SS

SKILLBUILDING WARMUP

alphabet	1	Jessie Quick believed the campaign frenzy would be exciting.
shift keys	2	L. K. Coe, M.D., hopes Dr. Lopez can leave for Maine in May.
3d row	3	We were quietly prepped to write two letters to Portia York.
easy	4	Kale's neighbor works with a tutor when they visit downtown.

| 1 | 2 | 3 | 4 | 5 | 6 | 7 | 8 | 9 | 10 | 11 | 12 |

14b ● 10'

SKILLBUILDING

Review high-frequency words

The words at the right are from the 100 most used words. Key each line once; work for fluency.

Top 100

5 a an it been copy for his this more no office please service

6 our service than the they up was work all any many thank had

7 business from I know made more not me new of some to program

8 such these two with your about and have like department year

9 by at on but do had in letter most now one please you should

10 their order like also appreciate that there gentlemen letter

11 be can each had information letter may make now only so that

12 them time use which am other been send to enclosed have will

---

TABLE BASICS

OBJECTIVES

1. Create tables using the Table function.

2. Format and edit tables and apply decimal tabs.

3. Improve speed and accuracy.

Module 7

LESSON 53

Create Tables

53a • 6'

GETTING started

each line 3 times SS; DS
between 3-line groups

SKILLBUILDING WARMUP

alphabet	1	Jim Ryan was able to liquefy frozen oxygen; he kept it very cold.
figures	2	Flight 483 left Troy at 9:57 a.m., arriving in Reno at 12:06 p.m.
direct reaches	3	My brother served as an umpire on that bright June day, no doubt.
easy	4	Ana's sorority works with vigor for the goals of the civic corps.

| 1 | 2 | 3 | 4 | 5 | 6 | 7 | 8 | 9 | 10 | 11 | 12 | 13 |

53b • 5'

NEW FUNCTION

Tables

Tables consist of columns and rows of data—either alphabetic, numeric, or a combination of both. Use correct terminology for the components of a table.

Column: Vertical list of information. Columns are labeled alphabetically from left to right.

Row: Information arranged horizontally. Rows are labeled numerically from top to bottom.

Cell: An intersection of a column and a row. Each cell has its own address consisting of the column letter and the row number.

	Column A	Column B	Column C
Row 1	Cell A1		
Row 2			Cell C2

Learn 1 and 8
each line once SS

Note: The digit "1" and the letter "l" have separate values on a computer keyboard. Do not interchange these characters.

1 Reach *up* with *left fourth* finger.

8 Reach *up* with *right second* finger.

SKILLBUILDING

Improve figure keyreaches
Control your reading speed; read only slightly ahead of what you are keying. Key each line once DS; repeat lines 23, 25, and 27.

SKILLBUILDING

Build skill
each sentence twice

Goals for 1':
14-15 *gwam*, acceptable
16-17 *gwam*, good
18-21 *gwam*, very good
  22+ *gwam*, excellent

Abbreviations
Do not space after a period within an abbreviation, as in Ph.D., U.S., C.O.D., a.m.

1

13 1 1a a1 1 1; 1 and a 1; 1 add 1; 1 aunt; 1 ace; 1 arm; 1 aye
14 1 and 11 and 111; 11 eggs; 11 vats; Set 11A; May 11; Item 11
15 The 11 aces of the 111th Corps each rated a salute at 1 p.m.

8

16 8 8k k8 8 8; 8 kits; ask 8; 8 kites; kick 8; 8 keys; spark 8
17 OK 88; 8 bags; 8 or 88; the 88th; 88 kegs; ask 88; order 888
18 Eight of the 88 cars score 8 or better on our Form 8 rating.

all figures learned

19 She did live at 818 Park, not 181 Park; or was it 181 Clark?
20 Put 1 with 8 to form 18; put 8 with 1 to form 81. Use 1881.
21 On May 1 at 8 a.m., 18 men and 18 women left Gate 8 for Rio.

22 The 188 men in 8 boats left Docks 1 and 18 at 1 p.m., May 1.

23 *On August 18, I saw 81 mares and 18 foals in fields 1 and 8.*

24 The 8 boxes on Pier 1 left on Ship 18 at 8 p.m. on March 11.

25 *Jane and Paul are 18; Sean and Harry are 81; Jake is now 18.*

26 Our 188 trucks moved 1881 tons on August 18 and December 18.

27 *Send Mary 181 No. 188 panes for her home at 8118 Oak Street.*

28 Did their form entitle them to the land?
29 Did the men in the field signal for us to go?
30 I may pay for the antique bowls when I go to town.
31 The auditor did the work right, so he risks no penalty.
32 The man by the big bush did signal us to turn down the lane.

| 1 | 2 | 3 | 4 | 5 | 6 | 7 | 8 | 9 | 10 | 11 | 12 |

Activity eight

Explore search engines

The World Wide Web contains millions of pages of information and is growing rapidly. Search engines are used to locate specific information. Just a few examples of search engines are AltaVista, Excite, Infoseek, Dogpile, Metacrawler, LookSmart, Lycos, and Yahoo!.

To go to a search engine, click on the Search or Net Search button on your Web browser. (**Note:** *Web browsers will vary.*)

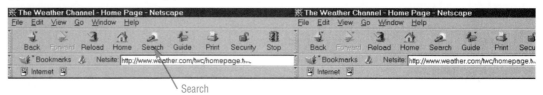

Search

Practice

1. Click the **Search** button in your Web browser. This will bring up a screen that shows several different search engines. Click the first search engine. Browse the hyperlinks available (i.e., Maps, People Finder, News, Weather, Stock Quotes, Sports, Games, etc.).

2. Click each search engine and explore the hyperlinks.

3. Conduct the following search using Dogpile, a multi-threaded search engine that searches multiple databases:
   a. Open the Web site for Dogpile (http://www.dogpile.com).
   b. In the Search entry box, key the keywords **American Psychological Association publications**; click **Fetch**.

Activity nine

Search Yellow Pages

Searching the Yellow Pages for information on businesses and services is commonplace, both in business and at home. Get your computer do the searching for you the next time. Several search engines provide a convenient hyperlink to the Yellow Pages.

Practice

1. Click the **Search** button in your Web browser. Browse the search engines to locate the hyperlinks for the Yellow Pages; click to open this valuable site.

2. Determine a city that you would like to visit. Assume you will need overnight accommodations. Use the Yellow Pages to find a listing of hotels in this city.

3. Your best friend lives in (*you provide the city*); you want to send him/her flowers. Find a listing of florists in this city.

4. You create a third scenario and find listings.

LESSON 15

5 and 0

15a ● 7'

GETTING started

For a series of capital letters press CAPS LOCK with the left little finger. Press again to release.

15b ● 7'

SKILLBUILDING

Improve response patterns

each line once SS; repeat if time permits

alphabet 1 John Quigley packed the zinnias in twelve large, firm boxes.

1/8 2 Idle Motor 18 at 8 mph and Motor 81 at 8 mph; avoid Motor 1.

caps lock 3 Lily read BLITHE SPIRIT by Noel Coward. I read VANITY FAIR.

easy 4 Did they fix the problem of the torn panel and worn element?

| 1 | 2 | 3 | 4 | 5 | 6 | 7 | 8 | 9 | 10 | 11 | 12 |

word response: read word by word

5 el id la or by doe so am is go us it an me ox he of to if ah

6 Did the air corps hang a map of the glens on the big island?

stroke response: read stroke by stroke

7 up you be was in at on as oh are no ad pop fad pun cad hi ax

8 Face bare facts, we beg you; read a free tract on star wars.

combination response: vary speed but maintain rhythm

9 be a duty|as junk|to form|at rest|of corn|do work|he read it

10 Doria paid the taxes on six acres of rich lake land in Ohio.

15c ● 12'

Learn 5 and 0

each line twice SS

5 Reach *up* with *left first* finger.

0 Reach *up* with *right fourth* finger.

5

11 5 5f f5 5 5; 5 fans; 5 feet; 5 figs; 5 fobs; 5 furs; 5 flaws

12 5 o'clock; 5 a.m.; 5 p.m.; is 55 or less; buy 55; 5 and 5 is

13 Call Line 555 if 5 fans or 5 bins arrive at Pier 5 by 5 p.m.

0

14 0 0; ;0 0 0; skip 0; plan 0; left 0; is below 0; I scored 0;

15 0 degrees; key 0 and 0; write 00 here; the total is 0 or 00;

16 She laughed at their 0 to 0 score; but ours was 0 to 0 also.

all figures learned

17 I keyed 550 pages for Invoice 05, or 50 more than we needed.

18 Pages 15 and 18 of the program listed 150, not 180, members.

19 On May 10, Rick drove 500 miles to New Mexico in car No. 08.

MODULE 6 ✓ checkpoint

Objective Assessment

Answer the questions below to see if you have mastered the content of this module.

1. The _____ command is used to delete blocks of text that are no longer needed. To place the deleted text in another location, simply click the _____ button.

2. The _____ command is used to repeat text from one location to another. To place the repeated text in the new location, simply click the _____ button.

3. To set margins, choose _____ from the _____ menu.

4. You have just added bold to text; now you have decided to delete the bold. You could click the Bold button or you could click the _____ button to reverse this recent action.

5. When copying selected text using Drag-and-Drop Editing, press and hold the _____ key; then drag and drop the text in the desired location.

6. Use _____ -point font for main headings.

7. Margins for unbound reports are _____ side margins, _____ top margin (first page), _____ top margin (second page), and _____ bottom margin.

8. Margins for leftbound reports are _____ side margins, _____ top margin (first page), _____ top margin (second page), and _____ bottom margin.

9. The _____ format displays the first line of text at the left margin and all other lines are indented to the first tab.

10. To number pages of a multipage report, choose _____ from the _____ menu.

11. To prevent a single line of a paragraph from printing at the bottom or top of a page, apply _____.

12. Use the _____ command to prevent a side heading from appearing alone at the bottom of the page.

13. Quotations of _____ or more lines should be _____ -spaced and indented from the _____. Click the _____ button to indent a quotation.

14. To center the title page vertically, choose the _____ tab from the _____ dialog box. Choose _____ in the Vertical Alignment box.

15. When formatting the title page for a leftbound report, use _____ left margin and _____ right margin.

Performance Assessment

Unbound report
1. Open *checkpt6*.
2. Make the necessary changes to convert it to a DS, unbound report.
3. Insert the ¶ at the right between ¶ 1 and ¶ 2.
4. Prepare a title page for **Altman Corporation**. Prepared by **Jason T. Forrest**.

A complete proposal is attached. The proposal includes the cost justification, the procurement alternatives; and the specifications of the system recommended. A brochure describing the system recommended is also attached.

15d ● 5'

Improve figure keyreaches

Work to avoid pauses; each line once DS; repeat lines 21 and 23.

20 After May 18, French 050 meets in Room 185 at 10 a.m. daily.

21 *Read pages 5 and 8; duplicate page 18; omit pages 50 and 51.*

22 We have Model 80 with 10 meters or Model 180 with 15 meters.

23 *Between 8 and 10 that night, 5 of us drove to 580 Park Lane.*

24 Flight 508 left Reno at 1 on May 10; it landed in Lima at 8.

15e ● 9'

SKILLBUILDING

Improve technique

Reach up or down without moving your hands; each line once; repeat drill.

direct reaches

25 fr ki aq lo sw ;p de ju bg ,k xs mj za .l cd njy cde mju xsw

26 za mj cd .l xs ,k vf jp xs jy bg ,ki zaq .lo xsw mjy cde juj

27 Decide before long the freedom needed to justify the switch.

adjacent reaches

28 as oil red ask wet opt mop try tree open shred operas treaty

29 were pore dirt stew ruin faster onion alumni dreary mnemonic

30 The opened red hydrants were powerful, fast, and very dirty.

outside reaches

31 pop zap cap zag wasp equip lazy zippers queue opinion quartz

32 zest waste paper exist parquet azalea acquaint apollo apathy

33 The lazy wasp passed the potted azalea on the parquet floor.

15f ● 10'

SKILLBUILDING

Build skill

Key ¶ 2 twice for 1'. Try to increase speed by 2 words the second time.

Optional:

1. Click the **Open Screen** button.
2. Take two 1' writings on ¶ 2. Note your *gwam.*
3. Take two 1' writings on ¶ 1. Try to equal ¶ 2 rate.
4. Take one 2' writing on both ¶s.

all letters/figures   *gwam*   2' | 3'

•   4   •   8   •

I thought about Harry and how he had worked for me for   6 | 4

12   •   16   •   20   •

10 years; how daily at 8 he parked his worn car in the lot;   12 | 8

24   •   28   •   32   •

then, he left at 5.   Every day was almost identical for him.   18 | 12

•   4   •   8   •

In a quiet way, he did his job well, asking for little   23 | 15

12   •   16   •   20   •

attention. So I never recognized his thirst for travel. I   29 | 19

24   •   28   •   32   •

didn't expect to find all of those maps near his workplace.   35 | 23

2' | 1 | 2 | 3 | 4 | 5 | 6 |
3' | 1 | 2 | 3 | 4 |

words

UNTAPPED RESOURCES

Document 1
Leftbound report with references

1. Format the report DS.
2. Number the pages correctly.
3. On the text Americans with Disabilities Act (¶4), insert a hyperlink to http://www.civilrights.com/disability.html.
4. Save as **52c-d1**.

Document 2
Unbound report

1. Open *present.* Save as **52c-d2**.
2. Convert this leftbound report to an unbound report; DS.
3. Format main, side, and paragraph headings correctly. Be alert to a widow line on page 1.
4. Insert Page Number command.

Document 3
Title page for leftbound report

Prepare a title page for Document 1.

1. Assume the report was prepared for **Ms. Leslie Chafee** and prepared by **Julian Houser, Project Director.**
2. Use the current date.

Directors of company personnel have important responsibilities, 17
among the most important being the acquisition of dedicated, conscien- 31
tious workers to carry out the daily functions of our businesses. 44

Staff Resources 47

Generally, we each have developed our own sources, which range 60
from local educational institutions, through employment offices, news- 74
papers, and on down to walk-ins, from which we find new employees. 87
But we always welcome new sources. 95

One supply often overlooked--though not by the more ingenious of 108
us--is the pool of available workers who have one or more noticeable or 122
definable "disabilities" or "handicaps." Occasionally, a supply of these 137
potential workers will go untapped in an area for a long period of time; 151
when discovered, they become a genuine treasure trove for a wide variety 166
of jobs. 168

Performance Level 172

Since the passage of the Americans with Disabilities Act in 1990, 185
studies have shown that disabled workers, while perhaps restricted 198
to the exact jobs they can do, perform well above the minimum require- 212
ments on jobs not beyond their capabilities. Limitations vary with 226
individuals; but once reasonable accommodations are made, these workers 240
become uniquely qualified employees. 248

Abrahms, writing of the reluctance of some employers to hire 260
handicapped workers, says that "workers with handicaps have high 273
rates of production, often higher than those achieved by other workers" 288
(Abrahms, 1998, 61). Munoz goes one step further by reminding us that 302
disabled workers "have high work-safety histories with low job-changing 316
and absentee records" (Munoz, 1999, 37). 325

From a practical as well as a personal point of view, then, hiring 338
workers who are physically or mentally handicapped can provide a 351
positive occupational impact for a company as well as a very rewarding 365
experience for its human resource director. One such director says: 379

Recently, I told a potential employee who was sitting in my 391
office in her wheelchair of our success with handicapped workers. 405
"That's great," she said. "You know, most of us rarely think about 418
things we can't do. There are too many things we can do and can 431
do well." I hired her (Belli, 1999, 78). 440

And so say all of us who sit in the employer's chair. 451

REFERENCES 453

Abrahms, Hollin C. "Searching for Employees." *The Human Services* 467
Monthly, January 1998, pp. 61-68. 474

Belli, L. R. "An Investment in Social Action." *Human Resources Quarterly.* 489
1999. <http://www.sainc.org/article/> (20 April 1999). 500

Munoz, Hector. "Changing Aspects of the American Workforce at the Close 515
of the Twentieth Century." *National Vo-Tech News,* May 1999, pp. 15-37. 529

LESSON 16

2 and 7

16a ● 7'

GETTING started

each line twice SS

16b ● 14'

Learn 2 and 7

each line twice SS

2 Reach *up* with *left third* finger.

7 Reach *up* with *right first* finger.

16c ● 5'

SKILLBUILDING

Improve keying techniques

fingers curved, wrists low; each line once; repeat as time permits

SKILLBUILDING WARMUP

alphabet 1 Perry might know I feel jinxed because I have missed a quiz.
figures 2 Channels 5 and 8, on from 10 to 11, said Luisa's IQ was 150.
caps lock 3 Ella Hill will see Chekhov's THE CHERRY ORCHARD on Czech TV.
easy 4 The big dog by the bush kept the ducks and hen in the field.
   | 1 | 2 | 3 | 4 | 5 | 6 | 7 | 8 | 9 | 10 | 11 | 12 |

2

5 2 2s s2 2 2; has 2 sons; is 2 sizes; was 2 sites; has 2 skis
6 add 2 and 2; 2 sets of 2; catch 22; as 2 of the 22; 222 Main
7 Exactly at 2 on August 22, the 22d Company left from Pier 2.

7

8 7 7j j7 7 7; 7 jets; 7 jeans; 7 jays; 7 jobs; 7 jars; 7 jaws
9 ask for 7; buy 7; 77 years; June 7; take any 7; deny 77 boys
10 From May 7 on, all 77 men will live at 777 East 77th Street.

all figures learned

11 I read 2 of the 72 books, Ellis read 7, and Han read all 72.
12 Tract 27 cites the date as 1850; Tract 170 says it was 1852.
13 You can take Flight 850 on January 12; I'll take Flight 705.

caps lock

14 Our OPERATOR'S HANDBOOK says to use either AC or DC current.

adjacent reaches

15 He said that poised talk has triumphed over violent actions.

direct reaches

16 Murvyn must not make any decisions until Brad has his lunch.

double letters

17 He will tell all three cooks to add a little whipped butter.

combination

18 Kris started to blend a cocoa beverage for a shaken cowhand.

52

Assessment

52a ● 7'

GETTING started

each line 3 times SS (work for fewer than 3 errors per group); DS between 3-line groups

SKILLBUILDING WARMUP

alphabet 1 Jacki might analyze the data by answering five complex questions.

figures 2 Memo 67 asks if the report on Bill 35-48 is due the 19th or 20th.

double letters 3 Aaron took accounting lessons at a community college last summer.

easy 4 Hand Bob a bit of cocoa, a pan of cod, an apricot, and six clams.

| 1 | 2 | 3 | 4 | 5 | 6 | 7 | 8 | 9 | 10 | 11 | 12 | 13 |

52b ● 10'

SKILLBUILDING

Assess straight-copy skill

1. Key one 3' writing.
2. Key one 5' writing.

all letters

gwam 3' 5'

		3'	5'
Subtle differences exist among role models, mentors, and		4	2 32
sponsors. A role model is a person you can emulate, or one who		8	5 35
provides a good example to follow. A mentor is one who will		12	7 37
advise, coach, or guide you when you need information about your		16	10 40
job or your organization. A sponsor is a person who will support		21	12 42
you or recommend you for a position or a new responsibility.		25	15 45
One person may fill all three roles, or several people may		30	18 48
serve as role models, mentors, or sponsors. These individuals		34	20 50
usually have higher ranks than you do, which means they will be		38	23 53
able to get information that you and your peers may not have.		42	25 55
Frequently, a mentor will share information with you that will		46	28 58
enable you to make good decisions about your career.		50	30 60

3' | 1 | 2 | 3 | 4 |
5' | 1 | 2 | 3 |

52c ● 33'

Assessment: Unbound and leftbound reports and title page

Time schedule

Planning time . . . . 3'
Timed production . . . . . 25'
Final check; proofread;
  determine g-*pram* . . . . . 5'

1. Organize your desktop.
2. On the signal to begin, key the documents in sequence. Check spelling after keying each document. Preview before printing.

3. Proofread all documents; count errors; determine g-*pram*.

$$\text{g-}pram = \frac{\text{total words keyed}}{25'}$$

Improve figure reaches
each line twice; DS between
2-line groups

19 Both towns bid for six bushels of produce down by the docks.

20 *The cowl of the formal gown is held down by a bow.*

21 I work 18 visual signals with 2 turns of the lens.

22 Did he fix the shape of the hand and elbow of the clay form?

23 *The ivy bowl is a memento of their visit to Japan.*

24 Did 7 of them fix the signals for the 50 bicycles?

16e ● 10'

SKILLBUILDING

Review high-frequency words
The words at the right are
from the 200 most used
words. Key each line once;
work for fluency.

Top 200

25 above again before call cost day feel further good how get

26 line meet opportunity per possible report since take today

27 account amount before check could sure hope cost used give

28 days find future help however its mail might every because

29 percent present request see special then through necessary

30 under well additional area being city could due get number

31 help insurance just mail month need plan interested return

32 state those upon what after complete present wish same its

33 available best course during form hope interest let matter

34 materials much next people policy prices receives possible

35 school want forward above into information letters however

16f ● 5'

SKILLBUILDING

Reach for new goals
Key each line twice. Work to
increase your speed by 2
words the second time.

	30"	20"
36 If they wish, she may make the form for the disks.	20	30
37 Did the chap focus the lens on the airy downtown signs?	22	33
38 The formal gowns worn by the girls hang in the civic chapel.	24	36
39 Di paid us to go to town to bid for an authentic enamel owl.	26	39
40 Busy firms burn coal; odor is a key problem in the city air.	28	42

51e ●

Leftbound report with references

Document 1
Challenge Activity

1. Open *reference* and format the report as a leftbound report; DS. Make the revisions as shown. Refer to p. 55 for proofreaders' marks.

2. Insert the following side headings:

   The First Step
   after ¶ 1

   The Correct Style
   after ¶ 2

   The Finished Product
   after ¶ 3

3. Format all headings correctly.

4. Insert page number; do not print on the first page.

5. Format references using hanging indent and italicize book titles. Be sure to check for widow/orphan lines.

6. In the reference section, create hyperlink to American Psychological Association (http://www.apa.org/publications/). Be sure to check for widow/orphan lines.

Document 2

1. Prepare a title page for:
   Dr. Mary E. Compton, Business Communication Instructor, Holcombe Community College.

2. Assume the paper was prepared by **Skyler Atencio**. Use current date.

Optional: Place border with shading on title page.

Basic Steps in Report Writing   6

the effective writer makes certain that reports that   17
leave her or his desk are technically usable in content,   24
correct in style, and attractive in format.   37

Information is gathered about the subject; the effective   51
writer takes time to outline the data to be used in the report. 64
This approach allows the writer to establish the organization of 77
the report. When a topic outline is used order of presenta- 90
tion, important points, and even various headings can be deter- 102
mined and followed easily when writing begins.   112

The purpose of the report often determines it's style.   126
Most academic reports (term papers, for example) are double- 138
spaced with indented paragraphs. Most business reports, how- 151
ever, are single-spaced, and paragraphs are blocked.   161

When a style is not stipulated, general usage may be   172
followed. The most capable writer will refrain from making   188
a report deliberately *impressive*, especially if doing so   200
makes it less *expressive*.   205

follow the outline. The writer does, however, follow   216
the outline carefully as a first draft is written. Obvious   228
error are ignored momentarily.   234

edit the draft. Refinement comes later, after all the   245
preliminary work is done. The finished product will then be 257
read and reread to ensure it is clear, concise correct, and   289
complete. Effective writers use the on line thesaurus, and   300
spelling tool of the software. In addition, they will keep
in easy reach an up-to-date desk reference and manuscript
style manual. Examples of these resources is listed in the   309
reference section below.   315

References   317

Publication Manual of the American Psychological   328
Association. 4th ed. Washington, D.C.: American   336
Psychological Association, 1999.   343

"APA-Style Helper." Version 1.0. <http://www.apa.org/   354
apa-style/> (22 Dec. 1998).   360

Fowler, H. Ramsey. The Little, Brown Handbook. 2nd ed.   372
Boston, MA: Little, Brown and Company, 1998.   380

17a ● 7'

GETTING started

each line twice

alphabet 1 Bob realized very quickly that jumping was excellent for us.

figures 2 Has each of the 18 clerks now corrected Item 501 on page 27?

space bar 3 Was it Mary? Helen? Pam? It was a woman; I saw one of them.

easy 4 The men paid their own firms for the eight big enamel signs.
| 1 | 2 | 3 | 4 | 5 | 6 | 7 | 8 | 9 | 10 | 11 | 12 |

17b ● 14'

Learn 4 and 9

each line twice SS

4 Reach *up* with *left first* finger.

9 Reach *up* with *right third* finger.

4

5 4 4f f4 4 4 4; if 4 furs; off 4 floors; gaff 4 fish; 4 flags
6 44th floor; half of 44; 4 walked 44 flights; 4 girls; 4 boys
7 I order exactly 44 bagels, 4 cakes, and 4 pies before 4 a.m.

9

8 9 9l l9 9 9 9; fill 9 lugs; call 9 lads; Bill 9 lost; dial 9
9 also 9 oaks; roll 9 loaves; 9.9 degrees; sell 9 oaks; Hall 9
10 Just 9 couples, 9 men and 9 women, left at 9 on our Tour 99.

all figures learned

11 Memo 94 says 9 pads, 4 pens, and 4 ribbons were sent July 9.
12 Study Item 17 and Item 28 on page 40 and Item 59 on page 49.
13 Within 17 months he drove 85 miles, walked 29, and flew 490.

17c ● 5'

SKILLBUILDING

Improve figure keyreaches

each line twice; DS between 2-line groups

14 My staff of *18* worked *11* hours a day from May *27* to June *12*.

15 There were *5* items tested by Inspector *7* at *4* p.m. on May *8*.

16 Please send her File *10* today at *8*; her access number is *97*.

17 Car *47* had its trial run. The qualifying speed was *198* mph.

18 The estimated score? *485*. Actual? *190*. Difference? *295*.

Drill 1

1. Open *Hyperlink* (shown below). Save as **51d-d1**.
2. Create hyperlinked text to a file:
   a. Select the text *50d* in the left column of the table; click the **Insert Hyperlink** button.
   b. Click **Browse for File**. Locate 50d created in Lesson 50; click **OK.**
3. Repeat Steps 2a-b for *College Comparison.xls*, an *Excel* file saved on formatting template.
4. Create hyperlinked text to a Web page:
   a. Select the text *South-Western's College Keyboarding*; click the **Insert Hyperlink** button.
   b. Key **http://www.swep.com/keyboarding/index.html** as the Web page name; click **OK.**
5. Create hyperlinked object to a Web page:
   a. Select the picture of the sun; click the **Insert Hyperlink** button.
   b. Key **http://www.weather.com** in the entry box. Click **OK.**
6. Create hyperlink to your favorite Web page; follow instructions shown in file.

HYPERLINK ACTIVITY

Hyperlinks are an easy way to send online readers to other files and to Web pages. Create the following hyperlinks in the table below.

Files/Web Pages	Hyperlink
50d	This hyperlink is to the Word file (50d) that you created in Lesson 50. Use *Browse for File* to locate this file.
College Comparison.xls	Hyperlink to Excel file saved on formatting template (College Comparison.xls). Use *Browse for File* to locate this file.
South-Western's *College Keyboarding*	Hyperlink to Web page. Key http://www.swep.com/keyboarding/index.html.
	Hyperlink to Web Page. Select image. Key http://www.weather.com.
My Favorite Web Site	Hyperlink to Web Page. Use *Browse for Web Page* to locate your favorite Web page. When Web site is located, use taskbar to return to this document; the Web address you selected will display.

Step 2-3 Document link

Step 4 Web link

Step 5 Object link

Step 6

Drill 2

1. Open *51c-d1* and save it as **51d-d2**.
2. Add the following sentence in Paragraph 4; key the name of your student organization and create a hyperlink to its Web page.

Visit the Web page of Student's Organization (insert hyperlink) to review its benefit.

17d ● 10'

SKILLBUILDING

Improve keying technique

key smoothly; strike the keys at a brisk, steady pace

first finger

19 buy them gray vent guy brunt buy brunch much give huge vying
20 Hagen, after her July triumph at tennis, may try volleyball.
21 Verna urges us to buy yet another of her beautiful rag rugs.

second finger

22 keen idea; kick it back; ice breaker; decide the issue; cite
23 Did Dick ask Cecelia, his sister, if she decided to like me?
24 Suddenly, Micki's bike skidded on the Cedar Street ice rink.

third/fourth finger

25 low slow lax solo wax zip zap quips quiz zipper prior icicle
26 Paula has always allowed us to relax at La Paz and at Quito.
27 Please ask Zale to explain who explores most aquatic slopes.

17e ● 14'

SKILLBUILDING

Reach for new goals

1. Key each ¶ in the Open Screen for a 1' writing. Save the timings; print the best one.

2. Set the Timer for **2'**. Take two 2' writings on all ¶s. Reach for a speed within 2 words of 1' *gwam*. Save both timings; print the best one.

3. Take a 3' writing on all ¶s. Reach for a speed within 4 words of 1' *gwam*. Print.

A all letters   *gwam* 2' | 3'

We consider nature to be limited to those things, such   6 | 4
as air or trees, that we humans do not or cannot make.   11 | 7

For most of us, nature just exists, just is. We don't   17 | 11
question it or, perhaps, realize how vital it is to us.   22 | 15

Do I need nature, and does nature need me? I'm really   28 | 19
part of nature; thus, what happens to it happens to me.   33 | 22

2' | 1   2   3   4   5   6
3' | 1   2   3   4

LESSON 17   4 AND 9   43

Hyperlinks

Hyperlinks allow the online reader to view the contents of another file or a Web page without leaving the *Word* document. It is easy to recognize a hyperlink because hyperlinked text is displayed in another color. Images such as clipart, charts, and other graphics, may contain a hyperlink to another document. When the mouse is pointed at a hyperlink, a pointing hand displays. To go to the hyperlinked document, just click on the hyperlinked text or object.

Some advantages of creating hyperlinks are (1) disk space is saved because the hyperlinked document is not saved with the document, (2) the reader does not have to know the filename or Web address of the hyperlink, and (3) the reader has quick access to this new document.

To create a hyperlink:

1. Select the text or object to be displayed as a hyperlink.
2. Click **Insert Hyperlink** button.
3. Click **Existing File or Web Page**.
4. Select filename or Web page by using either of the following methods:
   a. Key the filename or Web address.
   b. Select file from displayed list. Click the category tabs (Recent Files, Browsed Pages, and Inserted Links) to display various files.
   c. Click **Browse for File** or **Browse for Web Page** to locate desired file if name is not known.
5. Click **OK.**

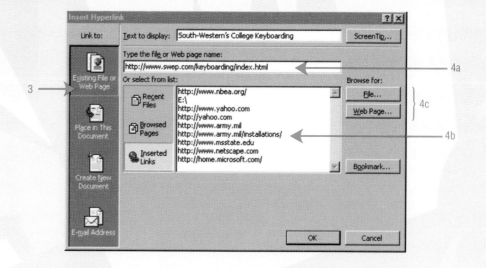

LESSON 18

3 and 6

18a ● 7'

GETTING
started

each line twice SS

18b ● 14'

Learn 3 and 6
each line twice SS

3 Reach *up* with *left second* finger.

6 Reach *up* with *right first* finger.

18c ● 7'

SKILLBUILDING

Improve keying techniques
each line once; repeat drill

SKILLBUILDING WARMUP

alphabet	1	Jim Kable won a second prize for his very quixotic drawings.
figures	2	If 57 of the 105 boys go on July 29, 48 of them will remain.
caps lock	3	Captain Jay took HMS James and HMS Down on a Pacific cruise.
easy	4	With the usual bid, I paid for a quantity of big world maps.

| 1 | 2 | 3 | 4 | 5 | 6 | 7 | 8 | 9 | 10 | 11 | 12 |

3

5 3 3d d3 3 3; had 3 days; did 3 dives; led 3 dogs; add 3 dips
6 we 3 ride 3 cars; take 33 dials; read 3 copies; save 33 days
7 On July 3, 33 lights lit 33 stands holding 33 prize winners.

6

8 6 6j 6j 6 6; 6 jays; 6 jams; 6 jigs; 6 jibs; 6 jots; 6 jokes
9 only 6 high; on 66 units; reach 66 numbers; 6 yams or 6 jams
10 On May 6, Car 66 delivered 66 tons of No. 6 shale to Pier 6.

all figures learned

11 At 6 p.m., Channel 3 reported the August 6 score was 6 to 3.
12 Jean, do Items 28 and 6; Mika, 59 and 10; Kyle, 3, 4, and 7.
13 Cars 56 and 34 used Aisle 9; Cars 2 and 87 can use Aisle 10.

caps lock

14 The USS San Simon sent an SOS; the USS McVey heard it early.

adjacent reaches

15 Ersa Polk sang three hymns before we lads could talk to her.

direct reaches

16 Brace Oxware hunted for a number of marble pieces in Greece.

double letters

17 Tell the cook to add eggs and cheese to Ann's dinner entree.

combination

18 Jimmy's drab garage crew tests gears fastest, in my opinion.

PROFESSIONAL AFFILIATIONS

DS

A survey of our employees indicated that approximately 20 percent are members of professional associations. However, technical employees were more likely to belong to these organizations than were individuals in other occupational groups.

Senior managers expressed a strong desire to have a high percentage of all employees affiliate with professional organizations. This study focused on ways to encourage employees to join professional associations.

Reasons for Not Joining Associations

Side heading

The primary reasons cited for not joining organizations were lack of time, cost, unawareness of associations for field, and never giving organizations much thought.

Reasons for Joining Associations

The major reasons cited for belonging to professional associations were the opportunity to network with other professionals, availability of literature addressing current issues in the field, and commitment to the profession.

Company Incentives

Employees indicated that with more company incentives they would join professional associations. Incentives desired were dues paid by company, recognition of employees who participate, and establishment of company chapters.

> Note: When reports are double-spaced, ¶s are indented. Extra space is not added between ¶s.

LEFTBOUND REPORT—DOUBLE-SPACED

18d ● 8'

SKILLBUILDING

Improve response patterns

each line once SS; DS between 2-line groups; repeat

18e ● 14'

SKILLBUILDING

Build staying power

1. Key the ¶ as directed in Step 2. Remember to save each timing with its own name (18e-t1, 18e-t2, etc.). If you finish the ¶ before time is up, repeat the ¶ until the Timer stops. Print a timing at each speed.
2. Key two 1' writings, then a 2' writing, and a 3' writing. Work for good rhythm.

Goals:

1', 17-23 *gwam*
2', 15-21 *gwam*
3', 14-20 *gwam*

Optional:

Return to the Numeric Lesson menu. Click the **Diagnostic Writings** button. Key the ¶ as a 3' *Diagnostic Writing.*

---

word response: *think* and *key* words

19 he el id is go us it an me of he of to if ah or bye do so am
20 Did she enamel emblems on a big panel for the downtown sign?

stroke response: *think* and *key* each stroke

21 kin are hip read lymph was pop saw ink art oil gas up as mop
22 Barbara started the union wage earners tax in Texas in July.

combination response: vary speed but maintain rhythm

23 upon than eve lion when burley with they only them loin were
24 It was the opinion of my neighbor that we may work as usual.

E all letters   *gwam* 2' | 3'

	2'	3'
• 4 • 8 • I am something quite precious. Though millions of people	6	4
12 • 16 • 20 • in other countries might not have me, you likely do. I have	12	8
24 • 28 • 32 • 36 a lot of power. For it is I who names a new president every	18	12
• 40 • 44 • 48 four years. It is I who decides if a tax shall be levied.	24	16
• 52 • 56 • 60 I even decide questions of war or peace. I was acquired at	30	20
• 64 • 68 • 72 a great cost; however, I am free to all citizens. And yet,	36	24
• 76 • 80 • 84 sadly, I am often ignored; or, still worse, I am just taken	42	28
• 88 • 92 • 96 for granted. I can be lost, and in certain circumstances I	48	32
• 100 • 104 • 108 can even be taken away. What, you may ask, am I? I am your	54	36
• 112 • 116 right to vote. Don't take me lightly.	58	39

2' | 1 | 2 | 3 | 4 | 5 | 6 |
3' | 1 | 2 | 3 | 4 |

Leftbound Reports and Hyperlinks

51a • 3'

GETTING started

each line once

SKILLBUILDING WARMUP

alphabet 1 Jayne Cox puzzled over workbooks that were required for geometry.

figures 2 Edit pages 308 and 415 in Book A; pages 17, 29, and 60 in Book B.

one hand 3 Plum trees on a hilly acre, in my opinion, create no vast estate.

easy 4 Did the foal buck? And did it cut the right elbow of the cowhand?

| 1 | 2 | 3 | 4 | 5 | 6 | 7 | 8 | 9 | 10 | 11 | 12 | 13 |

51b • 7'

SKILLBUILDING

Reach for new goals

1. Take two 1' writings.
2. Take a 2' writing. Try to maintain your 1' rate.

all letters   *gwam* 1' 2'

The value of an education has been a topic discussed many	12	6 48
times with a great deal of zest. The value is often measured in	25	12 54
terms of costs and benefits to the taxpayer. It is also judged	37	19 61
in terms of changes in the individuals taking part in the	49	24 67
educational process. Gains in the level of knowledge, the	61	30 72
development and refinement of attitudes, and the acquiring of	73	36 79
skills are believed to be crucial parts of an education.	84	42 84

1' | 1 | 2 | 3 | 4 | 5 | 6 | 7 | 8 | 9 | 10 | 11 | 12 | 13 |
2' | 1 | 2 | 3 | 4 | 5 | 6 |

51c • 15'

FORMATTING

Leftbound reports
Read the information at the right.

Document
Key the leftbound report on p. 143.

Formatting leftbound reports
The binding on a report usually takes about one-half inch of space; therefore, on a left-bound report, a 1.5" left margin should be used on all pages.

The same right side, top, and bottom margins are used for both unbound and leftbound reports. Reports may be either single-spaced or double-spaced. Paragraphs must be indented when double spacing is used.

1.5"

PROFESSIONAL AFFILIATIONS

A survey of our employees indicated that approximately 20 percent are members of professional associations. However, technical employees were more likely to belong to these organizations than were individuals in other occupational groups.

Senior managers expressed a strong desire to have a high percentage of all employees affiliate with professional organizations. This study focused on ways to encourage employees to join professional associations.

1.5"
Reasons for Not Joining Associations

The primary reasons cited for not joining organizations were lack of time, cost, unawareness of associations for field, and never giving organizations much thought.

Reasons for Joining Associations

The major reasons cited for belonging to professional associations were the opportunity to network with other professionals, availability of literature addressing current issues in the field, and commitment to the profession.

Company Incentives

Employees indicated that with more company incentives they would join professional associations. Incentives desired were dues paid by company, recognition of employees who participate, and establishment of company chapters.

$ and -, Number Expression

19a • 7'

GETTING started

each line twice SS

alphabet 1 Why did the judge quiz poor Victor about his blank tax form?

figures 2 J. Boyd, Ph.D., changed Items 10, 57, 36, and 48 on page 92.

3d row 3 To try the tea, we hope to tour the port prior to the party.

easy 4 Did he signal the authentic robot to do a turn to the right?

| 1 | 2 | 3 | 4 | 5 | 6 | 7 | 8 | 9 | 10 | 11 | 12 |

19b • 14'

Learn $ and - (hyphen)

each line twice SS; DS between 2-line groups

$ Shift; then reach *up* with *left first* finger.

- (hyphen) Reach *up* with *right fourth* finger.

- = hyphen
-- = dash
Do not space before or after a hyphen or a dash.

$

5 $ $f f$ $ $; if $4; half $4; off $4; of $4; $4 fur; $4 flats

6 for $8; cost $9; log $3; grab $10; give Rolf $2; give Viv $4

7 Since she paid $45 for the item priced at $54, she saved $9.

- (hyphen)

8 - -; ;- - - -; up-to-date; co-op; father-in-law; four-square

9 pop-up foul; big-time job; snap-on bit; one- or two-hour ski

10 You need 6 signatures--half of the members--on the petition.

all symbols learned

11 I paid $10 for the low-cost disk; high-priced ones cost $40.

12 Le-An spent $20 for travel, $95 for books, and $38 for food.

13 Mr. Loft-Smit sold his boat for $467; he bought it for $176.

19c • 5'

SKILLBUILDING

Practice troublesome pairs

Key at a controlled rate without pauses.

e/d 14 Edie discreetly decided to deduct expenses in making a deed.

w/e 15 Working women wear warm wool sweaters when weather dictates.

r/e 16 We heard very rude remarks regarding her recent termination.

s/d 17 This seal's sudden misdeeds destroyed several goods on land.

v/b 18 Beverley voted by giving a bold beverage to every brave boy.

FORMATTING

Title page/center

Document 1

1. Prepare a title page for the unbound report completed in 50d. Prepared for: **National Commerce Bank**. Prepared by: **Teresa DuChaine, Manager**.
2. Use bold and 14 point.
3. Center all lines horizontally.
4. Center the page vertically. Save as **50e-d1**.

Document 2
Challenge

Enhance the appearance of 50e-d1 by adding a border with shading. Follow the directions at the right.

Title page

The title page should convey to the reader a concise title that identifies the report. A **title page** includes the title of the report, the name and title of the individual or organization for whom the report was prepared, the name and title of the writer, and the date the report was completed.

Center items on a title page horizontally. Vertical placement depends on the amount of copy contained on the title page. The information should be positioned so that it is attractive and easy to read.

Creating border with shading

1. The title page *50e-d1* should be open.
2. Press ENTER to add blank lines above the title and below the "Current date." (Enter the same number above and below the text.)
3. Click **Edit, Select All** to select title page.
4. Choose *Format* then *Borders* and *Shading*.
5. From the Borders tab, click first on **Shadow.** Choose a single line as the *Style* and make the *Width* 1½ pt..
6. From the Shading tab, click **5%**. Click **OK**.

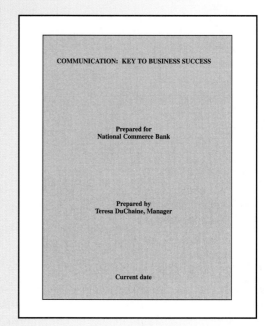

S E L F ✔
c h e c k

Answer the True/False questions at the right to see whether you have mastered the material presented in this lesson.

T F

1. A direct quotation that is two or more lines is single-spaced and indented .5" from the left margin.
2. To indent a direct quotation, click Increase Indent button.
3. An ellipsis (...) means quoted text is included.
4. Use the Layout tab of the Page Setup menu to center a page vertically.
5. The Click and Type feature requires a double click to begin.

Build fluency

Key each line once, working for fluid, consistent stroking. Repeat at a faster speed.

- Key the easy words as "words" rather than stroke by stroke.
- Key each phrase (marked by a vertical line) without pauses between words. ▧

easy words

19 am it go bus dye jam irk six sod tic yam ugh spa vow aid dug
20 he or by air big elf dog end fit and lay sue toe wit own got
21 six foe pen firm also body auto form down city kept make fog

easy phrases

22 it is|if the|and also|to me|the end|to us|it it|it is|to the
23 if it is|to the end|do you wish|to go to|for the end|to make
24 lay down|he or she|make me|by air|end of |by me|kept it|of me

easy sentences

25 Did the chap work to mend the torn right half of the ensign?
26 Blame me for their penchant for the antique chair and panel.
27 She bid by proxy for eighty bushels of a corn and rye blend.

19e ● 14'

Learn number-usage rules

1. Study the rules at right.
2. Key the sample sentences 28-33.
3. Change figures to words as needed in sentences 34-36.

Numbers expressed as words

Good writers know how to use numbers in their writing. The following rules illustrate when numbers should be expressed as words. Key as words:

- a number that begins a sentence.
- numbers ten and lower, unless they are part of a series of numbers any of which is over ten.
- the smaller of two adjacent numbers.

- isolated fractions and approximate numbers.
- round numbers that can be expressed as one or two words.
- numbers that precede "o'clock."

Note: Hyphenate spelled-out numbers between 21 and 99 inclusive. Also, hyphenate fractions expressed as words.

28 **Six** or **seven** older players were cut from the **37**-member team.
29 I have **2** of **14** coins I need to start my set.   Kristen has **9.**
30 Of **nine 24**-ton engines ordered, we shipped **six** last Tuesday.
31 Shelly has read just **one-half** of about **forty-five** documents.
32 The **six** boys sent well over **two hundred** printed invitations.
33 **One** or **two** of us will be on duty from **two** until **six** o'clock.
34 The meeting begins promptly at 9.   We plan 4 sessions.
35 The 3-person crew cleaned 6 stands, 12 tables, and 13 desks.
36 The 3d meeting is at 3 o'clock on Friday, February 2.

Two-page report with direct quotations
Apply the skills you have learned so far.

Review steps for "Formatting a report" in
49b if necessary.

words

COMMUNICATION: KEY TO   5
BUSINESS SUCCESS   8

Probably no successful enterprise   15
exists that does not rely for its success upon   24
the ability of its members to communicate   33
with   each   other   and   with   third   39
parties.   The role that effective communica-   48
tion plays in business success cannot be   56
stressed too strongly; it is essential that   65
strict attention be paid to the application,   74
implementation,   and   administration   of   81
communication within a business venture.   90

Effective communication results   96
when information is transmitted from   103
a sender to a receiver, and the   110
message is understood.   It is not nec-   117
essary that the message result in any   125
specific outcome, only that it be sent,   133
received, and understood (Higgason,   140
1999, 39).   143

Business communication falls into two   150
main categories: written and verbal.   More   159
time is spent by most business firms   166
studying and perfecting their written com-   175
munications.   It is verbal communication,   183
however, that makes up a major portion of   191
all   communication   and   deserves   more   199
attention than is typically the case.   "Suc-   207
cessful businesses have long known the   215
importance of good verbal communication,   223
yet many of them still give written com-   231
munication   greater   emphasis"   (Catlette,   239
1999, 29).   242

Written communication confirms facts   249
and intentions, and any important verbal   257
conversation   should   be   confirmed   in   265
writing.   Written   communication   also   272
constitutes proof; a letter signature can have   281
the same effect as a contract signature.   Fur-   291
ther, written communications can be retained   300

words

for later reference, affirmation being as close as   310
a hard copy in a file folder or an electronic file   320
on a computer server.   Written communication   329
avoids some of the natural barriers of verbal   339
communication.   Shyness,   speech   problems,   347
and other distractions are not found in a writ-   356
ten document.   359

Since verbal communication often involves   368
encounters on a one-on-one basis, it can bring   377
quicker results.   Misunderstandings are avoided;   387
questions are answered.   It is usually less   396
formal and friendlier; moods, attitudes, and   405
emotions are more easily handled.   Verbal com-   414
munication is augmented with facial expressions   424
and gestures, assuring greater clarity of the   433
message.   Words and phrases can be given special   442
emphasis not possible in a written message,   451
where emphasis is given by the receiver, not the   461
sender.   463

Schaefer points out the importance of   470
communication: 474

Make no mistake; both written and   480
verbal communication are the stuff upon   488
which success is built. . . . Both forms   496
deserve careful study by any business   504
that wants to grow.   Successful business-   512
people must read, write, speak, and listen   521
with skill (Schaefer, 1998, 28).   528

REFERENCES   530

Catlette, Darby.   *Communicating Effectively in*   540
the Next Millennium.   San Francisco: 547
Thomas Publishers, Inc., 1999.   554

Higgason, Carol.   "The Art of Communicating in   563
Business." *New Age Magazine*, July 1999,   572
pp. 39-43.   574

Schaefer, Adam.   "Tools for Executive Success."   584
Executive Minutes. 1998. <http://www.en.   592
edu/executivenews/ToolsforExecutive   600
Success.htm> (19 May 1998).   605

LESSON 20

and /

20a ● 7'

GETTING started

each line twice SS

SKILLBUILDING WARMUP

alphabet 1 Freda Jencks will have money to buy six quite large topazes.

symbols 2 I bought 10 ribbons and 45 disks from Cable-Han Co. for $78.

home row 3 Dallas sold jade flasks; Sal has a glass flask full of salt.

easy 4 He may cycle down to the field by the giant oak and cut hay.

| 1 | 2 | 3 | 4 | 5 | 6 | 7 | 8 | 9 | 10 | 11 | 12 |

20b ● 14'

Learn # and /

each line twice SS

Shift; then reach *up* with *left second* finger.

/ Reach *down* with *right fourth* finger.

= number sign, pounds
/ = diagonal, slash

#

5 # #e e# # # #; had #3 dial; did #3 drop; set #3 down; Bid #3

6 leave #82; sold #20; Lyric #16; bale #34; load #53; Optic #7

7 Notice #333 says to load Car #33 with 33# of #3 grade shale.

/

8 / /; ;/ / / /; 1/2; 1/3; Mr./Mrs.; 1/5/94; 22 11/12; and/or;

9 to/from; /s/ William Smit; 2/10, n/30; his/her towels; 6 1/2

10 The numerals 1 5/8, 3 1/4, and 60 7/9 are "mixed fractions."

all symbols learned

11 Invoice #737 cites 15 2/3# of rye was shipped C.O.D. 4/6/95.

12 B-O-A Company's Check #50/5 for $87 paid for 15# of #3 wire.

13 Our Co-op List #20 states $40 for 16 1/2 crates of tomatoes.

20c ● 7'

SKILLBUILDING

Reach for new goals

Key 30" writings on both lines of a pair. Try to key as many words on the second line of each pair. Work to avoid pauses.

gwam 30"

14 She did the key work at the height of the problem. 20

15 Form #726 is the title to the island; she owns it. 20

16 The rock is a form of fuel; he did enrich it with coal. 22

17 The corn-and-turkey dish is a blend of turkey and corn. 22

18 It is right to work to end the social problems of the world. 24

19 If I sign it on 3/19, the form can aid us to pay the 40 men. 24

Two-Page Report with Title Page

50a • 7'

GETTING started

each line twice SS; DS between groups

SKILLBUILDING WARMUP

alphabet 1 Dave Cagney alphabetized items for next week's quarterly journal.
figures 2 Close Rooms 4, 18, and 20 from 3 until 9 on July 7; open Room 56.
up reaches 3 Toy & Wurt's note for $635 (see our page 78) was paid October 29.
easy 4 The auditor is due by eight, and he may lend a hand to the panel.

| 1 | 2 | 3 | 4 | 5 | 6 | 7 | 8 | 9 | 10 | 11 | 12 | 13 |

50b • (optional)
SKILLBUILDING

Building staying power
Take a 3' writing.

  all letters   gwam 1' | 3'

When you write, how does the result portray you? Some of us   12 | 4 | 38
seem to take on some unique personality when we write. We forget   25 | 8 | 42
writing is just another way of talking, and what we write may   38 | 13 | 47
project an image that is not natural. Some writers, on the other   51 | 17 | 51
hand, try to humanize what they write so that it extends genuine   64 | 22 | 56
warmth and makes one want to read it. Apparently, correct format   77 | 26 | 60
and language, common sense, and some idea that a writer is still   90 | 30 | 64
among the living can add up to be very fine writing.   101 | 34 | 68

1' | 1 | 2 | 3 | 4 | 5 | 6 | 7 | 8 | 9 | 10 | 11 | 12 | 13 |
3' | 1 | | 2 | | 3 | | 4 |

50c • 5'

Review
Key the first two lines of the report DS (12-point font). Change to SS. Increase Indent. Press TAB to indent the first line of the ¶ an additional 0.5".

Review Indent:
Increase Indent
Decrease Indent

attention be paid to the application, implementation, and administration of communication within a business venture.

Effective communication results when information is transmitted from a sender to a receiver, and the message is understood. A response is not required, only that the message be sent, received, and understood (Higgason, 1999, 39).

20d • 8'

COMMUNICATION

Review number usage

DS; decide whether the circled numbers should be keyed as figures or as words and make needed changes. Check your finished work with 19e, p. 47.

```
20 Six or (7) older players were cut from the (37)-member team.
21 I have (2) of 14 coins I need to start my set.  Kristen has (9).
22 Of (9) 24-ton engines ordered, we shipped (6) last Tuesday.
23 Shelly has read just (1) half of about (45) documents.
24 The (6) boys sent well over (200) printed invitations.
25 (1) or (2) of us will be on duty from (2) until (6) o'clock.
```

20e • 14'

SKILLBUILDING

Improve speed

1. From the Lesson menu, click the **Open Screen** button.
2. Follow the procedures at the right for increasing your speed by taking guided writings.
3. Take a 3' writing without the guide on the complete writing.

Guided writing procedures

1. In the Open Screen, take a 1' writing on ¶ 1. Note your *gwam*.
2. Add 4 words to your 1' *gwam* to determine your goal rate.
3. Set the Timer for 1'. Set the Timer option to beep every 15".
4. From the table below, select from Column 4 the speed nearest your goal rate. Note the 1/4' point at the left of that speed. Place a light check mark within the ¶s at the 1/4' points.
5. Take two 1' guided writings on ¶s 1 and 2. Do not save.
6. Turn the beeper off.

1/4'	1/2'	3/4'	1' *gwam*
4	8	12	16
5	10	15	20
6	12	18	24
7	14	21	28
8	16	24	32
9	18	27	36
10	20	30	40

all letters

	gwam 2'	3'	
Some of us think that the best way to get attention is	6	4	35
to try a new style, or to look quixotic, or to be different	12	8	39
somehow. Perhaps we are looking for nothing much more than	18	12	43
acceptance from others of ourselves just the way we now are.	24	16	47
There is no question about it; we all want to look our	29	19	50
best to impress other people. How we achieve this may mean	35	23	54
trying some of this and that; but our basic objective is to	41	27	58
take our raw materials, you and me, and build up from there.	47	31	62

2' | 1 | 2 | 3 | 4 | 5 | 6
3' | 1 | 2 | 3 | 4

Two-page report with references

1. DS the unbound report.
2. Insert Page Numbers command; clear the check mark so that the number does not print on page 1.
3. Switch to Print Layout view to verify page numbers.
4. Save, check spelling, and print.

words

SOME PEOPLE YOU CAN'T LIVE WITHOUT

7

Are you looking for a career that will challenge you to use your | 20
mind and skills and one that will give you rich and varied rewards? | 34
Some people we absolutely cannot live without today are health care | 47
professionals. As a health care professional, you're part of something | 62
needed, something special, something exciting, and something | 74
respected. | 76

Shortage of Health Care Workers

83

Rumors regarding a surplus of nurses have periodically circu- | 95
lated. A study of the employment market shows that in the last 20 | 108
years three periods of time have occurred when we have experienced a | 122
shortage of nurses! The surplus that some speak of occurs because | 136
of hiring freezes and cutbacks. Each time the economy picked up and | 149
employers began hiring, the surplus quickly became a shortage. | 162

The underlying demand for allied health practitioners is greater | 175
now than ever before. Increasing numbers of people are living longer, | 189
and as the population grows older, the need and demand for quality | 203
health care grows (Elliott, 1999, 64). Political leaders are talking | 217
about national health insurance and making health care available for | 231
all Americans. Due to the fact that health care is a national priority, | 245
it is a growth industry. | 250

Skills Required

254

Health care workers must possess skills in the following areas: | 267
command of the English language, including written and oral commu- | 280
nication skills; computer skills; conflict resolution; supervision/ | 293
delegation of tasks; and knowledge of cultural diversity (Sabella, 1999, | 308
42). Fluency in more than one language is a valuable asset. Medical | 322
professionals must be willing to continually improve their knowledge | 336
and skills and stay current of the latest technological developments in | 350
the field. | 353

REFERENCES

355

Elliott, Thomas A. "A Career in Allied Health." *National Occupational* | 369
Projection Handbook. Chicago: Chicago-Versaille Press, 1999. | 382

Sabella, Irene C. "Make a Difference with Your Life." *Health* | 394
Professionals in the Year 2000. Ann Arbor: Alexandria Press, 1999. | 408

21

% and !

21a ● 7'

GETTING started

each line twice SS

alphabet 1 Merry will have picked out a dozen quarts of jam for boxing.

fig/sym 2 Jane-Ann bought 16 7/8 yards of #240 cotton at $3.59 a yard.

1st row 3 Can't brave, zany Cave Club men/women next climb Mt. Zamban?

easy 4 Did she rush to cut six bushels of corn for the civic corps?

| 1 | 2 | 3 | 4 | 5 | 6 | 7 | 8 | 9 | 10 | 11 | 12 |

21b ● 14'

Learn % and !

each line twice SS

% Shift; then reach *up* with *left first* finger.

% = percent sign
Use % with business forms or where space is restricted; otherwise, use the word "percent."
Space twice after the exclamation point!

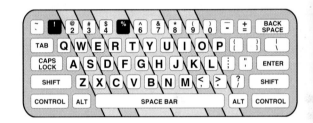

%

5 % %f f% % %; off 5%; if 5%; of 5% fund; half 5%; taxes of 5%

6 7% rent; 3% tariff; 9% F.O.B.; 15% greater; 28% base; up 46%

7 Give discounts of 5% on rods, 50% on lures, and 75% on line.

!: reach *up* with the *left fourth* finger

8 ! !a a! ! ! !; Eureka! Ha! No! Pull 10! Extra! America!

9 Listen to the call! Now! Ready! Get set! Go! Good show!

10 I want it now, not next week! I am sure to lose 50% or $19.

all symbols

11 The ad offers a 10% discount, but this notice says 15% less!

12 He got the job! With Clark's Supermarket! Please call Mom!

13 Bill #92-44 arrived very late from Zyclone; it was paid 7/4.

21c ● 5'

SKILLBUILDING

Improve response patterns

each line once; repeat

words: *think*, *say*, and *key* words

14 may big end pay and bid six fit own bus sit air due map lays

15 also firm they work make lend disk when rush held name spend

16 city busy visit both town title usual half fight blame audit

phrases: *think*, *say*, and *key* phrases

17 is the|to do|it is|but so|she did|own me|may go|by the|or me

18 it may|he did|but if |to end|she may|do so|it is|to do|is the

19 the firm|all six|they paid|held tight|bid with|and for|do it

Page numbers

The Page Number command automatically inserts the correct page number on each page. To enable the number not to print on the first page, you will remove the ✓ before Show number on first page box.

Print Layout view is designed to view page numbers and other features as they will print. Select Print Layout from the View menu to view page numbers.

Drill

1. Open *48c*.

2. Use Page Numbers command to insert number at top of page. Remove the ✓ in Show number on first page box.

3. Use Print Layout view to verify page numbers.

4. Save as **49c**.

To insert page numbers:

1. From the Insert menu, choose *Page Numbers*; the Page Numbers dialog box displays.

2. Select *Top of page (Header)* in the Position box.

3. Select *Right* in the Alignment box (default).

4. Remove the check (✓) in the Show number on first page box. Click **OK.**

5. Choose *Page Layout* from the View menu to view the page numbers.

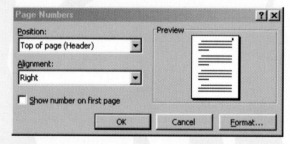

Drill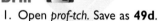

1. Open *prof-tch*. Save as **49d**.

2. Insert the page numbers. Do not show page number on the first page.

3. Select the heading "In Conclusion" and the ¶ that follows. Apply Keep with next.

4. Correctly format all headings.

5. Change to Print Layout view to verify page numbers and top margins.

6. Save and print. Compare your document to the model on the previous page.

Line and page breaks

Pagination or breaking pages at the appropriate location can be controlled easily using two features: Widow/Orphan control and the Keep with next.

• **Widow/Orphan control** prevents a single line of a paragraph from printing at the bottom or top of a page. A check displays in this option box indicating the default of Widow/Orphan control is "on."

• **Keep with next** prevents a page break from occurring between two paragraphs. Use this feature to keep a side heading from being left alone at the bottom of a page.

To use Keep with next:

1. Select the side heading and the paragraph that follows.

2. Click **Format,** then **Paragraph.**

3. From the Line and Page Breaks tab, select *Keep with next*. Click **OK.** The side heading moves to the next page.

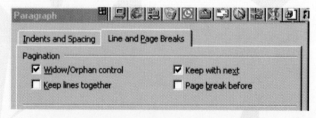

SKILLBUILDING

Improve finger reaches
Key each set of lines SS; DS between each group; fingers curved, hands quiet. Repeat if time permits.

1st finger

20 by bar get fun van for inn art from gray hymn July true verb
21 brag human bring unfold hominy mighty report verify puny joy
22 You are brave to try bringing home the van in the bad storm.

2d finger

23 ace ink did cad keyed deep seed kind Dick died kink like kid
24 cease decease decades kick secret check decide kidney evaded
25 Dedre likes the idea of ending dinner with cake for dessert.

3d finger

26 oil sow six vex wax axe low old lox pool west loss wool slow
27 swallow swamp saw sew wood sax sexes loom stew excess school
28 Wes waxes floors and washes windows at low costs to schools.

4th finger

29 zap zip craze pop pup pan daze quote queen quiz pizza puzzle
30 zoo graze zipper panzer zebra quip partizan patronize appear
31 Czar Zane appears to be dazzled by the apple pizza and jazz.

21e ● 4'

SKILLBUILDING

Practice speed runs with numbers
Take 1' writings; the last number you key when you stop is your approximate *gwam*.

1 and 2 and 3 and 4 and 5 and 6 and 7 and 8 and 9 and 10 and

11 and 12 and 13 and 14 and 15 and 16 and 17 and 18 and 19

and 20 and 21 and 22 and 23 and 24 and 25 and 26 and 27 and

on... One Space or Two?

VIEWS

Traditionally, two spaces follow end-of-sentence punctuation. In desktop publishing, one space generally follows end-of-sentence punctuation. As a result of desktop publishing and the proportional fonts of today's word processing programs, some users have suggested change.

With proportional fonts, characters use a varied amount of space depending upon their width. Monospace fonts such as Courier (also used by typewriters) use the same amount of space for each character; thus, two spaces are required after end-of-sentence punctuation for readability.

We believe the critical factors are readability and ease of retention, and not all fonts provide a distinct end-of-sentence look. End-of-sentence punctuation decisions will continue to be reevaluated with changing technologies. In this textbook, you will use two spaces after end-of-sentence punctuation for typical document production. In the Desktop Publishing module, however, you will use one.

Two-Page Reports

GETTING started

Use the drill lines in 45a, p. 123, to get started.

49b ● 5'

FORMATTING

Two-page reports

Read "Two-page reports."

Use the steps for formatting a two-page report after you learn to insert page numbers and control line and page breaks in 49c and 49d.

Two-page reports

The report format is widely used in various environments. Some basic considerations are:

- **Side margins**: Set according to binding.
- **Top margin**: 1.5" for first page of report, preliminary pages, reference page; 1" on other pages.
- **Page numbers**: Include page numbers for the second and succeeding pages of a report. Page numbers should be positioned in the right top margin.
- **Single lines:** Avoid single lines at the top or bottom of a report (called *widow/orphan lines*). Do not separate between pages a side heading from the paragraph that follows.

Formatting a report

1. Position the insertion point for an approximate 1.5" top margin.

2. Change line spacing to double and the font size to 12 point.

3. Insert page numbers; remove the ✓ so that the page number does not print on the first page.

4. Key and center the main heading. Select the heading and apply 14-point font.

5. Key the entire report, including the Reference section.

6. Protect side headings that may get separated from the related paragraph with Keep with next feature.

7. If the references must be formatted on a separate page, insert a manual page break. Position the heading REFERENCES at 1.5".

8. View the report from the Print Layout view.

1.5"

THE PROFESSIONAL TOUCH

Although its contents are of ultimate importance, a finished report's looks are of almost equal importance. If it is to achieve the goal for which it was written, every report, whether it serves a business or academic purpose, should be acceptable from every point of view.

Citations, for Example

No matter which format is used for citations, a good writer knows citations are inserted for the reader's benefit; therefore, anything the writer does to ease their use will be appreciated and will work on the writer's behalf. Standard procedures, such as those stated below, make readers comfortable.

Italicize titles of complete publications; use quotation marks with parts of publications. Thus, the name of a magazine is italicized, but the title of an article within the magazine is placed in quotation marks. Months and certain locational words used in the citations may be abbreviated if necessary (Mayr, 1996, 13).

And the Final Report

The final report should have an attractive, easy-to-read look.

The report should meet the criteria for spacing, citations, and binding that have been established for its preparation. "Such criteria are set up by institutional decree, by generally accepted standards, or by subject demands" (Chung, 1995, 27). A writer should discover limits within which he or she must write and should observe those limits with care.

1"   2

In Conclusion

Giving the report a professional appearance calls for skill and patience from a writer. First impressions count when preparing reports. Poorly presented materials are not read, or at least not read with an agreeable attitude.

REFERENCES

Chung, Olin. *Reports and Formats.* Cedar Rapids: Gar Press, Inc., 1995.

Hull, Brenda, and Muriel Myers. *Writing Reports and Dissertations.* 5th ed. New York: Benjamin Lakey Press, 1994.

Mayr, Polly. "Styles/Formats/Computers." *Business Weekly,* June 1996, p. 13.

(and)

22a ● 7'

GETTING
started

each line twice SS

alphabet 1 Avoid lazy punches; expert fighters jab with a quick motion.

fig/sym 2 Be-Low's Bill #483/7 was $96.90, not $102--they took 5% off.

caps lock 3 Report titles may be shown in ALL CAPS; as, BOLD WORD POWER.

easy 4 Do they blame me for their dismal social and civic problems?

| 1 | 2 | 3 | 4 | 5 | 6 | 7 | 8 | 9 | 10 | 11 | 12 |

22b ● 14'

Learn (and)
(parentheses)

each line twice SS

(Shift; then reach *up* with
the *right third* finger.

) Shift; then reach *up* with
the *right fourth* finger.

( ) = parentheses
Parentheses indicate off-
hand, aside, or explanatory
messages.

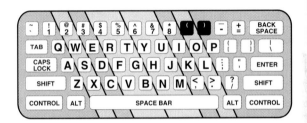

5 ((l l((; (; Reach from l for the left parenthesis; as, ((.

6)); ;))); Reach from ; for the right parenthesis; as,)).

( )

7 Learn to use parentheses (plural) or parenthesis (singular).

8 The red (No. 34) and blue (No. 78) cars both won here (Rio).

9 We (Galen and I) dined (bagels) in our penthouse (the dorm).

all symbols learned

10 The jacket was $35 (thirty-five dollars)--the tie was extra.

11 Starting 10/29, you can sell Model #49 at a discount of 25%.

12 My size 8 1/2 shoe--a blue pump--was soiled (but not badly).

22c ● 6'

SKILLBUILDING

Review numbers and
symbols

Key each line twice, keeping
eyes on copy. DS between
pairs.

13 Jana has one hard-to-get copy of her hot-off-the-press book.

14 An invoice said that "We give discounts of 10%, 5%, and 3%."

15 The company paid Bill 3/18 on 5/2/97 and Bill 3/1 on 3/6/97.

16 The catalog lists as out of stock Items #230, #710, and #13.

17 Elyn had $8; Sean, $9; and Cal, $7. The cash total was $24.

1. DS the unbound report.
2. SS quote, indenting from the left margin.
3. Insert a manual page break before the reference section since the references will not all fit on the first page. At this point, you have not learned to number pages, so do not number the second page.
4. Use Spelling and Grammar.
5. Save as **48c.**
6. View the document and check format before printing.

THE REFERENCE LIST
DS

When a report has been prepared, a list of references is often pro-   17
vided to clarify and/or support statements made in the report, to cite   31
sources, and to give the reader an opportunity to read more on the topic.   46
Conventions for references vary somewhat depending on the reference   60
manual that is used. Two popular style manuals are *A Manual for Writers*   75
of Term Papers, Theses, and Dissertations and the *Publication Manual of the*   89
American Psychological Association. A valuable Web site for referencing   103
formats is http://www.utexas.edu/depts/uwc/.html/citation.html.   117

The sample reference format shown at the end of this report illustrates   131
various types of references, including books, magazines, and electronic   145
citations. Note that references are (1) arranged alphabetically, usually by   161
last name of author, (2) formatted in hanging indent style, and (3) single-   176
spaced with a double space between each reference item.   187

To format references for documents retrieved electronically, Lehman,   201
Dufrene, Himstreet, and Baty (1999, B-9) offer the following guidelines: 216

The various referencing styles are fairly standardized as to the   229
elements included when citing documents retrieved electronically. . . .   241
Include the following items: author (if given), date of publication, title   258
of article and/or name of publication, electronic medium (such as on-   273
line or CD-ROM), volume, series, page, and path (Uniform Resource   286
Locator or Internet address) and date you retrieved or accessed the   300
resource.   302

If the entire list of references does not fit at the bottom of the last page   317
of the report, position them on the following page. However, if all references   333
fit on the last page of the report, separate the body of the report from the   348
references with a DS.   353

REFERENCES   355
DS

Journal → Altese, Rachel M. "Referencing Electronic Documents." *Multimedia*   368
Quarterly, April 1999, pp. 45-51.   375
DS

Online Journal → DePriest, J. Shanon. "WWW Citations." *Graduate Education Journal.*   390
(Spring 1998): <http://www.gej.edu/citations/wwwcitations.htm>   402
(23 July 1998).   406
DS

Book → Lehman, C. M., D. D. Dufrene, W. C. Himstreet, and W. M. Baty.   419
Business Communication. 12th ed. Cincinnati, OH: South-Western   432
Educational Publishing, 1999.   438
DS

E-mail → Thompson, John D. <jdt3@umt.edu>. "Electronic Citations Update."   452
E-mail to Matthew P. Crowson <mpcrowson@umt.edu> (23 January   464
1999).   465

COMMUNICATION

Learn number-usage rules

Study the rules at the right; then key lines 18-23.

Numbers expressed as figures

In most business communications, some numbers are expressed in figures, while others are expressed in words. The following guidelines indicate instances when writing numbers as figures is preferred practice. Key as figures:

- numbers coupled with nouns
- house numbers (except house number One) and street names (except ten and under); if street name is a number, separate it from the house number with a dash (--)
- time when expressed with a.m. or p.m.
- a date following a month; a date preceding the month (or standing alone) is expressed in figures followed by "d" or "th"

- money amounts and percents, even when approximate (use the $ symbol and/or the words "cents" or "percent")
- round numbers in the millions or higher with their word modifiers (with or without a dollar sign)

Note: When speaking or writing numbers (as in writing numbers on a check), the word "and" should be used only to signify a decimal point. Thus, 850 is spoken or written as "eight hundred fifty," not "eight hundred and fifty."

18 Ask **Group 1** to read **Chapter 6** of **Book 11** (**Shelf 19, Room 5**).

19 All **six** of us live at **One Bay Road**, not at **126--56th Street**.

20 At **9 a.m.** the owners decided to close from **12 noon** to **1 p.m.**

21 Ms. Vik leaves **June 9**; she returns the **14th or 15th of July**.

22 The **16 percent** discount saves **$115**. A stamp costs **35 cents**.

23 Elin gave **$3 million** to charity; our gift was only **75 cents**.

SKILLBUILDING

Build staying power

1. Take two 1' timings on each ¶.
2. Take a 3' timing on all ¶s. Determine *gwam*.

Goal: 17 *gwam*

all letters   *gwam*   3"

| | | 4 | | 8 | | |
Most people will agree that we owe it to our children   4 | 28
12   •   16   •   20   •
to pass the planet on to them in better condition than we   7 | 32
24   •   28   •   32   •
found it.   We must take extra steps just to make the quality   12 | 36
36   •
of living better.   13 | 37

•   4   •   8   •
If we do not change our ways quickly and stop damaging   16 | 41
12   •   16   •   20   •
our world, it will not be a good place to live.   We can save   21 | 45
24   •   28   •   32   •
the ozone and wildlife and stop polluting the air and water.   25 | 49

3' | 1 | 2 | 3 | 4 |

Unbound report with references

Read "Report documentation." Key and format the document on the next page.

Report documentation

Reports must include the sources of all information included in the report. Within the report, the writer uses either footnotes, endnotes, or internal citations to cite sources. A complete list of references is included at the end of the report.

Internal citations

Internal citations are an easy and practical method of documentation. The last name of the author(s), the publication date, and the page number(s) of the cited material are shown in parentheses within the body of the report (Gholston, 1999, 134). This information cues a reader to the name Gholston in the references listed at the end of the report.

Short direct quotations of three lines or fewer are enclosed within quotation marks. Long quotations of four lines or more are indented from the left margin and single-spaced. If a portion of the text referenced is omitted, use an ellipsis (. . .) to show the omission.

List of references

References cited in the report are listed at the end of the report in alphabetical order by authors' last names. The reference list may be titled REFERENCES or BIBLIOGRAPHY. Become familiar with the three types of references listed below:

- A book reference includes the name of the author (inverted), work (italicized), city of publication, publisher, and copyright date.

- A magazine reference shows the name of the author (inverted), article (in quotation marks), magazine title (italicized), date of publication, and page references.

- A reference retrieved electronically includes the author (inverted), article (in quotation marks), publication (italicized), publication information, Internet address (in brackets), and date the document was retrieved or accessed.

If the entire reference section does not fit at the bottom of the last page, insert a manual page break and position the entire reference section on the next page. Use the same margins as the first page of a report and number the page at the top right of the page. Single-space references in hanging indent format. DS between references.

If references are keyed on the last page of the report, separate the body of the report from the references with a DS.

1.5"

THE REFERENCE LIST

When a report has been prepared, a list of references is often provided to clarify and/or support statements made in the report, to cite sources, and to give the reader an opportunity to read more on the topic. Conventions for references vary somewhat depending on the reference manual that is used. Two popular style manuals are *A Manual for Writers of Term Papers, Theses, and Dissertations* and the *Publication Manual of the American Psychological Association*. A valuable Web site for referencing formats is http://www.utexas.edu/depts/uwc/.html/citation.html.

The sample reference format shown at the end of this report illustrates various types of references, including books, magazines, and electronic citations. Note that references are (1) arranged alphabetically, usually by last name of author, (2) formatted in hanging indent style, and (3) single-spaced with a double space between each reference item.

To format references for documents retrieved electronically, Lehman, Dufrene, Himstreet, and Baty (1999, B-9) offer the following guidelines:

The various referencing styles are fairly standardized as to the elements included when citing documents retrieved electronically. . . . Include the following items: author (if given), date of publication, title of article and/or name of publication, electronic medium (such as on-line or CD-ROM), volume, series, page, and path (Uniform Resource Locator or Internet address) and date you retrieved or accessed the resource.

If the entire list of references does not fit at the bottom of the last page of the report, position them on the following page. However, if all references fit on the last page of the report, separate the body of the report from the references with a DS.

1.5"   2

REFERENCES

Altese, Rachel M. "Referencing Electronic Documents." *Multimedia Quarterly*, April 1999, pp. 45–51.

DePriest, J. Shannon. "WWW Citations." *Graduate Education Journal*. Spring 1998. <http://www.gej.edu/citations/wwwcitations.htm> (23 July 1998).

Lehman, C. M., D. D. Dufrene, W. C. Himstreet, and W. M. Baty. *Business Communication*. 12th ed. Cincinnati, OH: South-Western Educational Publishing, 1999.

Thompson, John D. <jdt3@.umt.edu>. "Electronic Citations Update." E-mail to Matthew P. Crowson <mpcrowson@umt.edu> (23 January 1999).

& and :, Proofreaders' Marks

23a ● 7'

GETTING started

each line twice SS

alphabet 1 Roxy waved as she did quick flying jumps on the trapeze bar.
symbols 2 Ryan's--with an A-1 rating--sold Item #146 (for $10) on 2/7.
space bar 3 Mr. Fyn may go to Cape Cod on the bus, or he may go by auto.
easy 4 Susie is busy; may she halt the social work for the auditor?

| 1 | 2 | 3 | 4 | 5 | 6 | 7 | 8 | 9 | 10 | 11 | 12 |

23b ● 14'

Learn & and : (colon)

each line twice SS

& Shift, then reach *up* with *right first* finger.

: (colon) Left shift, then press key with *right fourth* finger.

& = ampersand, "and" sign
The ampersand is used only as part of company names.
Space twice after a colon.

& (ampersand)

5 & &j j& & & &; J & J; Haraj & Jay; Moroj & Jax; Torj & Jones
6 Nehru & Unger; Mumm & Just; Mann & Hart; Arch & Jones; M & J
7 Rhye & Knox represent us; Steb & Doy, Firm A; R & J, Firm B.

: (colon)

8 : :; ;: : : :; as: for example: notice: To: From: Date:
9 in stock: 8:30; 7:45; Age: Experience: Read: Send: See:
10 Space twice after a colon, thus: To: No.: Time: Carload:

all symbols learned

11 Consider these companies: J & R, Brand & Kay, Uper & Davis.
12 Memo #88-89 reads as follows: "Deduct 15% of $300, or $45."
13 Bill 32(5)--it got here quite late--from M & N was paid 7/3.

23c ● 9'

SKILLBUILDING

Improve response patterns

each line once; repeat

word response

14 Did the busy girl also fix the torn cowl of the formal gown?
15 Clement works with proficiency to make the worn bicycle run.
16 They may pay the auditor the duty on eighty bushels of corn.

stroke response

17 Lou served a sweet dessert after a caterer carved oily beef.
18 After noon, a battered red streetcar veers up a graded hill.
19 Jim gave up a great seat; give him a few cases of free soap.

| 1 | 2 | 3 | 4 | 5 | 6 | 7 | 8 | 9 | 10 | 11 | 12 |

Report with References

G ETTING
started

Function review

Hanging Indent: Drag
Hanging Indent marker to
1/2" mark on ruler. ■

SKILLBUILDING WARMUP

Dehlinger, Joyce E. "Policies to Monitor Internet Use." *Computer Weekly,*
April 1998, p. 34.

DePriest, J. Shannon. "WWW Citations." *Graduate Education Journal,*
Spring 1998. <http://www.gej.edu/citations/wwwcitations.htm>
(23 July 1998).

Shaffer, Helen. *Guidelines for Effective Use of Electronic Mail.* New York:
Concord International Press, Inc., 1999.

48b • 12'

NEW
FUNCTION

Manual page break

When a page is filled with copy, the software automatically inserts a *soft page break*, which is indicated with a dotted line across the page when you are in Normal view.

You may need to begin a new page, however, before the page is filled. To insert a manual page break, press CTRL + ENTER. The software inserts a dotted line across the screen with the words "Page Break." The insertion point moves to the next page; the status line at the bottom of the screen indicates this change. A manual page break will not move as text is inserted or deleted.

To remove a manual page break, position the insertion point on the Page Break line and press DELETE.

Drill

1. Key the text at right, using Increase Indent and Decrease Indent buttons.

2. Place the insertion point after the first set of goals. Insert a manual page break.

3. Continue keying page 2.

4. Save and print.

Increase Indent

Decrease Indent

GOAL 1: MEMBERSHIP DEVELOPMENT

Objective: To increase membership.

Indent ⟶ **Plan**
    A. Review and evaluate membership benefits.
    B. Study avenues for additional membership benefits.
    C. Develop new membership markets.

··· Insert page break.

GOAL 2: STAFF DEVELOPMENT

Objective: To enhance performance and motivation of staff.

Indent ⟶ **Plan**
    A. Review and evaluate previous staff development programs.
    B. Survey staff to determine needs.
    C. Implement relevant staff development program.

COMMUNICATION

Edit as you key
Read the information about proofreaders' marks. Key each line, making the revisions as you key.

Errors are often circled in copy that is to be rekeyed. More frequently, perhaps, the copy is marked with special symbols called "proofreaders' marks" that indicate desired changes.

Some commonly used proofreaders' marks are shown below. Study them. Read carefully. Concentrate on content of the copy as you key.

Symbol	Meaning	Symbol	Meaning
Cap or ═	Capitalize	⌗	Add horizontal space
∧	Insert	∕ or *lc*	Lowercase letters
ℛ	Delete	⌣	Close up space
⊏	Move to left	∼	Transpose
⊐	Move to right	*stet*	Leave as originally written
¶	Paragraph		

20 We miss 50% in life's rewards by refusing to new try things.

21 do it now--today--then tomorrow's load will be 100%% lighter.

22 Satisfying work--whether it pays $40 or $400-is the pay off.

23 Avoid mistakes: confusing a #3 has cost thousands.

24 Pleased most with a first-rate job is the person who did it.

25 My wife and/or me mother will except the certifi cate for me.

26 When changes for success are 1 in 10, try a new approach.

SKILLBUILDING

Build staying power
Key two 1' writings on each ¶; then two 3' writings on both ¶s; compute *gwams*.

Goals: 1', 20-27 *gwam*
3', 17-24 *gwam*

Ⓔ all letters   *gwam* 3'

```
          •          4          •          8          •
    Is  how  you  judge  my  work  important?    It  is,  of  course;    4 | 26
      12         •         16         •         20         •
I  hope  you  recognize  some  basic  merit  in  it.    We  all  expect    8 | 30
      24         •         28         •         32
to  get  credit  for  good  work  that  we  conclude.                     11 | 33
          •          4          •          8          •
    I  want  approval  for  stands  I  take,  things  I  write,  and      14 | 36
      12         •         16         •         20         •
work  I  complete.    My  efforts,  by  my  work,  show  a  picture  of   18 | 41
      24         •         28         •         32         •
me;  thus,  through  my  work,  I  am  my  own  unique  creation.          22 | 44
```

3' ⊢————1————⊢————2————⊢————3————⊢————4————⊣

Document 2

1. Open *report.*
2. Position main heading at approximately 1.5".
3. Set proper line spacing.
4. Format headings correctly.
5. Make other edits shown at the right.
6. Save as **47b-d2.**

Did you check...
Paragraph alignment?
Capitalization?
Heading format?
Font size?

Document 3

1. Read carefully "Unbound reports." Open template *heading.*
2. Edit main, side, and paragraph headings.
3. Save as **47b-d3.** Print a copy and compare it to the model on the previous page.

Document 4

1. Open *47b-d2.*
2. Move the section "Choosing a Typeface" above "Working with Blocks." Use either Cut and Paste or Drag-and-Drop Editing.
3. Save as **47b-d4.**

WHO CAN DESIGN A BETTER BROCHURE? — 7

Producing a brochure with a professional appearance — 17
requires careful creativity and planning. Not every one is — 29
an accomplished paste-up artist who is capable of creating — 41
a complex piece of printed art, but most skilled computer — 50
users can create an attractive layout for a basic brochure. — 62
Working with blocks — 66

Work with copy and illustration in blocks. Type body — 76
or text copy, leaving plenty of space for illustrations and — 87
headlines. The blocks should then be arranged in a orderly — 99
and eye appealing manner. — 101

Using a small a small size type (or font) is not recommended. — 112
In most cases, use a font that is 12 point or larger to — 122
make the document easy to read. Copy that is arranged in — 133
more than one column is also more attractive. Try not to key — 143
copy across the full width of a page Preferably break the — 147
page into smaller columns of copy and intersperse with photos or — 160
illustrations. — 163

Choosing a typeface — 167
Typeface refers to the style of printing on the page. — 178
Matching the style or "feeling" of the type with the purpose — 190
of the finished product is very important. For example, — 202
a layout include of
you would not want to use a gothic or "old style" typeface — 215
to promote a modern, high/tech product. Consider the bold- — 227
ness or lightness of the style, and the readability factor, and — 233
the decorativeness or simplicity. Mixing more than three — 251
different typefaces on a page should also be avoided. Vary — 271
the type sizes to give the effect of different type styles. — 275
ital.
Bold and italics can also be added for emphasis and vari- — 286
ety, especially when only one type style is being used. — 297

Other Symbols

LESSON 24

24a ● 7'

GETTING **started**

each line twice SS

alphabet 1 Pfc. Jim Kings covered each of the lazy boxers with a quilt.

figures 2 Do Problems 6 to 29 on page 175 before class at 8:30, May 4.

" 3 They read the poems "September Rain" and "The Lower Branch."

easy 4 When did the busy girls fix the tight cowl of the ruby gown?

| 1 | 2 | 3 | 4 | 5 | 6 | 7 | 8 | 9 | 10 | 11 | 12 |

24b ● 14'

Note location of <, >, [,], @, *, +, and =

each pair of lines once SS; DS between 2-line groups

These keys are less commonly used, but they are needed in special circumstances. Unless your instructor tells you otherwise, you may key these reaches with visual help.

* = asterisk, star
+ = "plus sign" (use a hyphen for "minus"; x for "times")
@ = "at sign"
= = "equals sign"
< = "less than"
> = "more than"
[= "left bracket"
] = "right bracket"

*: shift; reach *up* with *right second* finger to *

5 * *k k8* * *; aurelis*; May 7*; both sides*; 250 km.**; aka*

6 Note each *; one * refers to page 29; ** refers to page 307.

+: shift; reach *up* with *right fourth* finger to +

7 + ;+ +; + + +; 2 + 2; A+ or B+; 70+ F. degrees; +xy over +y;

8 The question was 8 + 7 + 51; it should have been 8 + 7 + 15.

@: shift; reach *up* with *left third* finger to @

9 @ @s s@ @ @; 24 @ .15; 22 @ .35; sold 2 @ .87; were 12 @ .95

10 Ship 560 lbs. @ .36, 93 lbs. @ .14, and 3 lbs. @ .07 per lb.

=: reach *up* with *right fourth* finger to =

11 = =; = = =; = 4; If 14x = 28, x = 2; if 8x = 16, then x = 2.

12 Change this solution (where it says "= by") to = bx or = BX.

<: shift; reach *down* with *right second* finger to <; >: shift; reach *down* with *right third* finger to >

13 Can you prove "a > b"? If 28 > 5, then 5a < x. Is a < > b?

14 Is your answer < > .05? Computer programs use < and > keys.

[ ]: reach *up* with *right fourth* finger to [and]

15 Mr. Wing was named. [That's John J. Wing, ex-senator. Ed.]

16 Mr. Lanz said in his note, "I am moving to Filly [sic] now."

| 1 | 2 | 3 | 4 | 5 | 6 | 7 | 8 | 9 | 10 | 11 | 12 |

About 1.5" top margin (Press ENTER)

DOCUMENT FORMAT

14 pt

DS

Effective page layout begins with the knowledge of basic document formatting guidelines. The format should enhance communication and create a consistent image.

DS

Side heading

Page Design

DS

Two simple formatting features related to page layout are the use of white space and appropriate use of attributes.

DS

Paragraph heading

White space. The first rule of page design is to provide adequate white space to avoid a cluttered page and to enhance reading. Formatting guides include (1) using side margins of 1" or more, (2) beginning the first page of the report 1.5" from the top edge of the paper, and (3) using appropriate line spacing.

Attributes. Applying various attributes such as bold, font size, and italic to text affects the physical appearance of a document. Bold adds emphasis to headings or selected words. Increasing the font size draws attention to parts of the document. Italic also adds emphasis as well as allowing the writer to follow established English rules. For example, titles of complete works can easily be italicized rather than underlined.

Default or 1"

Default or 1"

Typestyle

Another important decision of the page designer is choosing appropriate typestyles. A basic rule is to select typestyles that are appropriate to the type of communication and the audience to whom the communication is intended. A second rule is to limit typestyle changes within a document. Experts recommend using no more than two typestyles in one document.

UNBOUND REPORT

24c ● 10'

SKILLBUILDING

Review high-frequency words

The words at the right are from the 300 most used words. Key each line once; work for fluency.

Top 300

17 able attention bill card less concerning employees following
18 given him invoice list members note long recent until within
19 position provide several advise back board case free without
20 contract enclosing home items loan money offer payment where
21 public card regarding soon therefore making with application
22 basis book charge copies equipment free happy price hospital
23 job lock months period prices rate pay reply stock think own
24 where write association important both supply federal having
25 come credit full believe name paid personal products receipt
26 please increase past total attached better building customer
27 committee few general high increase life week while national
28 tax type property receive set system life able employees own

24d ● 7'

COMMUNICATION

Edit as you key

Read carefully and key each line twice at a controlled pace; edit as indicated by proofreaders' marks; compare your completed lines with those of 22d, p. 53.

29 Ask Group 1 to read Chater 6 of Book 11 (Shelf 19, Room 5).

30 All 6 of us live at One Bay road, not at 126-56th Street.
six

31 At 9 a.m. the owners decided to close form 12 noon to 1 p.m.

32 Ms. Vik leaves June 9; she returns the 14 or 15 of July.

33 The 16 per cent discount saves $115. A stamp costs 35 cents.

34 Elin gave $300,000,000; our gift was only 75 cents.
$3 million *to charity*

24e ● 12'

SKILLBUILDING

Build staying power

Keep eyes on copy, wrists low. Key a 1' writing on each ¶; then key two 3' writings on both ¶s.

all letters   *gwam* 3'

	•	4	•	8	•		

Why don't we like change very much? Do you think that   4 | 26

just maybe we want to be lazy; to dodge new things; and, as   8 | 30

much as possible, not to make hard decisions?   11 | 33

We know change can and does extend new areas for us to   14 | 36

enjoy, areas we might never have known existed; and to stay   18 | 40

away from all change could curtail our quality of life.   22 | 44

3' | 1 | 2 | 3 | 4 |

47a ● 10'

started

Functions applied:
- Margins
- Line spacing
- Preview
- Spelling

1. Open *report* from the template. Save as **47a**.
2. Use default side margins. Position the main heading with a 1.5" top margin.
3. Change line spacing to DS:
   - Select the entire document.
   - Choose *Paragraph* from the Format menu.

- Click **Indents and Spacing** tab; then select *Double* from the Line Spacing box.
- Click **OK**.
4. Check spelling and save.
5. Preview the document before printing. It should fit on one page.

47b ● 40'

FORMATTING

Unbound report format

Read carefully "Unbound reports" and study the illustration at the right: then, key the documents as directed.

Document 1

Key the model report on the next page.

1. Use default side margins. Position insertion point for a 1.5" top margin.
2. Set DS.
3. Key the main heading. Then select the heading and change the font size and style to 14 point and bold.
4. Bold side and paragraph headings.
5. Save as **47b-d1**.

Unbound reports

Reports prepared without covers or binders are called **unbound reports**. Pages may be attached with a staple or paper clip in the upper left corner.

Top margins: Approximately 1.5" for the first page; 1" for second and succeeding pages.

Side margins: 1" or default margins.

Bottom margins: Approximately 1"; last page bottom margin may be deeper.

Font size and spacing: Use 12-point size for readability. Double-space educational reports and indent paragraphs 0.5". Business reports are usually single-spaced; paragraphs begin at the left margin; DS between paragraphs.

Page numbers: The first page of a report is not numbered. The second and succeeding pages are numbered in the upper right corner.

Headings: Headings break a lengthy report into smaller, easy-to-understand parts. Reports will generally include side headings that are often further divided with paragraph headings. Format headings as follows:
- **Main headings:** Center title in ALL CAPS and bold. Use 14-point size.
- **Side headings:** Begin at left margin; bold heading. Capitalize first letters of main words; DS above and below headings.

- **Paragraph headings:** Begin text at the paragraph point. Bold the heading. Capitalize the first word only and follow heading with a period.

DOCUMENT FORMAT

Effective page layout begins with the knowledge of basic document formatting guidelines. The format should enhance communication and create a consistent image.

Page Design

Two simple formatting features related to page layout are the use of white space and appropriate use of attributes.

White space. The first rule of page design is to provide adequate white space to avoid a cluttered page and to enhance reading. Formatting guides include (1) using side margins of 1" or more, (2) beginning the first page of the report 1.5" from the top edge of the paper, and (3) using appropriate line spacing.

Attributes. Applying various attributes such as bold, font size, and italic to text affects the physical appearance of a document. Bold adds emphasis to headings or selected words. Increasing the font size draws attention to parts of the document. Italic also adds emphasis as well as allowing the writer to follow established English rules. For example, titles of complete works can easily be italicized rather than underlined.

Typestyle

Another important decision of the page designer is choosing appropriate typestyles. A basic rule is to select typestyles that are appropriate to the type of communication and the audience to whom the communication is intended. A second rule is to limit typestyle changes within a document. Experts recommend using no more than two typestyles in one document.

Assessment

GETTING started

each line twice SS

SKILLBUILDING WARMUP

alphabet 1 My wife helped fix a frozen lock on Jacque's vegetable bins.

figures 2 Sherm moved from 823 West 150th Street to 9472--67th Street.

double letters 3 Will Scott attempt to sell his bookkeeping books to Elliott?

easy 4 It is a shame he used the endowment for a visit to the city.

| 1 | 2 | 3 | 4 | 5 | 6 | 7 | 8 | 9 | 10 | 11 | 12 |

25b ● 10'

SKILLBUILDING

Assess straight copy
Key two 3' writings with controlled speed.

Goal: 3', 19-27 *gwam*

A   all letters   *gwam*   3'

The term careers can mean many different things to   3 | 51

different people.   As you know, a career is much more than a   8 | 55

job.   It is the kind of work that a person has through life.   12 | 59

It includes the jobs a person has over time.   It also involves   16 | 63

how the work life affects the other parts of our life.   There   20 | 67

are as many types of careers as there are people.   23 | 71

Almost all people have a career of some kind.   A career   27 | 74

can help us to reach unique goals, such as to make a living   31 | 79

or to help others.   The kind of career you have will affect   35 | 83

your life in many ways.   For example, it can determine where   39 | 87

you live, the money you make, and how you feel about yourself.   44 | 91

A good choice can thus help you realize the life you want.   47 | 95

3' | 1 | 2 | 3 | 4 |

⏱ 🔺 all letters   *gwam* 1' | 3'

Build staying power
Take two 3' writings on all ¶s.

In a recent show, a young skater gave a great performance. 12 | 4 | 69
Her leaps were beautiful, her spins were impossible to believe, 25 | 8 | 74
and she was a study in grace itself. But she had slipped during 38 | 13 | 78
a jump and had gone down briefly on the ice. Because of the high 51 | 17 | 82
quality of her act, however, she was given a third-place medal. 64 | 21 | 87

Her coach, talking later to a reporter, stated his pleasure 12 | 25 | 91
with her part of the show. When asked about the fall, he said 25 | 30 | 95
that emphasis should be placed on the good qualities of the per- 37 | 34 | 99
formance and not on one single blemish. He ended by saying that 50 | 38 | 104
as long as his students did the best they could, he would be 63 | 42 | 108
satisfied. 65 | 43 | 108

What is "best"? When asked, the young skater explained she 12 | 47 | 112
was pleased to have won the bronze medal. In fact, this perfor- 25 | 51 | 117
mance was a personal best for her; she was confident the gold 37 | 55 | 121
would come later if she worked hard enough. It appears she knew 50 | 60 | 125
the way to a better medal lay in beating not other people, but her 64 | 64 | 130
own personal best. 67 | 65 | 131

1' | 1 | 2 | 3 | 4 | 5 | 6 | 7 | 8 | 9 | 10 | 11 | 12 | 13 |
3' | 1 | | 2 | | 3 | | 4 |

on... **Trackballs**

NEWS

A traditional mouse works by moving the mouse casing, which contains a ball, across the desk on a mouse pad. A trackball is a type of pointing device that is similar to a mouse without a casing covering the ball. With a trackball, the thumb or finger is used to move the ball directly. Using a finger-activated trackball places less strain on the hand than using a traditional mouse repetitively. The ergonomic design of the trackball generally features buttons contoured to the shape of the hand. A trackball enables the user to control the pointer without hand or wrist movement. Trackballs range in price from less than $20 to more than $100 depending on the sophistication of the device.

SKILLBUILDING

Review reaches

Key smoothly, avoid pauses, and allow your fingers to work. Repeat if time permits.

symbols

5 He spent $25 for gifts, $31 for dinner, and $7 for cab fare.
6 As of 6/28, my code number is 1/k; Mona's, 2/k; John's, 3/k.

symbols

7 Bill #773 charged for us 4# of #33 brads and 6# of #8 nails.
8 He deducted 12% instead of 6%, a clear saving of 6%, not 7%.

outside reaches

9 When did Marq Quin go?   Did Quentin or Quincy Quin go?   Why?
10 We were quick to squirt a quantity of water at Quin and Wes.

long reaches

11 Barb Abver saw a vibrant version of her brave venture on TV.
12 Call a woman or a man who will manage Minerva Manor in Nome.

figures

13 On July 5, 54 of us had only 45 horses; 4 of them were lame.
14 Back in '90, Car 009 traveled 90 miles, getting 9 to 10 mpg.

| 1 | 2 | 3 | 4 | 5 | 6 | 7 | 8 | 9 | 10 | 11 | 12 |

25d • 13'

SKILLBUILDING

Assess figure skill

In the Open Screen, key two 1' writings and two 3' writings at a controlled speed.

Goal: 3', 16-24 *gwam*

all letters/figures   *gwam*   3'

Do I read the stock market pages in the news? Yes; and   4 | 35

at about 9 or 10 a.m. each morning, I know lots of excited   8 | 39

people are quick to join me. In fact, many of us zip right   12 | 43

to the 3d or 4th part of the paper to see if the prices of   16 | 47

our stocks have gone up or down. Now, those of us who are   19 | 51

"speculators" like to "buy at 52 and sell at 60"; while the   23 | 55

"investors" among us are more interested in a dividend we   27 | 59

may get, say 7 or 8 percent, than in the price of a stock.   31 | 62

3' | 1 | 2 | 3 | 4 |

Drag-and-Drop Editing

46d ● 10'

NEW FUNCTION

Drills 1-3

Repeat Drills 1-3 in 46b using Drag-and-Drop Editing.

Drag-and-Drop Editing allows selected text to be moved simply by (1) selecting the desired text and (2) dragging and dropping it in the new location. The mouse pointer will display a rectangle indicating Drag-and-Drop Editing.

To copy (or duplicate) the selected text, (1) select the text, (2) hold down the CTRL key, and (3) drag and drop. The mouse pointer will display a rectangle with a plus sign + when copying.

● If you should drop the text in the wrong location, click the Undo button and try again.

Window

46e ● 8'

NEW FUNCTION

More than one document can be open at a single time. Each document is displayed in its own window. To move from document to document, click the Window menu or click the document name shown in the Windows taskbar. The filename of each document that is open will display. A check mark is next to the active window. Text can be copied and pasted between documents.

Drill

1. Open the three drills completed in 46b.
2. Use the Window menu to go to each document.
3. Go to *46b-d2*. Copy the document.
4. Go to the bottom of document *46b-d1*. Click **Paste**.
5. Go to the bottom of document *46b-d3*. Click **Paste**.
● 6. Close all documents without saving.

46f ● (challenge)

Drag-and-Drop Editing between windows

Repeat drill in 46e and use Drag-and-Drop Editing.

Drag-and-Drop Editing can also be used to move and copy text to documents in other windows. To accomplish this, the windows must first be tiled. With two or more files open, follow these steps:

1. Right-click the background of the Windows taskbar.

Click here

2. Click **Tile Vertically.** All windows on the Windows desktop display.

3. Select the text to be moved or copied. (Using the left mouse button, click to drag; add CTRL key to copy text.)

4. Drag insertion point into the appropriate window; then drop text in desired location.

5. To undo tiling, right-click the Windows taskbar and choose **Undo Tile.**

EXTENDED SKILLBUILDING

OBJECTIVES

1. Improve speed and accuracy.

2. Key from rough-draft copy.

3. Key a 3' writing at 25 *wam* or higher.

LESSON 26

Skillbuilding

26a • 7'

GETTING started

The Skillbuilding Warmup is recorded on your software but not in the book. Key it and then progress to 26b in the usual manner.

26b • 13'

SKILLBUILDING

Practice reaches
each line at the right once;
avoid pauses

outside reaches

1 zap papaw was zipper quale paper axle zag aquas azure ataxia
2 apex wasp assay zip axial sassy pappy sassafras exit pallial
3 Was Polly acquainted with the equipped jazz player in Texas?

long reaches

4 ce cede cedar wreck nu nu nut punt nuisance my my amy mystic
5 ny ny any many company mu mu mull lumber mulch br br furbish
6 The absence of receiving my umbrella disturbed the musician.

figure reaches

7 Memo 461 dated May 20 was filed in drawer 85 and folder 397.
8 The November revenue of 836, 940, 271, and 573 averaged 655.
9 She purchased 62 pens, 139 stamps, 48 rulers, and 507 disks.

adjacent reaches

10 as we opt try web sad buy rest hurt tree join suit open trip
11 perk true union energy weave poster seeds backlog ergonomics
12 The opponent heard the treasurer read her opinion on unions.

| 1 | 2 | 3 | 4 | 5 | 6 | 7 | 8 | 9 | 10 | 11 | 12 |

46b, *continued*

To select the entire document, choose *Select All* from the Edit menu. (See Drill 3.) ▪

Drill 2   Copy and Paste

1. Open *select.* Save as **46b-d2**.
2. Select ¶ 1 and click **Copy**.
3. Move the insertion point to the blank line below the last ¶. Click **Paste**.
4. Save and print.

Drill 3   Copy and Paste

1. Open *copy.* Save as **46b-d3**.
2. Select the entire form. (See the Quick Tip.) Click **Copy**.
3. Move the insertion point below the form. Press ENTER 3 times. Click **Paste**.
4. Save and print.

46c ● 10'

NEW FUNCTION

Undo and Redo

Clicking the Undo button reverses the most recent action you have taken (i.e., inserting or deleting text, bolding, changing margins). To reverse several actions, first display a list of recent actions by clicking the arrow next to Undo. Then click the action you wish to reverse. However, remember all actions above the action selected will be reversed also. Commands such as Save and Print cannot be undone.

Redo reverses the last Undo and can be applied several times to redo the past several actions. Click on the arrow at the right of Redo to view all actions that can be redone.

Drill 1

1. Key the text SS.
2. After the document is keyed, center and bold the title.
3. Save as **46c-d1**.

CELLULAR PHONES

A car or cellular phone is essential in today's high-tech, fast-paced society. Secretaries, administrative support personnel, and managers are finding themselves dealing with critical, last-minute telecommunications.

Cellular phones provide safety as well as convenience. A person experiencing car trouble can solicit assistance without leaving the car. If medical assistance is needed, 911 can be called immediately.

Drills 2 and 3

With Drill 1 on your screen, complete Drills 2 and 3.

Drill 2

1. Change side margins to 2".
2. Click **Undo**:
   • to restore default margins.
   • again to return title to left margin.
   • again to remove bold.
3. Click **Redo** 3 times; watch as it restores each function.
4. Display the Undo drop list; click **Paragraph Alignment** to return the title to the left margin and change margins.

5. Display the Redo drop list and click **Page Setup**. This restores the margins and centers the title.

Drill 3

1. Select and bold "911." Click **Undo** to remove bold; restore the bold.
2. Select and italicize "solicit assistance." Use Undo to remove italic; restore the italic.
3. Delete the first sentence. Use Undo to restore the sentence.

26c • 5'

COMMUNICATION

Edit as you key
Read carefully; each line contains 2 errors, but only 1 is circled. Correct both errors as you key.

13 (i) asked Ty for a loan of $40; his interest rate is two high.

14 Please advice me how I can (spent) $18 for a second-hand book.

15 I'm sorry I lost (you) first-balcony tickers for the concert.

16 Linda saws 3659 Riley (rode) is her daughter-in-law's address.

26d • 8'

SKILLBUILDING

Practice opposite-hand reaches
each group once; repeat
Concentrate on the proper reach.

g/h

17 gag go gee god rig gun log gong cog gig agog gage going gang
18 huh oh hen the hex ash her hash ah hush shah hutch hand ache
19 ugh high ghoul rough ghosts cough night laugh ghee bough ghi
20 Hush; Greg hears rough sounds. Has Hugh laughed or coughed?

r/u

21 row or rid air rap par rye rear ark jar rip nor are right or
22 cut us auk out tutu sun husk but fun cub gun nut mud tug hug
23 rut aura run your rub cure rum our rue cur rug urn true pure
24 Ryan is sure you should pour your food from an urn or cruet.

| 1 | 2 | 3 | 4 | 5 | 6 | 7 | 8 | 9 | 10 | 11 | 12 |

26e • 17'

SKILLBUILDING

Check speed
Key two 3' writings.

Optional:
Diagnostic Writing
1. Return to the Lesson menu and click the **Diagnostic Writings** button.
2. From the list of writings, select *26e*. Set the Timer for **3'**.
3. Key the timing from the textbook.
4. Review your results on the Summary Report, Diagnostic Writings Summary.

  all letters   *gwam* 1' | 3'

I have a story or two or three that will carry you away   11 | 4
to foreign places, to meet people you have never known, to   23 | 8
see things you have never seen, to feast on foods available   35 | 12
only to a few. I will help you to learn new skills you want   47 | 16
and need; I will inspire you, excite you, instruct you, and   59 | 20
interest you. I am able, you understand, to make time fly.   71 | 24

I answer difficult questions for you. I work with you   11 | 27
to realize a talent, to express a thought, and to determine   23 | 31
just who and what you are and want to be. I help you to   35 | 35
know words, to write, and to read. I help you to comprehend   47 | 40
the mysteries of the past and the secrets of the future. I   59 | 44
am your local library. We ought to get together often.   70 | 47

1' | 1 | 2 | 3 | 4 | 5 | 6 | 7 | 8 | 9 | 10 | 11 | 12 |
3' | 1 | 2 | 3 | 4 |

LESSON **46**

Editing Text

46a ● 10'

FORMATTING

Review

1. Key the drill, indenting the rules only.
2. Practice selecting text:
   - The line containing "SELECTING TEXT"; bold and choose 14 point.
   - The word "quickly" in ¶ 1; bold.
   - The last sentence in ¶ 1; press DELETE.
   - ¶ 1; italicize.
   - Text from "Paragraph" to end of document; press DELETE.

SELECTING TEXT

Most people learn to use a mouse, but many do not learn to use the mouse efficiently. Let's practice using the mouse to select text quickly. Follow these rules in selecting the following text:

Word:	Double-click on the word.
Line of text:	Click in selection bar to the left of the line.
Sentence:	Hold down the CTRL key and click anywhere in the sentence.
Paragraph:	Double-click in the selection bar or triple-click in the paragraph.
Multiple lines:	Drag in the selection bar to the left of lines.

Now watch your friends and colleagues marvel at your efficiency in editing documents using smart mouse selection techniques.

46b ● 12'

NEW FUNCTION

Cut

Cut is used to delete blocks of text not needed. The Cut feature is preferred over using the DELETE key because the cut text remains on the Clipboard (temporary storage location) and can be retrieved once deleted. To use the Cut feature, select the text and then click the Cut button.

Paste

Paste is often used with Cut to move selected text in the document. First, cut the selected text; then, move the insertion point to the new location and click the Paste button. The text has now moved to the new location.

Copy

Text can be copied from one location to another within a document. The software will "copy" the text and "paste" the copy in a new location. The original copy remains in its place. If another copy is needed, click Paste again. The same text is pasted because the copied text remains on the Clipboard until new text is copied.

Drill I   Cut and Paste

1. Open *cutpaste*. Save as **46b-d1**.
2. Select the text beginning with the side heading "Cut and Paste" to the end of the file (two paragraphs). Click **Cut**.
3. Move the insertion point to the top of the document.
4. Click **Paste**. Press ENTER as needed to insert blank lines.

Skillbuilding

27a ● 7'

GETTING started

each line twice SS;
(slowly, then faster)

alphabet 1 Hose Wevs and Bruce Fox kept Zaney Quigly in Mexico in June.

figures 2 Do Problems 7 to 18 on page 264 before class at 9:30, May 5.

quotes 3 "I know the book is ready," she said, "to be shipped today."

easy 4 If she is not going with us, why don't we plan to leave now?

| 1 | 2 | 3 | 4 | 5 | 6 | 7 | 8 | 9 | 10 | 11 | 12 |

27b ● 10'

SKILLBUILDING

Practice opposite-hand reaches

Key at a controlled rate; concentrate on the reaches.

i/e
5 ik is fit it sit laid site like insist still wise coil light
6 ed he ear the fed egg led elf lake jade heat feet hear where
7 lie kite item five aide either quite linear imagine brighter
8 Imagine the aide eating the pears before the grieving tiger.

u/r
9 uj use jut jug dust sue duel fuel just sun tuna usual vacuum
10 rf red jar ear for rag over czar rose yarn real friend broom
11 fur urn run user turn pure utter under bursar course furnace
12 The younger bursar turned the ruined urns under the furnace.

w/o
13 ws we way was few went wit law with weed were week gnaw when
14 ol on go hot old lot joy odd comb open tool upon money union
15 bow owl word wood worm worse tower brown toward wrote weapon
16 The workers lowered the brown swords toward the wood weapon.

y/t
17 yj my say may yes rye yarn eye lye yap any relay young berry
18 tf at it let the vat tap item town toast right little attire
19 yet toy yogurt typical youth tycoon yacht tympani typewriter
20 Yesterday a young youth typed a cat story on the typewriter.

b/n
21 bf but job fibs orb bow able bear habit boast rabbit brother
22 nj not and one now fun next pony month notice runner quicken
23 bin bran knob born cabin number botany nibble blank neighbor
24 A number of neighbors banked on bunking in the brown cabins.

| 1 | 2 | 3 | 4 | 5 | 6 | 7 | 8 | 9 | 10 | 11 | 12 |

45c, continued

Drill 2

1. Drag the Hanging Indent marker 1/2"; then key the references.

2. Turn Hanging Indent off by dragging the Hanging Indent marker back to left margin.

Drill 3

1. Key the glossary.

2. Select all the entries and drag the Hanging Indent marker 1/2" to the right.

3. Center the main heading **GLOSSARY** a DS above the first item.

Busch, J. Austin. "Using the Internet Effectively in the Employment Search." *Surfing the Information Highway*. Boston: University Press, 1999.

Humphries, Peggy T. "Is Creativity Required of Today's Successful Executive?" *The New Management Quarterly*. Chicago: Quinton Press, 1999.

Hanging indent: A hanging indent places the first line of a paragraph at the left margin and indents remaining lines to the first tab.

Header: Text or graphic that is printed at the top of a page in a document.

Insert mode: Opposite of overstrike or typeover mode, the insert mode moves existing text to the right as you insert new characters.

45d ● 12'

Setting margins

Drill 1

1. Set 1" side margins.

2. Key the ¶ below right. Save as **45d-d1**; preview document.

3. Position insertion point at the beginning of Sentence 3. Press ENTER twice.

4. With insertion point in ¶ 2, change the top and side margins to 2". Preview document.

5. At the end of Sentence 3, press ENTER twice.

6. Key and complete this sentence with the better response: *The margin command affects the appearance of the a) entire document b) paragraph containing the insertion point.*

Drill 2

1. Set 1.5" left, right, and top margins. Apply margin settings to whole document. Key the ¶.

2. Save as **45d-d2**.

Margins

Margins are the distance between the edge of the paper and the print. The default settings are 1.25" side margins and 1" top and bottom margins. Default margins stay in effect until you change them.

To change the margins:

1. Click **File,** then click **Page Setup**.

2. From the Margins tab, click the up or down arrows to increase or decrease the default settings.

3. Apply margins to the *Whole document* unless directed otherwise. Click **OK**.

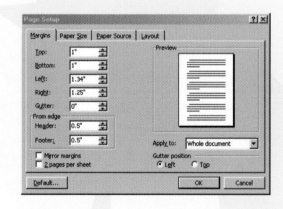

Drills 1 and 2

Documents are more attractive when the margins are set an equal distance from the left and right edges of the paper. This gives the document the appearance of being balanced. How the copy looks is just as important as what you key.

Build skill
Key the easy, balanced-hand copy without hesitation. Repeat at a faster pace.

25 is if he do rub ant go and am pan do rut us aid ox ape by is
26 it is | an end | it may | to pay | and so | aid us | he got | or own | to go
27 Did the girl make the ornament with fur, duck down, or hair?

28 us owl rug box bob to man so bit or big pen of jay me age it
29 it | it is | time to go | show them how | plan to go | one of the aims
30 It is a shame they use the autobus for a visit to the field.

| 1 | 2 | 3 | 4 | 5 | 6 | 7 | 8 | 9 | 10 | 11 | 12 |

27d ● 5'

COMMUNICATION

Key edited copy
Make corrections as indicated by proofreaders' marks.

There was once a rich man, *but unhappy,* who was not very happy. He had
spent large sums of *money* for fancy clothes, a *lovely* beautiful home,
luxurious cars --even his own plane --but none of it brought
him happiness. his psychiatrist, after weeks of therapy,
finally explained that happiness can't be bought; it must
be found. And--you guessed it--the unhappy man paid for
these words of wisdom with another large sum.
stet

27e ● 14'

SKILLBUILDING

Check speed
Key two 3' writings.

Optional:
Diagnostic Writing
1. Return to the Lesson menu and click the **Diagnostic Writings** button.
2. From the list of writings, select 27e. Set Timer for **3'**.
3. Key the timing from the textbook.

 all letters   *gwam* 1' | 3'

    The computer is the basic teaching tool to use in distance   12 | 4 | 43
education.   You quickly learn to work in the class as though   24 | 8 | 47
you were in the same room in a school house.   33 | 11 | 50

    In distance education, you can take the class at a local   44 | 15 | 53
school.   Class times are not so rigid.   The class does not   56 | 19 | 57
have a certain time to stop.   All of the communication can be   68 | 23 | 62
kept in the computer.   73 | 24 | 63

    This type of education does not have face-to-face instruc-   84 | 28 | 67
tion.   The machines may not be known to those on the job.   96 | 32 | 71
Too much data may be realized.   The cost can be high.   As   108 | 36 | 75
networks grow, so will distance education.   116 | 39 | 77

| 1' | 1 | 2 | 3 | 4 | 5 | 6 | 7 | 8 | 9 | 10 | 11 | 12 |
| 3' | | 1 | | | 2 | | | 3 | | | 4 | |

Indent

Indent moves all lines of a paragraph to the next tab. The tab moves only the first line of a paragraph to the next tab. Indent sets off a paragraph from the remainder of the document by indenting it from the side margins. Indent is a paragraph command.

To indent text from the left margin:
1. Click the **Increase Indent** button on the toolbar.
2. Key the paragraph and press ENTER. The left indent will continue until you click on the **Decrease Indent** button.

Indent can also be applied to text that has already been keyed by selecting the text and then clicking Increase Indent.

Drill 1

1. DS ¶ 1.

2. At the left margin, click the **Increase Indent** button to indent ¶ 2. Change to SS. Key ¶ 2.

3. Click the **Decrease Indent** button; change to DS. Key ¶ 3.

However, the thrust to use e-mail almost exclusively is causing a tremendous challenge for both e-mail recipients and companies.

Indent → With the convenience of electronic mail resulting in its widespread use, many users are forsaking other forms of communications--face-to-face, telephone (including voice mail), and printed documents. Now companies are challenged to create clear e-mail policies and to implement employee training on effective use of e-mail (Ashford, 1998, 2).

Communication experts have identified problems that may occur as a result of misusing e-mail. Two important problems include information overload (too many messages) and inappropriate form of communication.

Increase Indent

Decrease Indent

Hanging Indent

Hanging Indent places the first line of a paragraph at the left margin and indents all other lines to the first tab. Hanging Indent is commonly used to format bibliography entries, glossaries, and lists. Hanging Indent can be applied before text is keyed or after.

To use Hanging Indent:
1. Display the Horizontal Ruler (click **view**, then **ruler**).
2. From the Horizontal Ruler, drag the Hanging Indent marker to the position where the indent is to begin.

Hanging Indent marker

3. Key the paragraph. The second and subsequent lines are indented beginning at the marker.

LESSON 28

Skillbuilding

28a ● 7'

**G E T T I N G
s t a r t e d**

each line twice (slowly, then faster)

alphabet 1 A quaint report was given that amazed Felix, Jack, and Boyd.
figures 2 Do read Section 4, pages 60-74 and Section 9, pages 198-235.
fig/sym 3 Invoice #384 for $672.91, plus $4.38 tax, was due on 5/20/97.
easy 4 Do you desire to continue working on the memo in the future?

| 1 | 2 | 3 | 4 | 5 | 6 | 7 | 8 | 9 | 10 | 11 | 12 |

28b ● 8'

SKILLBUILDING

Practice specific rows

each line once; repeat
Work for smooth, continuous stroking.

5 Sarah Hall had a half dish of hash as she asked for a glass.
6 The lass had to wash half of the tall glasses in the washer.

7 Calvin named the excited zebra Zabic as the men boxed it in.
8 Can Nancy Cox be amazed by winning six dozen boxes of cocoa?

9 You are trying to type every top row key with a quick touch.
10 Put your power to rest if you are not trying to win the bet.

11 On May 19-23, the 72 employees worked from 6:30 to 8:45 a.m.
12 His social security number is 247513086; it arrived on 7/27.

28c ● 12'

SKILLBUILDING

Improve rhythm

each line twice; do not pause at the end of the lines

words: *think, say,* and *key* words
13 is do am lay cut pen dub may fob ale rap cot hay pay hem box
14 box wit man sir fish also hair giant rigor civic virus ivory
15 laugh sight flame audit formal social turkey bicycle problem

phrases: *think, say,* and *key* phrases
16 is it|is it|if it is|if it is|or by|or by|or me|or me|for us
17 and all|for pay|pay dues and|the pen|the pen box|the pen box
18 such forms|held both|work form|then wish|sign name|with them

easy sentences
19 The man is to do the work right; he then pays the neighbors.
20 Sign the forms to pay the eight men for the turkey and hams.
21 The antique ivory bicycle is a social problem for the chair.

| 1 | 2 | 3 | 4 | 5 | 6 | 7 | 8 | 9 | 10 | 11 | 12 |

SIMPLE REPORTS

OBJECTIVES

1. Format two-page unbound and leftbound reports.

2. Format long references and title pages.

3. Learn additional word processing functions.

4. Change the format of existing documents.

5. Improve speed and accuracy.

LESSON 45

Skillbuilding/Formatting Text

45a ● 8'

GETTING started

Key each line twice at a slow but steady pace. DS between 2-line groups. Rekey twice lines having more than one error.

SKILLBUILDING WARMUP

1 Few beavers, as far as I'm aware, feast on cedar trees in Kokomo.

2 A plump, aged monk served a few million beggars a milky beverage.

one-hand sentences

3 Johnny, after a few stewed eggs, ate a plump, pink onion at noon.

4 In regard to desert oil wastes, Jill referred only minimum cases.

5 Link agrees you'll get a reward only as you join nonunion racers.

| 1 | 2 | 3 | 4 | 5 | 6 | 7 | 8 | 9 | 10 | 11 | 12 | 13 |

45b ● 12'

SKILLBUILDING

Reach for new goals

1. Key 1' guided writings; determine *gwam*.
2. Take two 2' writings; try to maintain your best 1' rate.
3. Take a 3' writing. Use your *gwam* in Step 1 as your goal.

  all letters

	gwam	2'	3'

If you believe that office management is a viable objective 6 | 4

on your horizon, maybe you envision how essential it is that you 13 | 8

learn to work with others. As a leader, for example, you should 19 | 13

quickly become part of the company team. You will learn much by 26 | 17

working closely with your fellow workers; at first, you actually 32 | 21

depend on them to give you a better idea of how everyone fits in 39 | 26

the overall picture and how best to improve on office efficiency. 45 | 30

| 2' | 1 | 2 | 3 | 4 | 5 | 6 |
| 3' | | 1 | 2 | 3 | 4 |

COMMUNICATION

Key edited copy
Make corrections as indicated
by proofreaders' marks.

take time to evaluate your completed work. Look

caefully at what you havee done. Would be you impressed

with it if you wre a reader? Is it attractive in form and

accurate in content? Does it look like something you would

pick up because it looks interesting? Does the title

attract you? Do the first couple of lines catch your atten-

tion? Personal appraisal of your own work is very

important. For if it does not impress you, it

will not impress any one else.

SKILLBUILDING

Check speed
Key two 1' writings on ¶ 1.

Optional:

1. Set the Timer in the Open Screen for **2'**.
2. Take a 2' writing on ¶ 1. Note your *gwam*.
3. Take two 2' writings on ¶ 2. Try to equal your *gwam* on ¶ 1.
4. Take a 3' writing on both ¶s.

Ⓔ all letters

gwam | 1' | 2' | 3'

Good health is a matter not so much for its contribution 11 | 6 | 4

to a longer life but for a better life. Good health is attain- 24 | 12 | 8

able now to all. A few can measure up better than those who 36 | 18 | 12

are whole and sound in body but lacking in mind and spirit. 48 | 24 | 16

Learning to live and to live well is the highest concept. 60 | 30 | 20

How can we affect our future health? It is quite obvious 12 | 36 | 24

quite once at that there are some limit that we must accept. We 24 | 42 | 28

must learn to make the most of what we have. We can take 35 | 48 | 32

steps to hazards from with out and to control dangers 47 | 53 | 36

from within. WITH good health, we expect expect to live a just 59 | 59 | 39

life. 60 | 60 | 40

| 1 | 2 | 3 | 4 | 5 | 6 | 7 | 8 | 9 | 10 | 11 | 12 |

6. Review the entire registration form and submit it. You will be notified immediately that your e-mail account has been established. (If your e-mail name is already in use by someone else, you may be instructed to choose a different name before your account can be established.)

Send e-mail message

To send an e-mail message, you must have the address of the computer user you want to write. Business cards, letterheads, directories, etc., now include e-mail addresses. Often a telephone call is helpful in obtaining e-mail addresses. An e-mail address includes the user's login name followed by @ and the domain: sthomas@yahoo.com or sdt3@jn.ndu.edu.

Creating an e-mail message is quite similar to preparing a memo. The e-mail header includes TO, FROM, and SUBJECT. Key the e-mail address of the recipient on the TO line, and compose a subject line that concisely describes the theme of your message. Your e-mail address will automatically display on the FROM line.

Practice
1. Open the search engine used to set up your e-mail account. Click **E-mail**, **Free E-mail**, or **Get E-mail**. (*Terms will vary.*)
2. Enter your e-mail name and password when prompted.
3. Enter the e-mail address of your instructor or another student.
4. Compose a brief message. Be sure to include a descriptive subject line.
5. Send the message.

Read e-mail messages

Reading one's e-mail messages and responding promptly are considered important rules of netiquette (etiquette for the Internet). However, avoid responding too quickly to sensitive situations.

Practice
1. Open your e-mail account if it is not open.
2. Read your messages and respond immediately. Click **Reply** to answer the message. (*E-mail programs may vary.*)

Forward e-mail messages

Received e-mail messages are often shared or forwarded to other e-mail users. Be considerate of others as you make decisions about forwarding messages.

Practice
1. Open your e-mail account if it is not open.
2. Forward a message received from a student to your teacher or another student.
3. Delete all read messages.

Attach a document to an e-mail message

Electronic files can be attached to an e-mail message and sent to another computer electronically. Recipients of attached documents can transfer these documents to their computers and then open for use.

Practice
1. Open your e-mail account if it is not open.
2. Create an e-mail message to your teacher that states your homework is attached. The subject line should include the specific homework assignment (*44b-d1*, for example).
3. Attach the file by clicking **Attach**. Use the browser to locate the homework file. (*E-mail programs may vary.*)
4. Send the e-mail.

Skillbuilding

29a ● 7'

GETTING started

each line twice SS

alphabet	1	Juni, Vec, and Zeb had perfect grades on weekly query exams.
shift	2	Give a monetary prize to J. W. Fuqua and B. K. Charles next.
figures	3	Her grades are 93, 87, and 100; his included 82, 96, and 54.
combination	4	You should be interested in the special items on sale today.

| 1 | 2 | 3 | 4 | 5 | 6 | 7 | 8 | 9 | 10 | 11 | 12 |

29b ● 8'

SKILLBUILDING

Practice figures
each line once; repeat

8/1	5	line 8; Book 1; No. 88; Seat 11; June 18; Cart 81; date 1881
2/7	6	take 2; July 7; buy 22; sell 77; mark 27; adds 72; Memo 2772
3/9	7	feed 3; bats 9; age 33; Ext. 99; File 39; 93 bags; band 3993
4/0	8	set 0; push 4; Car 00; score 44; jot 04; age 40; Billet 4004
6/5	9	April 6; lock 5; set 66; fill 55; hit 65; pick 56; adds 5665
all	10	Do Problems 6 to 29 on p. 175 before class at 8:30 on May 4.

29c ● 10'

SKILLBUILDING

Improve reaches
each line once; fingers curved
and relaxed; wrists low

3d/1st	11	cry tube wine quit very curb exit crime ebony mention excite
	12	Remember to be invited to petition the men in the hot tower.
1st/2d	13	bad fun nut kick dried night brick civic thick hutch believe
	14	The huge knight began to certify everything in the gem tray.
3d/4th	15	pop was lap pass slaw wool solo swap apollo wasp load plaque
	16	Sally saw the son-in-law pass the wool and plaque proposals.
top	17	1 1a 11; 8 8k 88; 5 5f 55; 0 0; 00; 2 2s 22; 7 7j 77; 9 9l 9
	18	3 3d 33; 6 6j 66; 4 4f 44; 777 East 747 West; 3:40 on 3/5/97

| 1 | 2 | 3 | 4 | 5 | 6 | 7 | 8 | 9 | 10 | 11 | 12 |

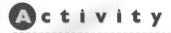

Activity

six   **Surf the Net with hyperlinks**

A **hyperlink** is used to link one Web document to another Web document. The hyperlink inserted in the Web site may be a link to another page in the Web site or to another Web site. For example, the Web page for a university may include hyperlinks to the various academic departments within the university (pages within the Web site) and a hyperlink to the local visitors' and convention center (another Web site).

A hyperlink may be applied to either text or images. Hyperlinked text displays in a different color and is underlined. When the mouse is pointed at hyperlinked text or images, the mouse pointer changes to a pointing hand. Click the hyperlink, and the new Web document displays. Remember to click the Back button to return to the original Web site.

Practice
1. At http://www.army.mil, click the following hyperlinked text: Installations.
2. From that page, click the database hyperlinked text.
3. Click the **Back** button twice to return to the original Web page.
4. At http://www.yahoo.com, click on the following hyperlinked text and images:
    a. **E-mail**
    b. **People Search**
    c. **Image for What's New**
5. Open a Web site for a university or college of your choice.
    a. List two hyperlinked images.
    b. List two examples of hyperlinked text.
    c. Which text or image is linked to another Web document within the Web site?
    d. Which text or image is linked to another Web site?

Activity

   **Electronic mail**

Electronic mail or *e-mail* refers to electronic messages sent by one computer user to another computer user. To be able to send or receive e-mail, you must have an e-mail address, have an e-mail program, and have access to the Internet or an Intranet (in-house network).

Set up e-mail addresses
Many search engines such as Yahoo!, Excite, Lycos, AltaVista, and others are now providing free e-mail via their Web sites. These e-mail programs allow users to set up an e-mail address and then send and retrieve e-mail messages. To set up an account and obtain an e-mail address, the user must (1) agree to the terms of agreement, (2) complete an online registration form, and (3) compose an e-mail name and password.

Practice
1. Click the **Search** button on the browser's toolbar. Click a search engine that offers free e-mail.
2. Click **Free E-mail**, **E-mail**, or **Get E-mail**. (*Terms will vary.*)
3. Read the Terms of Agreement and accept.
4. Enter an e-mail name. This name will be the login-name portion of your e-mail address.
5. Enter a password for your e-mail account. For security reasons, do not share your password, do not leave it where others can use it, and avoid choosing pet names or birth dates. Use number and letter combinations that make no sense.

(continued)

29d ● 8'

Improve figures/symbols
Key the paragraph once; keep wrists low and hands quiet.

Optional:
Take a 3' writing in the Open Screen.

 all letters/figures/symbols

gwam 3'

At your request, you just sold on 2/18/97 125 shares | 4 | 34 |
of stock for $34.96 a share. The stock was purchased on | 7 | 38 |
7/08/93 for $26.43 a share and that during the current year | 11 | 42 |
you realized $1.95 a share in cash dividends. You have a | 15 | 46 |
capital gain of $1,066.25 ($34.96/share - $26.43/share x 125 | 19 | 50 |
shares) and $243.75 in dividend income ($1.95 x 125 shares). | 23 | 54 |
If you were in a 31% group, your dividends would be subject | 27 | 58 |
to a 31% tax rate ($243.75 x .31 = $75.56 in taxes). | 31 | 62 |

3' | 1 | 2 | 3 | 4 |

29e ● 12'

Check speed
Key two 3' writings.

Optional:
1. In the Open Screen, take two 1' guided writings on ¶ 1.
2. Take a 2' writing; try to maintain 1' rate.
3. Take a 3' writing; try to maintain 1' rate.
(See p. 49 for instructions on taking a guided writing.)

all letters

gwam 2' 3'

A wise man once said that we have two ears and one | 5 | 3 | 33 |
tongue so that we may hear more and talk less. Therefore, | 11 | 7 | 37 |
we should be prepared to talk less quickly and exert more | 17 | 11 | 41 |
effort to listen carefully to what others have to offer. | 22 | 15 | 45 |
Most people do not realize that when we listen, we use | 28 | 19 | 48 |
not just our ears, but our eyes and mind as well. To form | 34 | 23 | 52 |
the art of listening well, show interest in what is said, | 40 | 26 | 56 |
pay attention, ask questions, and keep an open mind. | 45 | 30 | 60 |

2' | 1 | 2 | 3 | 4 | 5 | 6 |
3' | 1 | 2 | 3 | 4 |

29f ● 5'

Improve number speed
Take 1' writings; the last number you key when you stop is your approximate *gwam*.

1 and 2 and 3 and 4 and 5 and 6 and 7 and 8 and 9 and 10 and 11 and 12 and 13 and 14 and 15 and 16 and 17 and 18 and 19 and 20 and 21 and 22 and 23 and 24 and 25 and 26 and 27 and

Netsite entry box:	Displays the active URL or Web site address.
Back:	Moves to Web sites or pages visited since opening the browser.
Forward:	Moves forward to sites visited prior to using the Back button. (The Forward button is ghosted if the Back button has not been used.)
Print:	Prints a Web page.
Home:	Returns to the Web page designated as the Home or Start Page.
Stop:	Stops computer's search for a Web site.
Search:	Opens one of the Internet search engines.
Bookmarks:	Moves to list of Web sites marked for easy access.

Practice
1. Open the following Web sites:
   a. http://www.nike.com
   b. http://www.adidas.com
   c. http://www.reebok.com
   d. a site of your choice
2. Click the **Back** button twice. The _____ Web site displays.
3. Click the **Forward** button once. The _____ Web site displays.
4. Print the active Web page.
5. Key **http://www.msstate.edu** in the Netsite or Location entry box. Stop the search before the Web site is located.
6. Click the **Search** button.

Activity
five

Bookmark a favorite Web site

When readers put a book aside, they insert a bookmark to mark the place. Internet users also add bookmarks to mark their favorite Web sites or ones of interest for later browsing.

To add a bookmark:
1. Open the desired Web site.
2. Click **Bookmarks** and then **Add Bookmark**. (Browsers may vary on location and name of Bookmark button.)

To use a bookmark:
1. Click **Bookmarks** (or **Communicator, Bookmarks** or **Window Bookmarks**).
2. Select the desired bookmark. Click or double-click, depending on your browser. The desired Web site displays.

Practice
1. Open these favorite Web sites and bookmark them on your browser.
   a. http://www.weather.com   c. http://www.usps.gov
   b. http://www.cnn.com   d. Add one of your choice.
2. Use the bookmark to go to the following Web sites:
   a. The Weather Channel   c. The United States Postal Service
   b. CNN   d. The Web site you bookmarked

Skillbuilding

30a ● 7'

GETTING started

each line twice SS

SKILLBUILDING WARMUP

alphabet 1 Jewel quickly explained to me the big fire hazards involved.

– (hyphen) 2 Pam has an up-to-the-minute plan to lower out-of-town costs.

fig/sym 3 Pay Invoice #378 and #9605 by 6/21 to receive a 4% discount.

easy 4 Susie is busy; may she halt the social work for the auditor?

| 1 | 2 | 3 | 4 | 5 | 6 | 7 | 8 | 9 | 10 | 11 | 12 |

30b ● 8'

SKILLBUILDING

Practice long reaches
each line once; repeat;
keep hands quiet

n/y 5 deny many canny tiny nymph puny any puny zany penny pony yen

6 Jenny Nyles saw many, many tiny nymphs flying near her pony.

b/r 7 bran barb brim curb brat garb bray verb brag garb bribe herb

8 Barb Barber can bring a bit of bran and herbs for her bread.

c/e 9 cede neck nice deck dice heck rice peck vice erect mice echo

10 Can Cecil erect a decent cedar deck? He erects nice condos.

n/u 11 nun gnu bun nut pun numb sun nude tuna nub fun null unit gun

12 Eunice had enough ground nuts at lunch; Uncle Launce is fun.

30c ● 9'

SKILLBUILDING

Improve rhythm
work for even, continuous
stroking

double letters 13 feel pass mill good miss seem moons cliffs pools green spell

14 Assets are being offered in a stuffy room to two associates.

balanced hand 15 is if of to it go do to is do so if to to the it sign vie to

16 Pamela Fox may wish to go to town with Blanche if she works.

one hand 17 date face ere bat lip sew lion rear brag fact join eggs ever

18 get fewer on; after we look; as we agree; add debt; act fast

combination 19 was for|in the case of|they were|to down|mend it|but pony is

20 They were to be down in the fastest sleigh if you are right.

combination 21 I need to rest for an hour in my reserve seat in my opinion.

22 Look at my dismal grade in English; but I guess I earned it.

| 1 | 2 | 3 | 4 | 5 | 6 | 7 | 8 | 9 | 10 | 11 | 12 |

A Web address may also include a directory path and filenames separated by slashs: http://msstate.edu/athletics/. The Web document named *athletics* resides at this site.

Practice
1. Identify the high-level domain for the following Web sites:
   a. http://www.senate.gov
   b. http://www.fbla-pbl.org
   c. http://www.army.mil
   d. http://www.ibm.com

2. Identify the filenames for the following Web sites:
   a. http://www.reebok.com/soccer/
   b. http://www.espn.com/golf/
   c. http://www.cnn.com/QUICKNEWS/
   d. http://www.nike.com/participate

Activity three

Open a Web site

To open a Web site from your browser, click Open or Open Page from the File menu (or click the Open button if it is available on your browser's toolbar). Key the URL http://www.weather.com as shown below, and click Open. The home page for The Weather Channel displays.

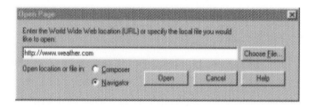

Shortcut: Click inside the Netsite, Location, or Address entry box, key the URL, and press ENTER.

Practice
Open the following Web sites:
1. http://weather.com
2. http://www.abc.com
3. http://www.cnn.com/QUICKNEWS/
4. http://www.espn.com/golf/
5. http://www.usps.gov/ctc/welcome.htm

Activity four

Explore the browser's toolbar

The browser's toolbar is very valuable when surfing the Internet. Become familiar with your browser's toolbar by studying the screen below. Browsers may vary slightly.

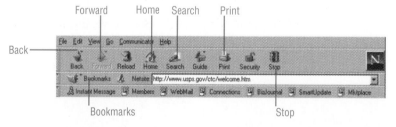

Check number usage
Change words to figures or figures to words as needed.

23 32 of the graduates gave $9,431 to the charity.
24 Luis lives at 23 West 57 Street, not 23 West 58 Street.
25 5 players were cut from our 21-player soccer roster.
26 We invited 6 girls and 5 boys to the dinner party.
27 Only 5 of 35 people who were invited actually attended.
28 2 of us will be working here until after six o'clock.

30e • 6'

SKILLBUILDING

Check speed
Key a 1' and 2' writing.

 all letters *gwam* 1' | 2'

Teams are the basic unit of performance for a firm. 11 | 5 | 42
They are not the solution to all of the organizational needs. 23 | 12 | 48
They will not solve all of the problems, but it is known 35 | 17 | 54
that a team can perform at a higher rate than other groups. 47 | 23 | 60
It is one of the best ways to support the changes needed for 59 | 30 | 66
a firm. The team must have time in order to make 71 | 36 | 72
a quality working plan. 74 | 37 | 74

```
1' |  1  |  2  |  3  |  4  |  5  |  6  |  7  |  8  |  9  |  10  |  11  |  12
2' |     1     |     2     |     3     |     4     |     5     |     6
```

30f • 10'

SKILLBUILDING

Assess skill
Key two 3' writings.

 all letters *gwam* 1' | 3'

Do you know how to use time wisely? If you do, then its 11 | 4 | 51
proper use can help you organize and run a business better. 24 | 8 | 55
If you find that your daily problems tend to keep you from 35 | 12 | 59
planning properly, then perhaps you are not using time well. 48 | 16 | 63
You may find that you spend too much time on tasks that are 60 | 20 | 67
not important. Plan your work to save valuable time. 70 | 24 | 70

A firm that does not plan is liable to run into trouble. 12 | 27 | 74
A small firm may have trouble planning. It is important 23 | 31 | 78
to know just where the firm is headed. A firm may have a 35 | 35 | 82
fear of learning things it would rather not know. To say 46 | 39 | 86
that planning is easy would be absurd. It requires lots of 58 | 43 | 90
thinking and planning to meet the expected needs of the firm. 70 | 47 | 94

```
1' |  1  |  2  |  3  |  4  |  5  |  6  |  7  |  8  |  9  |  10  |  11  |  12
3' |        1        |        2        |        3        |        4
```

internet activities

Activity

one **Open Web browser**

Word users can quickly access the Internet while in *Word* by using the Web toolbar. Display the Web toolbar by right-clicking on any toolbar and then choosing *Web* from the list of choices.

Start Page

Open your Web browser by clicking the Start Page button on the Web toolbar. The Web page you have designated as your Home or Start Page displays.

Practice

1. Begin a new *Word* document.
2. Display Web toolbar.
3. Click **Start Page** button to open your Web browser.

Note: You may also open your Web browser from the *Windows* desktop or from the Web toolbar located in any *Microsoft Office* application.

Activity

two **Understand Web addressing**

A **Web address**—commonly called the *URL* or *Uniform Resource Locator*—is composed of one or more domains separated by periods: http://www.house.gov or http://www.li.suu.edu. A domain name is the name given to a network or site that is connected to the Internet. As you move from left to right in the address, each domain is larger than the previous one. For example, in the Web address http://www.house.gov, *gov* (United States government) is larger than *house* (House of Representatives). The table below identifies the type of high-level domains.

.gov	Non-military government sites
.com	Commercial organizations
.edu	Educational institutions
.org	Other organizations
.mil	Military sites

Level 2

FORMATTING

BASIC

BUSINESS

DOCUMENTS

OBJECTIVES

Keyboarding

To key about 40 *wam* with good accuracy.

Formatting Skills

To format business letters, memos, reports, and tables.

Word Processing

To use the basic word processing functions with skill.

Communication Skills

To proofread and apply language art skills.

Objective Assessment

Answer the questions below to see if you have mastered the content of this module.

1. A _____ is a form of written communication that is used primarily for internal communication.

2. _____ is a method of transmitting documents and messages via the computer system.

3. An _____ is keyed at the end of the document when something is included with the correspondence.

4. If more than three people are to receive a copy of a memo, key a _____ list at the end of the memo.

5. The _____ contains the name and address of the person who will receive the letter.

6. The formal closing of the letter is called the _____ .

7. _____ allows you to check the layout of the document before it is printed.

8. The proper salutation for a letter addressed to Human Resources Director is _____ .

9. The proper salutation for a letter addressed to Computer-Tech Industries is _____ .

10. A _____ aligns copy at the decimal point.

11. The center point for a standard 8.5" x 11" paper is _____ .

12. A _____ indicates that a copy of the document has been sent to the person(s) named.

Performance Assessment

Document 1
Modified block letter
1. Estimate the letter length.
2. Include the letter address below. Use current date; add an appropriate salutation and closing. The letter is from **Alberto Valenzuela**.
3. Save as **ckpt5-d1**. Print.
   Ms. Shawna Olson
   Western Regional Manager
   Acune, Inc.
   5450 Signal Hill Rd.
   Springfield, OH 45504-5440

Document 2
Interoffice memo
1. Key the same message as a memo to **Ms. Sandra Habek** from **Alberto Valenzuela**. Use the current date and **May Seminar** as the subject line.
2. Add a copy notation to **Mark Roane**.

I have invited Lynda A. Brewer, P.L.D., Earlham College, Richmond, Indiana, to be our seminar leader on Friday afternoon, May 10.

Dr. Brewer, a well-known psychologist who has spent a lot of time researching and writing in the field of ergonomics, will address "Stress Management."

Please make arrangements for rooms, speaker accommodations, staff notification, and refreshments. I will send you Dr. Brewer's vita for use in preparing news releases.

ENTERING AND EDITING TEXT

OBJECTIVES

1. Enter, save, open, and print a document.

2. Learn simple character and paragraph formats.

3. Improve speed and accuracy.

LESSON 3I

Getting Started

31a ● 5'
GETTING
started

You are about to learn one of the leading word processing packages available today. You will learn to create and format documents that are professional in appearance. At the same time, you will continue to increase your keyboarding skill. You will use *Microsoft Word 2000* to create professional-looking documents. *Word* will make keying documents such as letters, tables, and reports easy and fun. Follow the steps in Drill 1 to create a new document in *Microsoft Word*.

If the *Microsoft Office* shortcut bar is displayed, click the **New Office Document** button to open the software. ■

Drill
1. Turn on computer and monitor.
2. The "Welcome to Windows" screen displays.
3. Click the **Start** button at the bottom of the screen.
4. Click **New Office Document**.
5. The New Office Document dialog box displays, as shown on the next page.

44c, *continued*
Document I
Memorandum
Save as **44c-d1**.

TO: Brenda Hull | FROM: Bruna Wertz | DATE: Current | SUBJECT: 13

Current Promotion   17

We have a problem, Brenda. I have learned that some of our distributors   31

are using older stock with our latest promotion. As you know, our older   46

boxes have no logos; but our refund plan asks for them.   57

I hope you will agree, however, that we must honor the coupons that arrive   72

without logos--hopefully there will not be too many of them. Please alert   87

your staff. | xx   90

Document 2
Business letter in block format

Supply an appropriate salutation. Save as **44c-d2**.

Current date | AMASTA Company, Inc. | 902 Greenridge Dr. | Reno,   12
NV 69505-5552   15

We sell your videocassettes and have since you introduced them. Follow-   33
ing instructions in your recent flyer, we tell customers who buy your   47
Super D videocassettes to return to you the coupon we give them; and you   62
will refund $1 for each cassette.   69

Several of our customers now tell us they are unable to follow the direc-   83
tions on the coupon. They explain, and we further corroborate, that there   98
is no company logo on the box to return to you as requested. We are not   113
sure how to handle our unhappy customers.   122

What steps should we take? A copy of the coupon is enclosed, as is a   136
Super D container. Please read the coupon, examine the box, and then   150
let me know your plans for extricating us from this problem.   162

Sincerely | John J. Long | Sales Manager | xx | Enc. 2   171

Document 3
Business letter in modified block format

Supply an appropriate salutation. Save as **44c-d3**.

Document 4

1. Open *Brackmun*. Save as **44c-d4**.
2. Replace the letter address with the following:
   **Viadex Corporation
   3945 Alexandria Blvd.
   Detroit, MI 48230-9732**
3. Supply a salutation.
4. Change the letter to block format.
5. Save; print.

Current date | Mr. John J. Long, Sales Manager | The Record Store | 12
9822 Trevor Ave. | Anaheim, CA 92805-5885   20

With your letter came our turn to be perplexed, and we apologize. When we   38
had our refund coupons printed, we had just completed a total   50
redesign program for our product boxes. We had detachable logos put on   65
the outside of the boxes, which could be peeled off and placed on a   80
coupon.   81

We had not anticipated that our distributors would use back inventories   96
with our promotion. The cassettes you sold were not packaged in our   110
new boxes; therefore, there were no logos on them.   120

I'm sorry you or your customers were inconvenienced. In the future,   134
simply ask your customers to send us their sales slips; and we will honor   149
them with refunds until your supply of older containers is depleted.   163

Sincerely yours | Bruna Wertz | Sales and Promotions Dept. | xx   174

6. Double-click the **Blank Document** icon.
(If you do not see the Blank Document icon on your screen, click the **General** tab to display it.)

7. *Word* names the first document that it opens as Document 1.

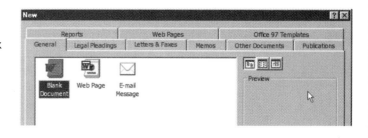

31b ● 12'

Review the screen shown at the right. Complete Drills 1 and 2.

Microsoft Word document screen

The *Microsoft Word* document screen contains many of the elements that you reviewed in the Welcome to Windows section.

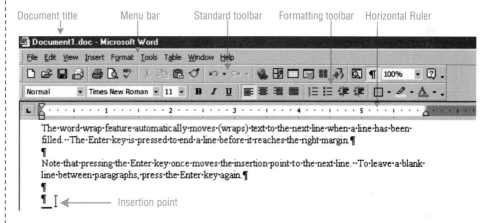

Title bar: Name of the application that is currently open.

Menu bar: Menus from which commands can be selected.

Standard toolbar and Formatting toolbar: Buttons that provide access to common commands. The name of each button displays when you point to it.

Horizontal Ruler: Use the Ruler to set tabs and indents within a document. To change the display of the Ruler, choose Ruler from the View menu.

Insertion point: Shows where the text you key will appear.

Drill 1

1. Point to each button on the Standard toolbar. Notice the name of each button as it displays.

2. Repeat for Step 1 for the Formatting toolbar.

Drill 2

1. Key ¶ 1 using wordwrap.

2. Press ENTER twice after keying ¶ 1 to DS between paragraphs. Key ¶ 2. Ignore the red and green wavy lines that may appear under text as you key.

3. Keep the document on the screen for the next exercise.

The wordwrap feature automatically moves (wraps) text to the next line when a line has been filled. The Enter key is pressed to end a line before it reaches the right margin.

(Strike ENTER twice.)

Note that pressing the Enter key once moves the insertion point to the next line. To leave a blank line between paragraphs, press the Enter key again.

LESSON 44

Assessment

44a ● 7'

GETTING **started**

each line twice SS; DS
between 2-line groups

44b ● 10'

SKILLBUILDING

**Assess
straight-copy skill**
Take two 3' writings; key
fluently, confidently; determine
gwam; proofread; count errors.

SKILLBUILDING WARMUP

alphabet 1 Two exit signs jut quietly above the beams of a razed skyscraper.
figures 2 At 7 a.m., I open Rooms 18, 29, and 30; I lock Rooms 4, 5, and 6.
direct reaches 3 I obtain many junk pieces dumped by Marvyn at my service centers.
easy 4 The town may blame Keith for the auditory problems in the chapel.

| 1 | 2 | 3 | 4 | 5 | 6 | 7 | 8 | 9 | 10 | 11 | 12 | 13 |

　all letters　　　　　　　　　　　　　　　　*gwam*　3'

Whether or not a new company will be a success will depend	4	62
on how well it fits into our economic system. Due to the demands	8	66
of competition, only a company that is organized to survive will	13	71
likely ever get to be among the best. Financial success, the	17	75
reason why most companies exist, rests on some unique ideas that	21	79
are put in place by a management team that has stated goals in	25	83
mind and the good judgment to recognize how those goals can best	30	88
be reached.	31	89
It is in this way that our business system tries to assure	34	92
us that, if a business is to survive, it must serve people in the	39	97
way they want to be served. Such a company will have managed to	43	101
combine some admirable product with a low price and the best ser-	47	106
vice--all in a place that is convenient for buyers. With no	52	110
intrusion from outside forces, the buyer and the seller benefit	56	114
both themselves and the economy.	58	116

3' | 1 | 2 | 3 | 4 |

44c ● 33'

FORMATTING

**Assess basic business
correspondence**
Time schedule
Planning time . . . . 3'
Timed production . . . . . . 25'
Final check; proofread;
    determine *g-pram* . . . . . 5'

1. On the signal to begin,
   key the documents in
   sequence; use the current
   date and your reference
   initials.
2. Repeat Document 1 if time
   allows.

3. Proofread all documents;
   count errors; determine
   g-pram.

$$g\text{-}pram = \frac{\text{total words keyed}}{25'}$$

1. Review the commands on the Menu bar.
2. Complete the drill.

Menu bar

The Menu bar contains nine menus of commands that are useful in formatting and editing documents. When a name on the Menu bar is clicked, a menu cascades or pulls down and displays the functions that are available. The File menu shown below illustrates many characteristics of pull-down menus.

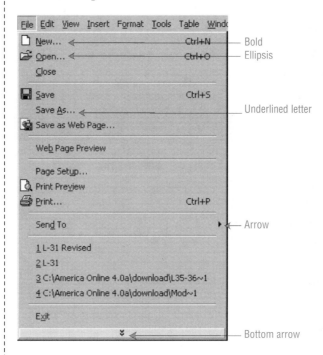

Ellipsis (…) following a command: A dialog box will display.

Arrow: Additional commands are available.

Bold: Command is available for use.

Dimmed command: Command is unavailable for use.

Underlined letter: Keying the underlined letter activates a command just as clicking the mouse on the command.

Bottom arrow: Additional commands are available.

Drill

1. Use the mouse to point to *File* on the Menu bar; click the left mouse button.
2. Use the mouse to point to the arrow at the bottom of the File menu; click the left mouse button. Note that additional commands display.
3. Click **Edit** on the Menu bar. Note that *Cut* is dimmed. Click **Cut.** Note that nothing happens because a dimmed command is not available.
4. Click **File** in the Menu bar again. Note that the Save As command is followed by an ellipsis (…).
5. Click **Save As** to display the *Save As* dialog box.
6. Click **Cancel** to close the *Save As* dialog box.

43c, *continued*

Document 2

Key the letter at the right in modified block format. Make corrections as marked. Save as **43c-d2** and print.

Current date — 3

Mr. Herbert *Brackmun* — 7
747 Myrtle Street — 10
Evansville, IN 47710 - *3277* — 15

Dear Mr. *Brackmun* — 19

Your recent letter has us more than a little intrigued. — 30

In it, you describe a back yard squirrel feeder you — 40
have built one that keeps out birds. This is certainly — 52
are the turnaround from the usual winter ~~animal~~ feeding *bird* — 61
situation, and we believe it may have some apeal for — 72
many of our customers. We are interested. — 81

We are interested enough, in ~~matter of~~ fact, to — 88
invite you to send or bring to our office plans for your — 100
new feeder. If it can be built at a reasonable cost, we — 111
want to talk with you about representation in the market — 123
place. — 124

Document 3

1. Open *43c-d2* and save as **43c-d3**.
2. Select the letter address and then delete it.
3. Address the letter to:
   **Mr. Charles B. Onehawk
   139 Via Cordoniz
   Santa Barbara, CA
   93015-0319**
4. Delete the final paragraph and the enclosure notation.
5. Save and print.

We have several agency plans that we ~~used~~ have with — 135
success in representing clients like you for a number of — 146
years. We shall be happy to explain them to you. — 156

A copy of our recent catalog is enclosed. — 165

sincerely
very ~~truly~~ yours — 169

Miss Debra Stewert — 173
Sales manager — 176

xx — *use your initials* — 176

Enclosured — 178

**Document 4
Challenge Document**

Follow the steps at the right to change *39c-d1* from a block letter to a modified block letter. Print and save as **43c-d4**.

Changing a letter from block to modified block format

1. Open the document (letter).

2. Select the entire letter.
3. Set a tab at 3".
4. Click the insertion point at the beginning of the line to be tabbed; press TAB.

Repeat Step 4 for each remaining line to be tabbed (closing lines).

1. Review the Save As information at the right.
2. Complete the drill to name and save a document.

Save/Save As

Saving a document preserves it so that it can be used again. If a document is not saved, it will be lost once the computer is shut off. The Save As command is used to save and name a new document or to rename an existing document. In this course, name documents as a lesson part (for example, **31d**).

To save a new document:

1. From the File menu, click **Save As.** The Save As dialog box displays.

2. Select the drive and folder.

3. Key the filename in the *File name* box.

4. Click **Save.**

Tip: To save the document in a different folder, choose a different folder in the *Look in* box. To save the document in a new folder, click **Create New Folder** .

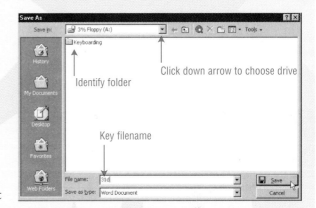

The Save As dialog box contains a *Save in* list box, a *File name* text box, and a *Save as type* list box. The text area may either be blank or have a list of files if previous documents have been saved on your disk.

Drill

1. Insert your storage disk in Drive A. A storage disk is a blank formatted disk. You will use this disk to save your files.

2. Select the *File* menu and click **Save As.**

3. Click the arrow in the *Save in* list box to display the list of drives available. Point to Drive A to highlight it; click the left mouse button to select it.

4. Use the mouse and point to the *File name* text box. Click the left button to place the insertion point in the *File name* text box.

5. Key **31d** as the filename.

6. Check to see that the default ("Word Document") is displayed in the *Save as type* list box. If not, click the arrow and select "Word Document."

● 7. Click **Save.**

Review Modified Block Letters

GETTING started

each line twice SS; DS between 2-line groups

SKILLBUILDING WARMUP

alphabet	1	Melva Bragg required exactly a dozen jackets for the winter trip.
figures	2	The 1903 copy of my book had 5 parts, 48 chapters, and 672 pages.
shift	3	THE LAKES TODAY, published in Akron, Ohio, comes in June or July.
easy	4	Did he vow to fight for the right to work as the Orlando auditor?

| 1 | 2 | 3 | 4 | 5 | 6 | 7 | 8 | 9 | 10 | 11 | 12 | 13 |

43b ● 10'

SKILLBUILDING

Build production skill

1. Arrange each drill line in correct modified block letter format.
2. Use default top and side margins; return 5 times between drills. Use your reference initials.
3. Repeat the drill using block format.

Optional: Key a 1' writing on each line.

gwam 1'

5 May 28, 200-   3

QS

Ms. Dora Lynn   6
128 Avon Ln.   9
Macon, GA 31228-1421 12

DS

Dear Ms. Lynn   15

gwam 1'

6 Sincerely   2

QS

Rebecca Dexter   5
Engineer   7

DS

xx   8

DS

Enclosures: Draft 251   13
              Area maps   15

7 February 4, 200-|Ms. Lilly Bargas|3945 Park Ave.|Racine, WI 53404-3822   14
8 Sincerely yours|Manuel Garcia|Council President|MG:xx|c Ron N. Nesbit   14
9 Yours truly|Ms. Loren Lakes|Secretary General|xx|Enclosure|c Libby Uhl   14

43c ● 33'

FORMATTING

Business letters: modified block
Document 1
Key the letter in modified block format; center vertically. Save, preview before printing, and print.

words

Current date | Dr. Burtram M. Decker | 800 Barbour Ave. | 10
Birmingham, AL 35208-5333 | Dear Dr. Decker   19

The Community Growth Committee offers you its sincere   30
thanks for taking an active part in the sixth annual Youth   41
Fair. We especially appreciate your help in judging the   53
Youth of Birmingham Speaks portion of the fair and for   64
contributing to the prize bank.   70

Participation of community leaders such as you makes this   81
event the annual success it has become. We sincerely hope   93
we can seek your help again next year.   101

Cordially | Grace Beebe Hunt | Secretary | HNJ:xx   110

Print

The Print button on the Standard toolbar is an efficient way to print an entire document.

Close and Exit

Close clears the screen of the document and frees it from memory. You will be prompted to save the document before closing if you have not saved it or if you have made changes to the document since the previous save.

To close a document, click **File** on the Menu bar; then click **Close**.

Exit saves all documents that are on the screen and then exits the software. You will be prompted to save before exiting if you have not already saved the document or if you have made changes to it since last saving.

To exit *Microsoft Word*, click **Exit** form the File menu.

Close and Exit Option ☒

Option: Close and Exit can also be accomplished using the buttons in the upper right corner. The Close button is on the right side the Menu bar. Exit is located at the top right of the document title bar. Click the Close button at the top right side of the document window.

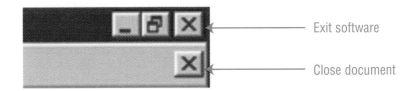

Exit software

Close document

Drill I

1. Locate the Print button on the Standard toolbar.
2. With Document **3Id** displayed on the screen, click the **Print** button to print the document.
3. Close **3Id**.
4. Exit *Microsoft Word*.

Drill 2

1. Start *Microsoft Word*.
2. Key the paragraph.
3. Insert a storage disk into Drive A and save the document as **3Ie**.
4. Close the document.
5. Exit *Microsoft Word*.

In Lesson 31, I have learned the basic operations of my word processing software. Today I opened the word processor, created a new document, saved the document, printed the document, closed the document, and exited the software. This new document that I am creating will be named 31e. I will save it so that I can use it in the next lesson to open an existing document.

All Business Communication

18950 Bonanza Way
Gaithersburg, MD 20879-1211
301-555-1256
301-555-1268 (FAX)

December 14, 200- QS

Ms. Mukta Bhakta
9845 Buckingham Rd.
Annapolis, MD 21403-0314 DS

Dear Ms. Bhakta DS

Thank you for your recent inquiry on our electronic bulletin service. The ABC BBS is an interactive online service developed by All Business Communication to assist the online community in receiving documents via the Internet.

All Business Communication also provides a *Customer Support Service* and a *Technical Support Team* to assist bulletin board users. The Systems Administrators will perform various procedures needed to help you take full advantage of this new software.

For additional information call: DS

Customer and Technical Support   Center-align
Telephone: 1-900-555-1212
9:00 a.m.-5:00 p.m., Monday-Friday, Eastern Time

Please look over the enclosed ABC BBS brochure. I will call you within the next two weeks to discuss any additional questions you may have.

Sincerely QS

Alex Zampich
Marketing Manager DS

xx DS
Enclosure DS
c Laura Aimes, Sales Representative

MODIFIED BLOCK LETTER

Create a Document

Reinforcement

1. Key the ¶s. Press ENTER twice between ¶s. Disregard keying errors.
2. Save the document with the name **32a**.
   - Click **Save As** in the File menu.
   - In the *Look in* list box, click Drive *A*.
   - Key **32a** in the *File name* text box.
   - Click **Save**.
3. Close the document.

Serendipity, a new homework research tool from Information Technology Company, is available to subscribers of the major online services via the World Wide Web.

Offered as a subscription service aimed at college students, Serendipity is a collection of tens of thousands of articles from major encyclopedias, reference books, magazines, pamphlets, and Internet sources combined into a single searchable database.

Serendipity puts an electronic library right at students' fingertips. The program offers two browse-and-search capabilities. Users can find articles by entering questions in simple question format or browse the database by pointing and clicking on key words that identify related articles. For more information, call 800-555-0174 or address e-mail to <<lab@serendipity.com>>.

32b ● 10'

NEW FUNCTION

1. Read the procedures for opening an existing document.
2. Complete the drill on p. 77.

Open

Documents that have been saved can be opened and used again. Choose Open from the File menu or click the Open button on the toolbar. The Open dialog box displays the name of the files within a folder.

To open a document:

1. From the File menu, click **Open.** The Open dialog box displays.
2. In the *Look in* box, click the down arrow and select the drive where your files are stored (Drive A).
3. Click the desired filename and click **Open.**

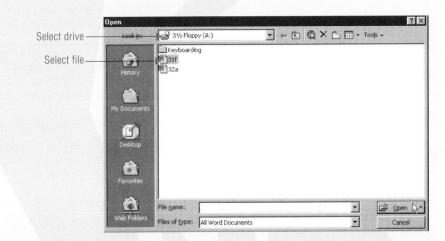

FORMATTING

Modified block letters

Study the information at the right and then key Documents 1 and 2.

Document 1

1. Study the modified block letter on the next page.
2. Set a tab at 3". Key the letter; press TAB before keying the dateline and closing lines.
3. Because of the many single lines, key the date at approximately 2.1" from the top.
4. Proofread, save, and print.

Document 2

Key Document 2 according to the directions in Document 1. Key the current date at 2.1" and supply an appropriate salutation. Preview before printing.

Modified block format

The **modified block format** is a variation of the block format. It is "modified" by moving the dateline and the closing lines from the left margin to the center point of the page. Set a tab so that the date and closing are keyed at center. Paragraphs may be indented, but it is more efficient not to indent them. Do not indent paragraphs in this module.

Reference initials: If the writer's initials are included with those of the keyboard operator, the writer's initials are listed first in ALL CAPS followed by a colon:

> **BB:xx**

Enclosure notation: If an item is included with a letter, an enclosure notation is keyed a DS below the reference initials. Acceptable variations include:

> **Enclosure**
> **Enclosures: Check #8331**
> **Order form**
> **Enc. 2**

Copy notation: A copy notation c indicates that a copy of the document has been sent to person(s) named. Key it a DS below reference initials (or enclosure notation):

> **c Andrew Wilkes**

Express Rapid Delivery

*1400 Broadway * Denver, CO 80203-2137*
*(303) 865-2405 * FAX: (303) 865-5839*

October 19, 200–

Miss Latanya Denny
208 Humboldt St.
Denver, CO 80218-8828

Dear Miss Denny

Today our delivery service tried unsuccessfully a second time to deliver at the above address the merchandise you ordered. The merchandise is now at our general warehouse at 8000 Iliff Avenue.

We regret that no further attempts at delivery can be made. You may claim your merchandise at the warehouse if you will show a copy of your order (a duplicate is enclosed) to John Kimbrough at the warehouse.

We shall hold your merchandise for 30 days. After that time, it will be transferred to our main warehouse at 218 Harvard Avenue, East; unfortunately, we must charge a rental fee for each day the goods are stored there.

Yours truly

Elizabeth A. LeMoyne
Dispatcher

BB:xx

Enclosure

c John Kimbrough

---

	words
opening	3

Mr. Jose E. Morales, Director | Flint Business Association | 584 Brabyn — 15
Ave. | Flint, MI 48508-5548 — 22

The Octagon Club is concerned about Baker House. — 35

As you know, Baker House was built on Calumet Rd. in 1797 by Zaccaria — 49
Baker; he and his family lived there for many years. It was home for vari- — 64
ous other families until 1938, when it became an attractive law and real — 79
estate office. Flint residents somehow assumed that Baker House was a — 93
permanent part of Flint. It wasn't. — 101

Baker House was torn down last week to make room for a new mall. It's — 115
too late to save Baker House. But what about other Flint landmarks? — 129
Shall we lose them too? Shopping malls may indicate that a community — 143
is growing, but need growth destroy our heritage? — 153

We ask for your help. Will you and Mr. Wilkes include 20 minutes on your — 168
January meeting agenda for Myrna Targlif, president of the Flint Octagon — 182
Club, to present our views on this problem? She has information that you — 197
will find interesting; a brief outline is enclosed. — 208

Sincerely yours | Barbara Brahms | Secretary, Octagon Club | BB:xx | — 220
Enclosure | c Andrew Wilkes — 225

32b, *continued*

In Lesson 31, you created a document, named it **31e**, and saved it on your storage disk. Follow the steps at the right to open that document and add a paragraph.

To rename and save an existing file, choose *Save As* from the File menu, instead of clicking the Save button on the Status bar. ▪

Drill

1. Place your storage disk in Drive A.
2. From the File menu, click **Open.**
3. If file *31e* does not show in the Open dialog box, click the arrow in the *Look in* box and select *Drive A.* Click the document named **31e** and then click **Open** (or double-click the document named **31e**).
4. Place your insertion point at the end of the paragraph by moving the I-beam or mouse pointer to the end of the paragraph and clicking. Press ENTER twice and then key the following paragraph:

    This paragraph modifies the document created for 31e in the last lesson. Documents that have been saved may be reused without any changes, or they may be modified.

5. Save the document as **32b**. Close the document.
6. Click **Open** on the File menu to display the Open File dialog box. Check to see that both files *31e* and *32b* are stored on your disk, as shown in the illustration below.

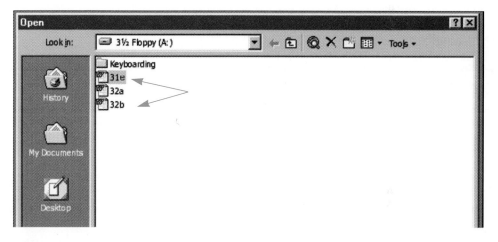

7. Open *32b*; check to see that the document contains the second paragraph that you just keyed. Close the document.
8. Open *31e*. Note that this is the original file you opened. It should contain only one paragraph.
9. Close the document.

32c ● 3'

NEW FUNCTION

1. Read about saving an existing document at right.
2. Open *32b*.
3. Key your name a double space below ¶ 2. Click the **Save** button on the toolbar.
4. Close the document.

Save an existing file with the same name

Whenever you want to save an existing document on screen with the same name, click the Save button on the toolbar. Since you are not renaming the file, the Save As dialog box does not appear.

Modified Block Letter Format

GETTING started

Review

1. Set line spacing to DS.
2. Set tabs for .5" and 2".
3. Bold and center the title; 1.5" top margin.
4. After keying the 4 single lines, select them and apply SS.
5. Save as **42a**. Print and close.

THRIVING IN A MULTICULTURAL WORKPLACE

To avoid conflict and misunderstanding in the workplace, we must be aware of the cultural differences that exist among peoples from other cultures. Become more sophisticated in your relationships by knowing some American customs that often prove confusing to persons from other countries.

Love of individualism
Informality of workers
Hierarchy and protocol
Directness

FORMATTING

Determine tab setting

Set tab at center

When formatting documents such as a modified block letter, you will need to set a tab at the center of the page. The center point of a standard sheet of 8.5" wide paper is 4.25". Tabs are measured in inches from the left margin.

To determine the tab setting for keying text at center, subtract the left margin setting from 4.25". For example, if the left margin is set at 1.25", set a tab at 3" to key text at center. See example.

4.25"	Center (or desired tab setting)
- 1.25"	Margin
3"	Tab setting

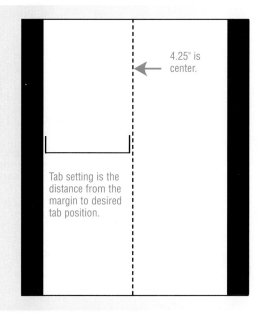

4.25" is center.

Tab setting is the distance from the margin to desired tab position.

Drill

Key the drill at the right using default margins. Set a tab at center for the closing lines.

We shall hold your merchandise for 30 days. After that time, it will be transferred to our main warehouse at 291 Harvard Ave., East; unfortunately, we must charge a rental fee for each day the goods are stored.

Sincerely yours

QS

Elizabeth A. LeMoyne
Dispatcher

Print using Print dialog box

In Lesson 31, you learned to print an entire document by clicking the Print button on the Standard toolbar. Additional options for printing a document are available in the Print dialog box accessed from the File menu.

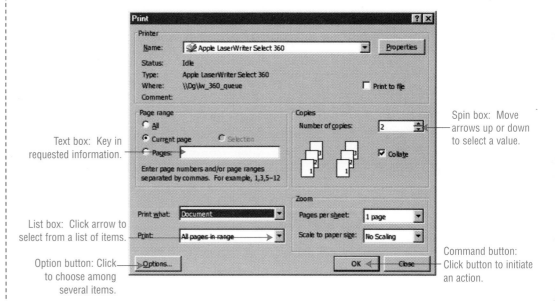

Text box: Key in requested information.

Spin box: Move arrows up or down to select a value.

List box: Click arrow to select from a list of items.

Option button: Click to choose among several items.

Command button: Click button to initiate an action.

Drill

1. Open *32a.* From the File menu, click **Print.**
2. Select the option button for *Current Page* under Page range.
3. Click the spin button to increase the number of copies to 2; click **OK.**
4. Check to see that two copies of the page print.
5. Keep the document open.

**Insertion point
movement**

1. Read the information at the right.
2. Complete the drill.

Moving within a document

Changes often need to be made to text after it has been keyed. To change or edit the text, you must move the insertion point around in the document. The insertion point (the blinking vertical bar) is where the text will appear when you begin to key. You can move to different parts of the document by using the mouse, the keyboard, or the scroll bars. In this lesson, you will learn to move by pointing the mouse and clicking the left mouse button.

Drill

1. Using the mouse, point to the beginning of the last sentence of *32a.*
2. Click the left mouse button to move the insertion point before the words *For more information;* then key the following sentence:

Articles can be printed in full.

3. Point the mouse at the beginning of the word *students* in the second sentence; click the left mouse button. Then key: **and high school.**
4. Close the document; do not save it.

Document 2
1. Bold, center, and key the title using a 14-point font.
2. Use bold and italic as shown.
3. After keying the second ¶, set tabs at 1.5" and 2.5" for the columns.
4. Preview, save, and print.

INTERNET NEWS GROUPS

<table>
<tr><td></td><td>4</td></tr>
</table>

The Internet has electronic discussion groups, called *news groups*, where people with similar interests can post or send in their opinions regarding specific topics. These articles that accumulate on a specific topic are called a *thread*.

A news group name may begin with a category name, which identifies the main topic of the group. For example, the news group comp.lang.c++ is a computer group formed to discuss use of the C++ computer language. Below is a list of other news group prefixes.

Name	Description	
comp	Computer topics	113
biz	Business groups	117
ieee	Electrical engineering groups	124
rec	Recreational topics	129
sci	Scientific topics	133

word counts for the paragraphs: 18, 32, 46, 52, 65, 77, 91, 105, 109

41d ● 5'

NEW FUNCTION

1. Read the information at the right.
2. Complete the drill.

Open a document as a copy

When you open a document as a copy, a new copy of the document is created in the folder that contains the original document. When you open a document as a copy, the original document is not changed. When you use the formatting template, open documents as a copy so that you will always have the original template document in case something happens to the document while you are working on it.

To open a document as a copy:
1. Click **File**; then **Open**.
2. Click on the file to select the one you want to open.
3. Click the arrow on the Open command button; then select *Open as Copy*.

Drill

The disk in the back of your textbook is a formatting template. It contains extra documents you will use in this course. Put the formatting template in Drive A and proceed.

1. Open the document *mercer* as a copy.
2. Remove the tab at center.
3. Reformat the letter in block format.
4. Center the page.
5. Save as **41d** and print.

The World Wide Web and Internet Usenet News groups are electronic fan clubs that offer users a way to exchange views and information on just about any topic imaginable with people around the world.

World Wide Web screens contain text, graphics, pictures, and, on some sites, real-time audio and video. Simple pointing and clicking on the pictures and links (underlined words) bring users to new pages or sites of information.

32g ● 5'

S E L F

c h e c k

Answer the True/False questions at the right to see whether you have mastered the material presented in this lesson.

T F

☐ ☐ 1. The quickest way to print an entire document is to click the Print button on the Standard toolbar.

☐ ☐ 2. When you save an existing document using the Save As command and a new name, both the original and the new document are saved.

☐ ☐ 3. The insertion point does not move to the position of the mouse pointer until the left mouse button is clicked.

☐ ☐ 4. Commands, such as printing the current page and multiple copies, can be accessed by clicking the Print button on the Standard toolbar.

N E W S on... **Netiquette**

With the growth of the Internet, it is becoming increasingly important for people to be aware of good online etiquette. Netiquette (Net etiquette) is the unwritten code of behavior for the Net, news groups, chat rooms, the World Wide Web, e-mail, and other networks. The basic premise of netiquette is to treat people with courtesy and consideration. Apply these basic rules of netiquette:

Stick to the subject, whether chatting in a theme room, posting to a news group, or answering e-mail. Posting an irrelevant message is considered rude and exposes you to being "flamed" or electronically abused by others. Also, don't send irrelevant e-mail messages; people don't have time for frivolous mail.

Use shortcuts with care. Emoticons, such as :- (for a sad face, :-) for a happy face, or ;-) for a wink for a joke or sarcasm, are sometimes fun to use. Some people believe, however, that emoticons are becoming obsolete. Acronyms such as IMO (in my opinion) are effective only if both parties know the meaning.

Write clearly and concisely. State exactly what you mean to reduce time and need for clarification. And, remember to use proper grammar. Avoid using ALL CAPS for emphasis, particularly in a chat room or news group; it is considered SHOUTING.

As the Internet evolves, so will its protocols, including netiquette. So stay "plugged in."

41b, *continued*

Drills 1 and 2

Follow the directions at the right. After setting the tabs for Drill 1, your Ruler should look similar to the one illustrated.

Drill 1
Set tabs

1. Display the Ruler.
2. Set a left tab at 0.5".
3. Change the Tab Alignment to a right tab. Set a tab at 2.5".
4. Change the Tab Alignment to a center tab. Set a tab at 3.5".
5. Set a decimal tab at 5".
6. Key the drill. Save and print; do not close.

Drill 2
Move tabs

1. Select Column 4. (Other columns will also be highlighted.) Move the decimal tab to 5.5".
2. Select Column 3. Move center tab to 4".
3. Select Column 2. Move right tab to 3".
4. Save, print, and close.

Almich	West	San Francisco	400.00
Cambridge	Midwest	Chicago	20.20
Langfield	Southeast	Miami	1,000.00

Almich	West	San Francisco	400.00
Cambridge	Midwest	Chicago	20.20
Langfield	Southeast	Miami	1,000.00

Drill 3

Set a center tab at 1.0", a decimal tab at 3.5", and a right tab at 5.5". DS. Key, save, and print.

Chicago	$1,112.00	100,000
Dallas	872.50	3,000
San Francisco	43.00	250

41c ● 23'

FORMATTING

Document 1

1. Key the memo in proper format.
2. After keying the second ¶, strike ENTER twice. Set a tab at 2.5" for the last 4 lines.
3. Save and print.

words

TO:	All Sunwood Employees	5
FROM:	Julie Patel, Human Relations	12
DATE:	Current	17
SUBJECT:	Eric Kershaw Hospitalized	24

We were notified by Eric Kershaw's family that he was admitted into the   38
hospital this past weekend. They expect that he will be hospitalized for   53
another ten days. Visitations and phone calls are limited, but cards and   68
notes are welcome.   72

A plant is being sent to Eric from the Sunwood staff. Stop by our office   87
before Wednesday if you wish to sign the card. If you would like to send   101
your own "Get Well Wishes" to Eric, send them to: 112

Eric Kershaw	114
County General Hospital	119
Room 401	121
Atlanta, GA 38209-4751	125

Enter and Edit Text

33a • 5'

GETTING started

Reinforcement

1. Key both ¶s SS; press ENTER twice between ¶s.
2. Practice moving the insertion point with the mouse.
3. Save as **33a**.
4. Print the document; close.

A wise man once said that we have two ears and one tongue so that we may hear more and talk less. Therefore, we should be prepared to talk less quickly and exert more effort to listen carefully to what others have to offer.

Most people do not realize that when we listen, we use not just our ears, but our eyes and mind as well. To form the art of listening well, show interest in what is said, pay attention, ask questions, and keep an open mind.

33b • 20'

NEW FUNCTIONS

Read about the features, then complete Drills 1–4. Follow these procedures for the remainder of textbook.

Insert, Delete, Overtype

The Insert, Delete, and Overtype features are often used when revising documents.

Insert

Microsoft Word is set for the Insert mode. To insert text, simply position the insertion point where the new text is to appear and key the text. Existing text moves to the right.

Delete

The DELETE key can be used to erase text that is no longer wanted.

> **To delete a character:** Position the insertion point to the left of the character to delete and press DELETE, or position the insertion point to the right of the character to delete and press BACKSPACE. Be careful not to hold down the DELETE or BACK-SPACE keys as they will continue to erase characters.

> **To delete a word:** Double-click the word to be deleted and press DELETE.

Overtype OVR

The Overtype feature replaces existing characters with text that is keyed. Double-click on OVR in the Status bar to turn on the Overtype feature.   Return to the Insert mode by double-clicking OVR again. OVR is dimmed when the feature is off.

Drill I

1. Open *32a*.
2. Click **File**, then **Save As** to save the file with a new name, **33b-d1**.
3. Make the corrections shown at right to ¶ 3. (Your text will be single-spaced.)
4. Click the **Save** button.
5. Print the document.

Serendipity puts an electronic library right at students' fingertips. The program offers two browse-and-search capabili-ties. Users can find articles *on just about any subject* by entering questions in simple question format or browse the database by pointing and clicking on key words that identify related articles. For more information, call 1-800-555-0174 or address e-mail to ‹1ab@serendipity.com›. *with just a computer and a modem.*

Tabs

Reinforcement
1. Edit as you key; DS.
2. Check spelling, save, print.
3. Proofread printed document; revise if necessary.

Someone has said, "you are what you eat" the speaker did not mean to imply that fast food make fast people, or that a hearty meal makes a person hearty or even that good food makes a person good On the other hand, though, a healthfull diet does indeed make person healthier;and good health is one of the most often over looked treasures within human existance.

Tabs

Tabs are useful for aligning text. Tabs move one line of text to the next tab stop. Default tabs are set every half inch; however, you can reset or change the tab stops. Setting a new tab removes the default tabs left of the custom tab.

Tabs may be set directly on the Horizontal Ruler or in the Tab dialog box. Using the Ruler is often faster, but the dialog box provides extra options. Tab settings are measured from the left margin. A tab set at 1" will indent text 1" from the margin.

Horizontal Ruler

When the Horizontal Ruler is displayed, tabs can be set and cleared with the mouse. The numbers on the Ruler indicate the distance in inches from the left margin. The small gray lines below each half-inch position are the default tab stops. The Tab Alignment button at the left edge of the Ruler indicates the type of tab. To change the tab type, click the Tab Alignment button.

J. Smith	R72	3,576	$2,305.89
B. Jones	R21	1,379	938.94

Tab Alignment   Left   Center   Right   Decimal

Tab	Symbol	Result
Left	L	Aligns text to the right of the tab. Default tab setting.
Center	⊥	Aligns text around the tab.
Right	⌐	Aligns text to the left of the tab.
Decimal	⊥	Aligns numbers at the decimal.

Working with tabs on the Ruler:

To display the Ruler: From the View menu, click **Ruler**.

To set a tab: Click the **Tab Alignment** button to display the desired tab type. Click on the Ruler where you want to set the tab.

To delete a tab: Point to the tab symbol, hold down the left mouse button, and drag the tab straight down off the Ruler.

To move an existing tab: Press the left mouse button and drag the tab to the new location. **Note:** The insertion point must be in the paragraph that will be affected. If a column tab is to be moved, select the entire column first.

Drill 2

1. Open *33b-d1*, if not already opened.
2. Delete the text at the right in ¶s 1 and 2.
3. Save as **33b-d2**.
4. Print, then close the document.

Serendipity, a ~~new homework~~ research tool from Information Technology Company, is available to subscribers of ~~the major~~ on-line services via the World Wide Web.

Offered as a subscription service aimed at ~~college~~ students, Serendipity is a collection of tens of thousands of articles from ~~major~~ encyclopedias, reference books, magazines, pamphlets, and Internet sources combined into a single searchable database.

Drill 3

Key the words in the first column, then use the Overtype feature to replace the words with the words in the second column. Close without saving.

can	may
November	December
decide on	determine

Drill 4

Follow the directions at the right.

1. Open *33a*.
2. Delete each occurrence of the word "talk" and insert "speak" in its place.
3. Use the Overtype feature to replace "may" with "can."
4. Correct any additional errors that you may have made in your document.
5. Save as **33b-d4**. Print. Close the document.

33c ● 15'

NEW FUNCTION

Drill

1. Open *32f*.
2. Click Show/Hide to display the nonprinting characters.
3. Delete the two ¶ markers separating ¶s 1 and 2. Insert spaces as needed.
4. Save as **33c**.
5. Print and close.

Show/Hide ¶

The Show/Hide button displays all nonprinting characters such as paragraph markers (¶) and spaces (.). While creating a document, it is often helpful to see these characters. Show/Hide makes it easy to check that you have keyed a space after a comma or to combine two paragraphs.

Click the Show/Hide button to display all nonprinting characters. The button will appear depressed (pressed down). To turn the nonprinting characters off, click the Show/Hide button again. The button will no longer appear depressed.

The·World·Wide·Web·and·Internet·Usenet·News·groups·are·electronic·fan·clubs·that· offer·users·a·way·to·exchange·views·and·information·on·just·about·any·topic·imaginable· with·people·around·the·world.¶ ←———— Paragraph marker

¶

World·Wide·Web·screens·contain·text,·graphics,·pictures,·and,·on·some·sites,·real-time· audio·and·video.··Simple·pointing·and·clicking·on·the·pictures·and·links·(underlined· words)·bring·users·to·new·pages·or·sites·of·information.¶

Space

COMMUNICATION

Read and apply the information on "Salutations" in the letters that you format.

Salutations

The **salutation** greets the person receiving the letter. A proper salutation consists of the title of the person and his/her last name. Do not greet someone on a first-name basis unless you have a personal relationship with the receiver.

Personal titles (such as Mr. or Ms.) should be included in the letter address and the salutation unless a professional title (Dr.) is appropriate. Use Ms. when the first name is feminine unless Miss or Mrs. is preferred by the recipient. Use salutations as recommended below:

	Receiver	Salutation
To an individual:	Mr. Alexander Gray	Dear Mr. Gray
	Dr. and Mrs. Thompson	Dear Dr. and Mrs. Thompson
	Ms. Mara Rena	Dear Mara (personal relationship)
To a corporation:	Esquire Electronics, Inc.	Ladies and Gentlemen
To the title of a person:	Advertising Manager	Dear Advertising Manager

FORMATTING

Block letter review
Document 1

1. Key the letter in block format. Use the current date. Proofread and spell-check.
2. Center the letter vertically on the page.
3. Preview the letter before printing; make additional changes if needed.
4. Save as **40e-d1** and print.

words

Current date | Mr. Trace L. Brecken | 4487 Ingram St. | Corpus Christi, TX 78409-8907 | Dear Mr. Brecken — 13 / 19

We have received the package you sent us in which you returned goods from a recent order you gave us. Your refund check, plus return postage, will be mailed to you in a few days. — 33 / 48 / 55

We are sorry, of course, that you did not find this merchandise personally satisfactory. It is our goal to please all of our customers, and we are always disappointed if we fail. — 70 / 85 / 92

Please give us an opportunity to try again. We stand behind our merchandise, and that is our guarantee of good service. — 105 / 116

Cordially yours | Mrs. Margret Bredewig | Customer Service Department | xx — 130

Document 2

Follow the same directions as in Document 1. Save as **40e-d2**.

Current date | Mrs. Rose Shikamuru | 55 Lawrence St. | Topeka, KS 66607-6657 | Dear Mrs. Shikamuru — 14 / 19

Thank you for your recent letter asking about employment opportunities with our company. We are happy to inform you that Mr. Edward Ybarra, our recruiting representative, will be on your campus on April 23, 24, 25, and 26 to interview students who are interested in our company. — 33 / 47 / 62 / 75

We suggest you talk soon with your student placement office, as all appointments with Mr. Ybarra will be made through that office. Please bring with you the application questionnaire the office provides. — 89 / 103 / 115

Within a few days, we will send you a company brochure and more information about our offices; plant; salary, bonus, and retirement plans; and the beautiful community in which we are located. We believe a close study of this information will convince you, as it has many others, that our company builds futures as well as small motors. — 128 / 143 / 158 / 172 / 183

If there is any other way we can help you, please write to me again. — 197

Yours very truly | Miss Myrle K. Bragg | Human Services Director | xx — 209

33d ● 10'

Office Assistant
1. Read the information at the right.
2. Complete the drill.

Help from the Office Assistant

You learned to use the Contents and Index features of Help in the Introduction to *Windows 98* section. Now you will learn an easy-to-use Help feature called the **Office Assistant**. Although you can access Office Assistant in many ways, the most efficient way is to click the Question button. This displays the Office Assistant and a message box. Key your question and click Search.

If the Office Assistant is already on your screen, click the Office Assistant icon to display the message box. If the Office Assistant icon is not displayed on your document screen, do the following:

- Click Help on the Menu bar.
- Then click Show the Office Assistant.

Selecting a different icon: Note the icon shown here is *Clipit,* the default Office Assistant icon; it is one of nine different animated Assistant icons you can select. To select a different Office Assistant icon, use the mouse to point to the *Clipit* icon. Click the right mouse button and select Choose Assistant. Use the Back and Next buttons to view the different Office Assistant icons. When you find the Office Assistant icon you wish to use (such as *Links* shown below), click OK.

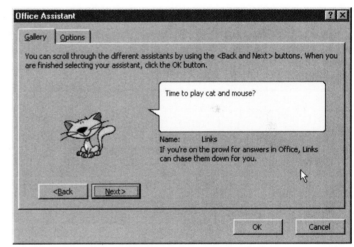

Drill
1. Display the Office Assistant icon if it is not already displayed on your screen.
2. Click the right mouse button over the icon.
3. Select *Choose Assistant* to display the Gallery of icons.
4. Choose an Office Assistant icon.
5. Click **OK**.

LESSON 33   ENTER AND EDIT TEXT   82

Review Block Letters

40a ● 7'

GETTING started

each line twice SS; DS between 2-line groups

alphabet 1 Jim Daley gave us in that box the prize he won for his quick car.

figures 2 Send 345 of the 789 sets now; send the others on April 10 and 26.

one hand 3 I deserve, in my opinion, a reward after I started a faster race.

easy 4 Enrique may fish for cod by the dock; he also may risk a penalty.

| 1 | 2 | 3 | 4 | 5 | 6 | 7 | 8 | 9 | 10 | 11 | 12 | 13 |

40b ● 8'

SKILLBUILDING

Key two 1' timings on each ¶. The second and third ¶s each contain 2 more words than the previous ¶. Try to complete each ¶ within 1'.

  all letters

	gwam	1'	3'

Have you thought about time? Time is a perplexing commodity. Frequently we don't have adequate time to do the things we must; yet we all have just the same amount of time.

12 | 4 | 40
25 | 8 | 45
35 | 12 | 48

We seldom refer to the quantity of time; to a great extent, we cannot control it. We can try to set time aside, to plan, and therefore, to control portions of this valuable asset.

12 | 16 | 52
24 | 20 | 56
37 | 24 | 60

We should make an extra effort to fill each minute and hour with as much quality activity as possible. Time, the most precious thing a person can spend, can never be realized once it is lost.

12 | 28 | 64
25 | 32 | 68
37 | 36 | 72
39 | 36 | 73

1' | 1 | 2 | 3 | 4 | 5 | 6 | 7 | 8 | 9 | 10 | 11 | 12 | 13 |
3' | 1 | 2 | 3 | 4 |

40c ● 12'

COMMUNICATION

Compose at the keyboard

1. Compose an answer to each question in 1 or 2 sentences. Join the sentences into 3 ¶s (as shown). Center the title **MY CAREER** over the ¶s.
2. Save as **40c** and print.
3. Edit the printed document, using proofreaders' marks to make corrections.
4. Revise, save, and print.

¶ 1 What is your present career goal?
2 Why do you think you will enjoy this career?

¶ 3 Where do you think you would most like to pursue your career?
4 Why do you think you would enjoy living and working in that area?

¶ 5 What civic, political, or volunteer activities might you enjoy?
6 What other careers may lie ahead for you?

33e • 10'

Review

1. Key the document, correcting errors as you key. Errors may be identified with wavy red lines.
2. Proofread and correct any errors that you made.
3. Save as **33e.**
4. Click the **Show/Hide** button. Combine ¶s 1 and 2. ¶
5. Click the **Save** button to save the file with the same name.
6. Print.

As the man says, I have some good news and some good news. Let me give you first the bad news.

Due to a badly pulled muscle, I have had to withdraw from the Eastern Racquet Ball tournament. As you know, I have been looking forward to the tournament for a long time and I had begun to hope that I might even win it. I've been working hard.

That's the bad news. The good news is that I have been picked to help officiating, so I'll be coming to Newport News any way. In fact, I'll arrive there a day earlier than I had planned originally.

So, put the racquet away; but get out the backgammon board. I'm determined to win something on this trip!

33f •

SKILLBUILDING

Use the remaining class time to build your skills using *Keyboarding Pro Skill Builder*. Follow the directions at the right.

Keyboarding Skill Builder

1. Open *Keyboarding Pro* or *Keyboarding Pro Multimedia*.
2. Open the Skill Builder module.
3. Insert your storage disk for *Keyboarding Pro* into Drive A.
4. Select *Lesson A* for speed practice.
5. Beginning with Keyboard Mastery, complete as much of the lesson as time permits.
6. Exit the software. Remove your storage disk. Store your materials as directed.

on... Ergonomic Keyboards

NEWS

Concerned about repetitive strain injuries (RSI), keyboard manufacturers now offer keyboards designed to improve hand posture and make keying more comfortable.

Ergonomic keyboards come in many different designs. Most of them, however, have several features in common: the standard QWERTY key layout, a split design with left and right banks of keys, and tilting or rotating features.

Ergonomic keyboards are curved and have either added or moved keys to different locations, such as the BACKSPACE key in the center of the keyboard between the right and left banks of keys.

Many people believe ergonomic keyboards are more comfortable than conventional keyboards. More research is needed to determine just how effective ergonomic keyboards are in preventing RSI and carpal tunnel syndrome.

39c, continued

Document 2
1. Key the letter in block letter style.
2. Add current date and your reference initials.
3. Center the letter vertically on the page.
4. Save but do not close.

Ms. Alice Ottoman
Premiere Properties Inc.
52 Ocean Drive
Newport Beach, CA 92747-6293
                                        DS
Dear Ms. Ottoman
                 DS
Internet Solutions has developed a new technique for you to market your properties on the World Wide Web. We can now create 360-degree panoramic pictures for your Web site. You can give your clients a virtual spin of the living room, kitchen, and every room in the house.
                                        DS
Call today for a demonstration of this remarkable technology. Give your clients a better visual understanding of the property layout--something your competition doesn't have.
                              DS
Sincerely
           QS
Lee Rodgers
Marketing Manager

39d ● 6'

NEW FUNCTION

Read "Print Preview." Complete the drill.

Print Preview

Print Preview shows how the page will look when it is printed. Use Print Preview to check the layout of your document, such as margins, line spacing, and tabs before printing. Print Preview is helpful for checking letter placement. A document can also be edited in the Print Preview mode.

The Preview toolbar has various options for viewing the document. The Magnifier button allows you to view the document at 100%. By clicking the Magnifier button on the Preview toolbar, the mouse pointer changes to a magnifying glass.

Drill
1. Document *39c-d2* should be displayed. Click the **Print Preview** button.
2. Preview *39c-d2*. Print when you are satisfied with the way it appears.

To preview a document:
- Click the **Print Preview** button to see the full-page version of the document. Print Preview will display the page where the insertion point is located.
- Click **Close** to return to the document screen.

on... **Address Protocol**

When addressing letters, follow the protocol of the reader's country. In many countries, the surname is listed first followed by the first name. In the following example, *Fan* is the surname and *Gexin* is the first name. The name of a foreign country is keyed in ALL CAPITALS as the last line of the address.

Mr. Fan Gexin
#93 South Huanghe St.
Huanggu District
Shenyang 110003
PEOPLE'S REPUBLIC OF CHINA

Mag. Helmut Kratky
Fasanenstrasse 5, D-10625
Berlin 12
GERMANY

Formatting Text

34a ● 12'

GETTING started

Reinforcement

1. Open *33e*.
2. Insert and delete text as marked in the first two paragraphs. Save as **34a**. Print and close.

As the man says, I have some good news and some ~~good~~ *bad* news. Let me give you (first) the bad news. Due to a badly ~~pulled~~ *strained* muscle, I have had to withdraw from the Eastern Racquet Ball tournament. As you know, I have been looking forward to the tournament for a long time, and I had begun to hope that I might even win it. I've been working hard.

That's the bad news. The good news is that I have been ~~picked~~ *Chosen* to help *with the* officiating, so I'll be coming to Newport News any way. In fact, I'll arrive ~~there~~ a day earlier than I had planned originally.

34b ● 8'

NEW FUNCTION

Drill

1. Open *33b-d4*.
2. Use the mouse to select each item; cancel the select function after each item:
   • The first sentence
   • The word "wise" in ¶ 1
   • The first line
   • The first ¶
3. Use the keyboard to select:
   • The word "attention" in the last sentence
   • ¶ 1
   • Both paragraphs
4. Move the insertion point to the top of the document. Key your name; press ENTER twice.
5. Save as **34b**; print; close the document.

Selecting text

Selecting text identifies the text that has been keyed so that it can be formatted. Selected text appears black on the screen. Text may be selected by using the mouse or keyboard.

To select text with the keyboard:

1. Position the I-beam on the first character. Press SHIFT + CTRL and → or ←.
2. To select large portions of text, press SHIFT + CTRL and ↑ or ↓ .
3. Cancel the select function by pressing an arrow key.

To select text with the mouse:

1. Position the I-beam on the first character to be selected.
2. Click on the left mouse button and drag the mouse over the text to be selected.
3. To cancel a selection, click the mouse button again or press any arrow key.

To select:	
A word	Double-click the word.
A line	Click in the area left of the line.
Multiple lines	Drag in the area left of the lines (selection bar).
A paragraph	Double-click in the selection bar next to the paragraph or triple-click anywhere in the paragraph.

Professional Office Consultants, Inc.

584 Castro St.
San Francisco, CA 94114-2201
415-555-8725
415-555-8775 (FAX)

Dateline

January 17, 200-
QS

Letter
address

Ms. Armanda Castillo, Office Manager
TeleNet Corporation
24 Technology Dr.
Irvine, CA 92865-9845
DS

Salutation

Dear Ms. Castillo
DS

Body

Thank you for selecting Professional Office Consultants, Inc. to assist with the setup of your new corporate office. You asked us for a recommendation for formatting business letters. We highly recommend the block letter style because it is easy to read, economical to produce, and efficient.
DS

This letter is keyed in block format. As you can see, all lines begin at the left margin. Most letters can be keyed using default side margins and then centered vertically on the page for attractive placement. The block letter format is easy to key because tabs are not required.

We think that you will be happy using the block letter format. Over 80 percent of businesses today are using this same style.
DS

Complimentary
close

Sincerely
QS

Writer's name

Anderson Cline

Title

OA & CIS Consultant
DS

Reference
initials

xx

BLOCK LETTER

34c ● 15'

NEW FUNCTION

Character formats on the Formatting toolbar

The Formatting toolbar provides an efficient way to apply character formats, such as bold, underline, italic, fonts, and font sizes. The basic commands on the Formatting toolbar also make it easy to align text. These formatting options can be applied while you are keying, or they can be applied to existing text.

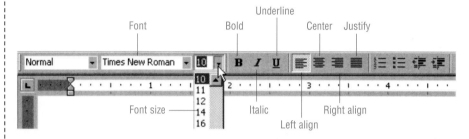

To apply character formats as you key:

1. Click the appropriate format button and key the text.
2. Click the same button again to turn off the format. When the formatting feature has been turned on, the button appears lighter and depressed.

To apply character formats to existing text:

1. Select the text.
2. Click the appropriate format button.

Font size

The size of the font is measured in points. One vertical inch is equal to 72 points. Most text is keyed in a 10-, 11-, or 12-point font, although a larger font may be used to emphasize headings. To change the size of the font, select the text to be changed and then click on the Font Size down arrow. A list of available font sizes displays; select the desired font size.

Drill 1

Key each of the sentences, applying the formats as you key. Save as **34c-d1**.

These words are keyed in bold.

These words are keyed in italic.

<u>These words are underlined.</u>

This line is keyed in 14 point.

Drill 2

Select the text and click the appropriate format button.

1. Open *34a;* save as **34c-d2**.
2. Bold the words "good," "win," and "day earlier."
3. Italicize the words "bad" and "badly."
4. Underline the last sentence in the third paragraph. Select the line and change it to 14 point.
5. Key your name and **34c-d2 Keyboarding** at the top of the document. Press ENTER 4 times. Save and print.

39b, *continued*

Block letter format

All lines begin at the left margin in **block format,** making this an efficient letter style. **Open punctuation** requires no punctuation following the salutation or the complimentary close.

Letter placement

Business letters are prepared on letterhead stationery, which has the company name, address, telephone number, and logo. The letterhead often includes the fax and/or e-mail address and company slogan. Most letterheads are between 1" and 2" deep. If a letter is printed on plain stationery, the sender's return address is keyed immediately above the date.

To be attractive, letters are positioned on the page according to their length (short, average, long). As the Letter Placement Table shows, the length of letters is determined by estimating the number of words in the letter or by the number of paragraphs. For example, short letters have only one or two paragraphs and fewer than 100 words.

Default margins are used regardless of the letter's length. Short or average letters may be positioned vertically by using the Center Page command. To avoid interfering with the letterhead, Center Page should not be used in long letters or average-length letters containing many extra letter parts. Instead, position the dateline on the appropriate line. Preview the letter before printing to check vertical placement.

Letter Placement Table		
Length	**Dateline Position**	**Margins**
Short: 1-2 ¶s	Center page or 3"	Default
Average: 3-4 ¶s	Center page or 2.7"*	Default
Long : 4 or more ¶s	2.3" (default + 7 hard returns)	Default

* Decrease for extra lines; position based on 12-point font.

Short Letter

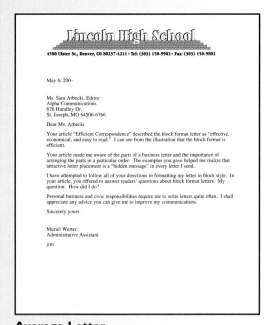

Average Letter

39c ● 20'

FORMATTING

**Block letters
Document 1**

1. Key the letter on p. 103.
2. Use Center Page to position the letter vertically.
3. Follow the "Proofreading procedures" listed in 37c, p. 96.
4. Save as **39c-d1** and print.

Alignment

Alignment refers to the way in which the text lines up. Paragraphs can be aligned at the left, center, right, or justified (lined up with both margins). Use the Alignment buttons on the Formatting toolbar to align paragraphs quickly.

To align existing text:

1. Place the insertion point in the paragraph to be changed. If more than one paragraph is affected, select the paragraphs to be aligned.
2. Click the appropriate Align button. (see page 85).

To align text as you key:

1. Click the appropriate Align button.
2. Key the paragraph. This alignment will remain in effect until you click the button again.

Drill

1. Key the document.
2. Format the headings in bold and align the paragraphs as shown.
3. Save as **34d**. Close and exit.

Left alignment

Left alignment is used for this first paragraph. When left alignment is used, each line in the paragraph begins at the same position on the left side. The right side may have a ragged margin. Left alignment is used most frequently.

Center alignment

Center alignment is useful for keying
invitations, announcements, and other documents
with a number of short lines.

Right alignment

Right alignment is used for this third paragraph. When right alignment is used each line in the paragraph ends at the same position on the right side. The left side may have a ragged margin. Right alignment is used frequently with figures.

Justify

Justify is used for this fourth paragraph. When justify is used, all lines begin and end at the same position at the left and right margins. To even out both the left and right margins, spaces are distributed automatically in the text. Justify is often used for reports.

Block Letter Format, Print Preview

GETTING started

Reinforcement
1. Edit the ¶ as marked. DS.
2. Save and print.

Writing ~~concise~~ responses, formulating ~~competitive~~ bids, creating ~~effective~~ business plans, answering ~~customer~~ feedback, composing messages ~~and letters~~ to clients, responding to customers and staff, maintaining relations with coworkers and supervisors, interpreting messages, and persuading customer these are just a few examples of ~~written and oral~~ communication that ~~is~~ are handled by everday every day by competent business people. ~~Communicating skills and a keen knowledge of business are valuable assets for anyone seeking success in business.~~

FORMATTING

Block letters
Study carefully the information about business letter parts and placement (at the right and on the next page).

Parts of a business letter
Business letters contain a variety of parts that serve very specific purposes. Listed below are basic parts of a typical business letter:

Dateline: The letter is dated the day it is mailed.

Letter address: The address of the person who will receive the letter begins a quadruple space (QS) below the dateline. Include a personal title (for example, Mr. or Ms.) unless a professional title (Dr.) is appropriate.

Salutation: Key the salutation, or greeting, a double space (DS) below the letter address. The salutation should correspond to the first line of the letter address. Use Ladies and Gentlemen when the first line of the address is a company name.

Body: The body is the message of the letter. Begin the body a double space (DS) below the salutation. Single-space the body and double-space between paragraphs.

Complimentary close: The complimentary close, which is the formal closing of the letter, begins a double space below the body.

Writer's name and title: Leave three blank lines (QS) for the writer's signature, keying the name on the fourth line. If the writer's title is short, it may follow the name; if the title is long, key it on the next line.

Reference initials: When business letters are keyed by someone other than the writer, the operator's initials are keyed in lowercase a double space below the writer's keyed name and/or title. Initials are not included when the writer keys the letter.

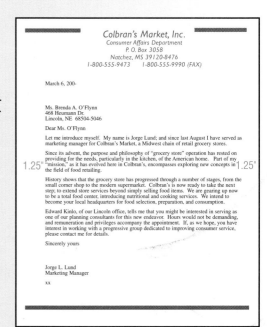

Long Letter

Spelling, Grammar, and Center Page

35a • 5'

GETTING started

Reinforcement
1. Key the paragraph. Disregard errors for now.
2. Save as **35a**.
3. Print and close.

35b • 20'

NEW FUNCTION

Accidents on the job can often be avoided if each employee is aware of the hazards involved in his or her duties. Employees should be informed of things that they may inadvertently do or leave undone that may jeopardize others. It is always better to play it safe when working with others. Remember, accidents don't just happen; they are caused.

AutoCorrect, Spelling and Grammar check

Spelling and grammar checking and other correcting features *assist* you in proofreading and editing documents; they do not *replace* editing and proofreading. *Microsoft Word* provides two options:

AutoCorrect
Common keying errors are corrected automatically as you key. For example, if you key *teh*, the AutoCorrect feature automatically corrects the spelling to *the*. You can customize the AutoCorrect feature by accessing AutoCorrect on the Tools menu.

Spelling and Grammar automatic check
Microsoft Word automatically checks the spelling and grammar of text as you key, placing a red wavy line under misspelled words and a green wavy line under potential grammar errors. By reviewing the document, you can quickly see where corrections are needed.

As an additional tool, the Spelling and Grammar Status button on the Status bar contains a ✓ when no errors are marked and an ✗ when errors are marked in the document. Clicking the right mouse button in a marked word will display a shortcut menu to correct the error.

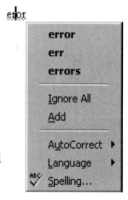

No Errors

Errors

Drill 1
1. Key the sentences as shown, including errors.
   Note: Errors in Sentences 1 and 2 are corrected automatically (Auto-Correct). Possible errors in Sentences 3 and 4 are marked.
2. Right-click the marked words and correct the errors.
3. Can you locate the error that is not marked?

i beleive alot of dissatisfied customers will not return.

a seperate comittee was formed to deal with the new issues.

please includ a self-addressed, stampted envelope with your letter.

if you don't receive a repsonse to you e-mail messige, call Robbins and Associates at 555-9870

FORMATTING

Electronic mail

Without Internet access: Complete the documents below as memos.

With an e-mail address: Complete the documents in your software and send.

With Internet access but no e-mail address: Refer to Internet Activity 7, p. 121, and set up a free e-mail address.

Electronic mail

An **e-mail message** is an informal message that is sent by one computer user to another computer user. Electronic mail is an increasingly popular means of communication that affords many advantages, including speed, convenience, and cost. To be able to send or receive e-mail, you must have an e-mail address, have an e-mail program, and have access to the Internet.

E-mail users are expected to use netiquette or "e-manners" that were developed as this technology became so widely used.

Companies are also developing policies for company electronic mail.

Heading: Key accurately the e-mail address of the receiver and supply a specific subject line for the message. The date and your e-mail address will display automatically.

Body: Single-space (SS) the body and DS between paragraphs. Do not indent ¶s.

Formatting: Do not add bold, italic, or vary fonts. Do not use uppercase letters for emphasis. Use emoticons or e-mail abbreviations with caution (e.g., ;-) for a wink or BTW for by the way).

Document 1
E-mail message

Before keying Document 1, complete *Send E-mail message,* p. 122.

1. Key e-mail message at right to your instructor.
2. Follow "Proofreading procedures" on p. 96.
3. Send the message.

E-Mail

| To: *(Your Instructor)* | | cc: | SRainey@tele.com |
| | | | FSanchez@tele.com |

| Subject: | *Extra Credit Assignment* |

| Attachment: |

Message:
Thank you for the opportunity to complete an extra credit assignment. I have attached an electronic copy of my completed assignment. A printed version of the assignment is in your mailbox.

Document 2

Key the memo at right as an e-mail to three students in your class. The memo is from **H. T. Hemphill**. Use current date, your reference initials, and the subject line, **Company Electronic-Mail Policy**. Be sure to order names alphabetically on separate lines. DS between listed items in the message.

Electronic mail is offering many advantages to our company. Your team members have reported the following advantages:

-- E-mail is a fast, convenient way to communicate internally.
-- Time is saved from telephone tag and telephone interruptions.
-- Time barriers are eliminated by the 24-hour, seven-days-per-week capability of e-mail.

With the use of e-mail comes a responsibility to follow guidelines for appropriate use. An official company policy will be distributed to all employees effective January 1. The policy covers areas such as appropriateness of choice of e-mail communication, composition of e-mail messages, personal privacy of e-mail sent at the company, and ethical and legal implications of e-mail.

Correcting errors

The Spelling and Grammar dialog box displays at each error. You have the option of changing or ignoring errors. You can also click the Add button to add correct words to the dictionary. The Ignore All and Change All buttons apply to the entire document.

Drill 2

1. Open *35a*.

2. Click the **Spelling and Grammar** button on the Standard toolbar to check the document.

3. Proofread and make additional corrections as needed.

4. Save as **35b-d2** and print.

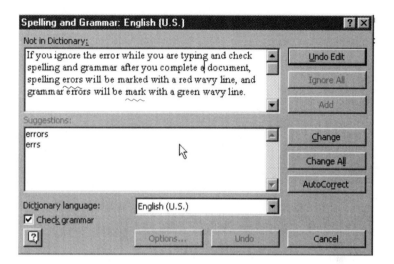

Drill 3

1. Key the ¶s exactly as shown; include the misspellings and abbreviations. Strike TAB to indent the ¶s.

2. Position the insertion point in the first word marked with an error.

3. Click the right mouse button; select the correct word from the menu.

4. Click the button on the Status bar to move to the next error; correct all errors.

5. Proofread for errors not found by the software. Correct any found.

6. Save as **35b-d3**.

7. Print and close the document.

These paragraph demonstrates errors that might be marked for analysiz. Note that once an error is marked, an x appears in the Grammar and Spelling status buttan on the status bar. Position the insertion point in the first marked error and click the rite mouse button. Note that this error is a grammar error and two alternatives are offered. The 2nd alternative is prefererable because this exercize has two paragraph. In some cases, a spelling suggestion is not available. Abbreviations (Mr.), acronyms (ABC), and names (VanHuss) are considered exceptions and are usually ignored.

Some errors are not detected by the software, which explains why you must proofred documents carefully. Some potential errors such as the last use of the passive form that is marked could be ignored if you chose to do so. However, active form is preferable.

Review Memo and E-Mail

38a ● 7'

GETTING started

fingers curved, hands quiet;
each line twice as shown

1st
1 My 456 heavy brown jugs have nothing in them; fill them by May 7.
2 The 57 bins are numbered 1 to 57; Bins 5, 6, 45, and 57 are full.

2d
3 Ed decided to crate 38 pieces of cedar decking from the old dock.
4 Mike, who was 38 in December, likes a piece of ice in cold cider.

3d/4th
5 Polly made 29 points on the quiz; Wex, 10 points. Did they pass?
6 Sally saw Ezra pass 200 pizza pans to Sean, who fixed 10 of them.

| 1 | 2 | 3 | 4 | 5 | 6 | 7 | 8 | 9 | 10 | 11 | 12 | 13 |

38b ● 20'

FORMATTING

Interoffice memos

Document 1
1. Add your reference initials.
2. Indent the names on the Distribution List to the first tab.
   Distribution:
   Allen Bejahan
   Janet James
   Terry Johnson
   Ray Lightfoot
3. Check spelling. Proofread carefully. Save as **38b-d1**.

words

TO: Team Leaders -- Distribution Below   8
             DS
FROM: J. Mac Chandler, Office Manager   15

DATE: May 14, 200-   19

SUBJECT: New Multimedia Lab Available June 12   29
                         DS

We are pleased to announce the opening of our new Multimedia Lab effec-   43
tive June 12. The lab is in the front office just beyond the Advertising   58
Department.   The lab has four new computers with full multimedia capa-   72
bility, two laser disc players, a VCR, two presentation projection devices, 87
two scanners, and various color and laser printers.   97

Use this lab if your computer is too small for your job, too slow, or too   112
limited to handle a specific job. Just complete the sign-up sheet located 127
adjacent to the equipment. Projection equipment and two laptop com-   141
puters may be checked out for presentations. Please reserve this equipment 156
twenty-four hours in advance.   162

                                                            closing 176

Document 2
Key the memo; make changes as shown. Use your reference initials.

TO: J. Ezra Bayh   4
FROM: Greta Sangtree   8
DATE: August 14, 200-   ⟩ DS   13
SUBJECT: Letter-Mailing Standards   20

                                              , because of
                                              the delay,

                       chk sp
Recently the post office delivered late a letter that   35
caused us some (embarassment). To avoid recurrence, please 47
ensure that all administrative assistants and mail person- 58
nel follow postal service guidelines.   67
         U.S.

Perhaps a refresher seminar on correspondence guidelines is 79
in order. Thanks for your help.   86

Center Page

The Center Page command centers a document vertically on the page. Should extra hard returns (¶) appear in a document, these are also considered to be part of the document. Be careful to delete extra hard returns before centering the document.

To use Center Page:

1. Position the insertion point on the page to be centered.
2. From the File menu, select *Page Setup.* The Page Setup dialog box displays.
3. Click the **Layout** tab.
4. Click the **Vertical alignment** down arrow.
5. Select *Center;* then click **OK.**

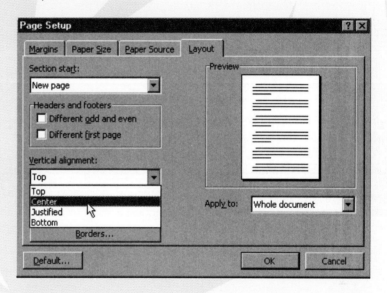

The topic of stress has received considerable attention over the past few years. Everyone experiences some stress during his or her lifetime. Stress results from happy events as well as from sad or frustrating events. Holidays are particularly stressful for many people.

People are affected by stress in many ways. A situation that causes stress may upset some people but may not have an effect on others. For some individuals stress is stimulating and enhances performance. Coping with stress will help you to live a full and happy life.

Drill

1. Key the ¶s, indenting each paragraph using the TAB key.
2. Bold each occurrence of the word "stress."
3. Center the page.
4. Save as **35c** and print.
5. Close and exit.

35d ● 15'

SKILLBUILDING

Use the remaining time to improve your speed using *Keyboarding Pro.*

FORMATTING

Distribution lists

Distribution lists

When memos are sent to more than one person, list their names after **TO:**. Generally the names are listed in alphabetical order; some organizations, however, list the names in order of rank. For readability, key the names on separate lines. When sending the memo to many people, refer to a distribution list at the end of the memo. Example: **TO:** Task Force Members--Distribution Below.

If you have any questions about these policies, please call me at any time.

xx

Distribution:
Allen Bejahan
Janet James
Terry Johnson
Ray Lightfoot

Document

Key the memo at the right. Add your reference initials. Indent the names on the Distribution List to the first tab. Check spelling and proofread carefully. Save as **37e.**

TO: TAB TAB Manufacturing Team--Distribution Below
DS

FROM: TAB Mei-Ling Yee, Administrative Assistant
DS

DATE: TAB April 14, 200-

SUBJECT: TAB Enrichment Seminar

As was stated by Robert Beloz in the January newsletter, *Focus for the New Year,* Foscari & Associates will be offering a series of enrichment seminars for its employees in the year ahead. If you have suggestions for seminars that would be beneficial to your team, please let me know.

We are proud to announce our first seminar offering, *First Aid and CPR.* Participants will be awarded CPR Certificates from the American Heart Association upon successful completion of this eight-hour course. If you are interested in taking this seminar, please call me at ext. 702 or send me an e-mail message by April 25.

Mark your calendar for this important seminar.

First Aid and CPR Enrichment Seminar
May 16 and 17
1:00-5:00 p.m.
Staff Lounge

xx

Distribution:
Eddie Barnett
Steve Lewis
Dinah Rice
Amy Sturdivant

Paragraph Formatting

Reinforcement
1. Open *35a*.
2. Edit as shown. DS between ¶s.
3. Center the page.
4. Save as **36a**. Print. Close.

Accidents on the job can often be (avoided) *italic* if each employee is aware of the hazards involved in his or her duties. Employees should be informed of things that they may (inadvertently) *italic* do or leave undone that may jeopardize others. ¶ It is always better to play it safe when working with others. Remember, accidents don't just happen; they are caused.

36b ● 5'

NEW
FUNCTION

Note: The new commands in this lesson are paragraph formats.

Paragraph formatting

Formatting can be applied to characters, lines, paragraphs, and the entire document. In Lesson 34, you learned to apply character formats, such as bold, indent, and underline and to align text. In this lesson, you will learn to apply paragraph formats. Paragraph formats apply to an entire paragraph and can be applied before or after a paragraph has been keyed. Alignment and line spacing are common paragraph formats.

Microsoft Word defines a paragraph as anything keyed that ends with a hard return. Thus, a heading or each item in a list is considered a paragraph. The Show/Hide button you learned to use in Lesson 33 displays paragraph markers, spaces, and other nonprinting characters. The paragraph mark at the end of a paragraph contains all of the formats of the paragraph that precedes it.

To apply any paragraph format to a paragraph that has already been keyed:
1. Place the insertion point in the paragraph to be changed. If more than one paragraph is affected, select the paragraphs to be formatted.
2. Apply the new paragraph format.

The·topic·of·stress·has·received·considerable·attention·over·the·past·few·

years. ··Everyone·experiences·some·stress·during·his·or·her·lifetime.¶ ——— { Double spacing 12-pt. font left-align

¶

→   People· are· affected· by· stress· in· many· different· ways. ··A· situation· that· causes·stress·may·upset·some·people·but·may·not·have·an·effect·on·others. ··Coping· with· stress· and· knowing· the· difference· between· productive· and· nonproductive· stress·will·help·you·to·live·a·full·and·happy·life.¶ ——— { Single spacing 10-pt. font full-align

37d, *continued*

**Document 1
Memo**

1. Press ENTER to position the insertion point for a 1.5" top margin.
2. Key the memo.
3. Follow "Proofreading procedures" in 37c.

1.5" Top margin

 Interoffice Memo

TO: TAB TAB Loretta Howerton, Office Manager

FROM: TAB Lawrence Schmidt, OA/CIS Consultant

DATE: TAB March 16, 200-

SUBJECT: TAB Memorandums for Internal Correspondence

A memorandum is an internal communication that is sent within the organization. It is often the means by which managers correspond with employees and vice versa. Memos provide written records of announcements, requests for action, and policies and procedures.

Templates, or preformatted forms, are often used for keying memos. Templates provide a uniform look for company correspondence and save the employee the time of having to design and format each memo. Word processing software also has memo templates that can be customized. An example of a template is attached.

xx

Attachment

---

words

Document 2
Key the document at the right. Save as **37d-d2**.

TO:	Lonny Ashmyer	4
	DS	
FROM:	Breton S. Vreede	9
	DS	
DATE:	January 11, 200-	13
SUBJECT:	Wheelchair Access	19

Recently, I explained to you my efforts on a variety of projects to facilitate 35
wheelchair entry into public buildings. I may have found a solution to one 50
problem, Lonny; that is, how does someone open a large public door from 64
a wheelchair? 67

The answer may lie in the installation of an electrical signal similar to a 83
garage door opener that can be activated from the chair. All signals would 98
be identical, of course, permitting universal application. 110

Please provide me with a rough estimate of the costs for conducting the 125
necessary preliminary search, equipping a wheelchair, and tooling our fac- 139
tory to manufacture this item. 146

xx 146

Line spacing

Single-spaced text normally is not indented. A blank line is placed between paragraphs to distinguish the paragraphs and to improve readability. Indent the first line of double-spaced text to indicate the beginning of the paragraphs. Do not place extra lines between double-spaced paragraphs. To indent the first line of a paragraph, press the TAB key. The default indention is .5".

To change line spacing:

1. Position the insertion point in the paragraph in which the line spacing will be changed.
2. Click **Format**; then **Paragraph**.
3. Select the *Indents and Spacing* tab.
4. Click the arrow in the *Line spacing* box and select *Double*.
5. Click **OK**.

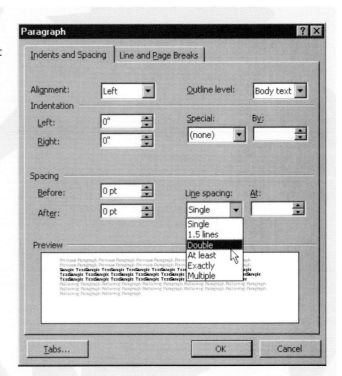

Drill I

1. DS the paragraph at the right. Indent the first line.
2. Rekey the paragraph SS; do not indent the first line.

Drill 2

1. Key the two paragraphs SS; do not indent them. Leave a blank line between them.
2. Select both paragraphs. Click **Format**; then **Paragraph**.
3. In the *Line spacing* box, change the spacing to double; indent paragraphs.
4. Print the document.
5. Change the spacing to 1.5 lines, print, and close.

Indenting paragraphs properly helps to enhance the appearance of the text and to make it more readable. Remember to indent paragraphs when double-spacing is used. Do not indent single-spaced paragraphs.

Commitment is an important concept that helps to build credibility. Commitment simply means following up on promises and doing what you said you would do. Many people think that commitments should be put in writing. Others feel that a verbal commitment is just as valid. DS

If circumstances make it impossible for you to keep a commitment, notify the individual to whom the commitment was made as quickly as possible so that other arrangements can be made for someone else to assume your commitment. Letting people down at the last minute puts them in an awkward position.

COMMUNICATION

Proofreading

Read the information at the right. Follow these steps for each document you key from now on.

Proofreading

Before documents are complete, they must be proofread, and errors must be corrected. Error-free documents send the message that you are detail-oriented and capable. Apply these procedures for all exercises in this textbook:

Proofreading procedures

1. Use Spelling and Grammar to check spelling when you have completed the document.
2. Proofread the document on screen to be sure that it makes sense. Errors of omission or repeated copy are easy to miss.
3. Verify the vertical position and overall appearance of the document using Print Preview. (See Lesson 39.)
4. Save the document again and print.
5. Proofread the printed document by comparing it to the source copy (textbook).
6. If errors are found on the printed copy, revise document, save, and print.
7. Verify the corrections and placement of the second printed copy.

FORMATTING

Interoffice memos

Read the information. Then key the three documents.

Interoffice memorandums

Messages sent to persons within an organization are called **memorandums** (memos for short). Memos include a heading, a body, and one or more notations. Addresses are not required, and use of default margins and tabs makes memos a streamlined, efficient means of communication. An increasingly popular form of internal communication is electronic mail, or **e-mail**. Users create and send the message on their computer.

Memos may be printed on plain paper or memohead. Memos are sent in plain envelopes or in interoffice envelopes, which can be reused several times.

Memo format

Headings: Double-space (DS), bold, and ALL CAPS. Job titles and department names of the sender and receiver are optional. Depending on formality or company style, courtesy titles (Mr., Ms.) of the receiver may be included. Generally courtesy titles are not used for the sender.

Body: Single-space (SS) the body and DS between paragraphs. Do not indent ¶s.

Reference initials: When the memo is keyed by someone other than the sender, the keyboard operator's initials are keyed in lowercase letters a DS below the body. Initials are not included when keying your own memo.

Notations: Items clipped or stapled to the memo are noted as *attachments*; items included in an envelope are *enclosures*. These notations are keyed a DS below the reference initials.

Side and bottom margins: Default or 1".

Top margin: Approximately 1.5". To position the first line of the heading, insert 3 hard returns from the default top margin.

Font size: Use 12 point for readability.

Interoffice Memo

TO: Loretta Howerton, Office Manager

FROM: Lawrence Schmidt, OA/CIS Consultant

DATE: March 16, 200-

SUBJECT: Memorandums for Internal Correspondence

A memorandum is an internal communication that is sent within the organization. It is often the means by which managers correspond with employees and vice versa. Memos provide written records of announcements, requests for action, and policies and procedures.

Templates, or preformatted forms, are often used for keying memos. Templates provide a uniform look for company correspondence and save the employee the time of having to design and format each memo. Word processing software also has memo templates that can be customized. An example of a template is attached.

xx

Attachment

36d ● 25'

THE INTERNET

Document 1
1. Key the text; apply paragraph and character formats as shown.
2. Center the page vertically.
3. Save as **36d-d1**. Do not close the document.

Full align ➤ The Internet is the greatest entertainment medium since television and the greatest business tool since the computer.   Don't be left wondering; cruise the Internet and find out for yourself.

DS — strike ENTER twice

Left align ➤ Each time you browse, you will find different places and different information.   Here are a few of the benefits the Internet offers you:

DS

Center align ➤
Interactive entertainment
A chance to meet people on the Net
Research sites
Business opportunities

DS

Left align ➤ <u>Even if you don't like computers, the Internet will be the catalyst that brings you into the computer age</u>.

DS

Right align ➤
For more information or help, contact:
THE INTERNET HELP DESK
301 Web Avenue
Seattle, WA 98543-3276

Left align ➤ (Your Name)

Document 2
The document *36d-d1* should be displayed. Follow the steps at the right to change the formatting.

1. Click the **Show/Hide** button to display non-printing characters.
2. Change the heading to 14-pt. bold font.
3. Position the insertion point in ¶ 1. Change line spacing to **1.5**. Note that ¶ 2 is not affected.
4. Italicize *Internet* in the first line of the first ¶.
5. Position the insertion point in ¶ 2. Change line spacing to **1.5**.
6. Select the 4 center-aligned lines and change the alignment to left align. Use single-spacing for these 4 lines. With the 4 lines still selected, click the **Bullet** button on the Formatting toolbar.

7. Select the ¶ that is underlined; change line spacing to **1.5**. Change the format from underline to bold. (With the ¶ selected, click the **Underline** button to remove underlining; then apply bold format.)
8. Add a blank line before the line: THE INTERNET HELP DESK.
9. Insert 4 blank lines before *your name*.
10. Compare your document to the illustration on the next page.
11. Save the document as **36d-d2** and close it.

BUSINESS CORRESPONDENCE

OBJECTIVES

1. Learn block and modified block letter formats.

2. Learn standard memorandum format.

3. Change the format of existing documents.

4. Improve speed and accuracy.

LESSON 37 Interoffice Memorandum

37a • 7'

GETTING started

each line twice SS; DS
between 2-line groups

SKILLBUILDING WARMUP

alphabet	1	The explorer questioned Jack's amazing story about the lava flow.
fig/sym	2	I cashed Cartek & Bunter's $2,679 check (Check #3480) on June 15.
adjacent reaches	3	As Louis said, few questioned the points asserted by the porters.
easy	4	The eighty firms may pay for a formal audit of their field works.

| 1 | 2 | 3 | 4 | 5 | 6 | 7 | 8 | 9 | 10 | 11 | 12 | 13 |

37b • 5'

SKILLBUILDING

Build staying power
Take a 1' writing on each ¶.

all letters   *gwam*   1'   3'

All of us can be impressed by stacks of completed work; yet, 12 | 4 39
we should recognize that quality is worth just as much praise, or 25 | 8 44
maybe even more, than the quantity of work done. 35 | 12 47

Logically, people expect a fair amount of work will be fin-12 | 16 51
ished in a fair amount of time; still, common sense tells us a 24 | 20 55
bucket of right is better than two wagonloads of wrong. 35 | 24 59

The logic of the situation seems lucid enough: Do the job 12 | 27 63
once and do it right.   If we plan with care and execute with 24 | 32 67
confidence, our work will have the quality it deserves. 35 | 35 70

1' | 1 | 2 | 3 | 4 | 5 | 6 | 7 | 8 | 9 | 10 | 11 | 12 | 13 |
3' | | 1 | | 2 | | 3 | | 4 |

36d, *continued*

How does your document compare to this solution?

THE INTERNET

The *Internet* is the greatest entertainment medium since television and the greatest business tool since the computer. Don't be left wondering; cruise the Internet and find out for yourself.

Each time you browse, you will find different places and different information. Here are a few of the benefits the Internet offers you:

- Interactive entertainment
- A chance to meet people on the Net
- Research sites
- Business opportunities

Even if you don't like computers, the Internet will be the catalyst that brings you into the computer age.

For more information or help, contact:
THE INTERNET HELP DESK DS
301 Web Avenue
Seattle, WA 98543-3276 QS

(Your Name)

Document 3
1. Key the text.
2. Format the document as shown at the right. Use 14-pt. bold for title.
3. Center page vertically.
4. Save as **36d-d3.** Print.

36e ●
SKILLBUILDING

Use remaining time to improve your speed using *Keyboarding Pro,* Skill Builder Module.

NEW MISSION FOR EDUCATION

In a time of increasing emphasis on diversity, schools must find a way to focus on conveying common human and democratic values and to validate their expressions in a multicultural context.

As reflected in our mission statement, the fundamental expectations of our schools are to develop:

Well-Informed Citizens

A Professional, Adaptive, World-Class Workforce

Objective Assessment

Answer the questions below to see whether you have mastered the content of this module.

1. An ellipsis following a command on a pull-down menu indicates that a _____ will display.

2. A _____ command on a menu indicates that it is not available for use.

3. To modify a document and save both the original version and the modified version, use the _____ command.

4. To print only page 2 of a document, use the Print command on the _____ menu.

5. The _____ command replaces existing characters with text that is keyed.

6. The _____ command is used to bring a previously stored document on the screen.

7. _____ refers to the way in which the characters or text lines up.

8. _____ displays all nonprinting characters.

9. To use the DELETE key to delete a character, place the insertion point to the _____ of the character to be deleted.

10. The Center Page command is accessed on the _____ dialog box.

Performance Assessment

1. DS the ¶s. SS the list.
2. Center-align the two headings. Use 14-point for GROUPWARE heading line.
3. Right-align your name and date a DS below the list.
4. Center the document vertically on the page.
5. Save as **ckpt4**.

GROUPWARE

What Is It?

The term *Groupware* has received a lot of publicity over the past few months. But ironically enough, a recent survey showed that the majority of the people could not define Groupware. *ital*

Groupware is software that allows people to work together; "it supports collaboration and the collaborative process by enhancing the productivity and effectiveness of a group of people." Groupware *ital* software gives the traveling executive the capability of being able to access their corporate databases, communicate with his employees, and schedule meetings while on the road.

The six categories of groupware *ital* include the following:

SS
center
align {
E-mail and communications
Calendaring and scheduling
Information sharing and conferencing
Meeting support and group decision-making
Shared document and image management
Word-flow management
}
DS

right
align [
Your Name
Current Date
]

Contents

KEYPAD DRILLS 1, 2, 3

Drill 1

Technique tip
Keep fingers curved and upright over home keys. Keep right thumb tucked under palm.

	a	b	c	d	e	f
	11	22	33	14	15	16
	41	52	63	36	34	35
	24	26	25	22	42	62
	27	18	39	30	20	10
	30	30	10	19	61	43
	32	31	21	53	83	71

Drill 2

	a	b	c	d	e	f
	414	141	525	252	636	363
	141	111	252	222	363	333
	111	414	222	525	333	636

Drill 3

	a	b	c	d	e	f
	111	141	222	252	366	336
	152	342	624	141	243	121
	330	502	331	302	110	432
	913	823	721	633	523	511
	702	612	513	712	802	823
	213	293	821	813	422	722

Drill 4

	a	b	c	d	e	f
	24	36	15	12	32	34
	115	334	226	254	346	246
	20	140	300	240	105	304
	187	278	347	159	357	158
	852	741	963	654	321	987
	303	505	819	37	92	10

Drill 5

	a	b	c	d	e	f
	28	91	37	22	13	23
	524	631	423	821	922	733
	15	221	209	371	300	25
	823	421	24	31	19	107
	652	813	211	354	231	187
	50	31	352	16	210	30

$appendix$ (A)

FILE MANAGEMENT

Windows Explorer

Files can be managed by using a program called *Windows Explorer.* To access *Windows Explorer,* click *Start,* then click *Programs,* and then *Windows Explorer. Windows Explorer* provides a very convenient way to set up folders (directories) and subfolders (subdirectories). Folders and subfolders can be set up on your hard disk drive or on a floppy disk. The example shown below provides folders for a keyboarding and an English class.

Creating folders and subfolders

Each folder has two subfolders—Classwork and Homework. To create the folders, click *Drive A,* then click *File.* From the cascading menu, click *New* and then *Folder.* Key **English** as the name of the folder. Repeat the process and name the new folder **Keyboarding**.

To create the subfolders for the folder named English, click *English,* then *New,* and then *Folder.* Name the folder **Classwork**. Repeat the process, naming the new folder **Homework**. To create the sub-

folders for Keyboarding, click *Keyboarding, New,* and *Folder.* Name the folder **Classwork**. Repeat the process, naming the new folder **Homework**.

Drill I

Using *Windows Explorer*

1. Insert your storage disk into Drive A or B.

2. Click on **Start.** Highlight *Programs.* Click on **Windows Explorer.**

3. Maximize the *Explorer* window. If Desktop is not the top object in the All Folders pane, click on the up scroll arrow until it is displayed.

4. If a plus sign (+) displays beside the My Computer icon, click the **+** to extend its sublevels.

5. Click on **3 1/2" Floppy (A: or B:).**

6. From the View menu, click **List** to display the contents of the folder in numerical and alphabetical order.

Drill 2

Create folders for this book

1. From the File menu, choose *New,* then *Folder.* A new folder icon labeled "New Folder" displays in the Contents pane.

2. Enter the folder name **Module 4** and press ENTER. A new folder appears on your disk.

3. Repeat Steps 1 and 2 to create new folders labeled Module 5, Module 6, Module 7, Module 8, and Appendix.

KEYPAD DRILLS 7, 8, 9

Drill 1

a	b	c	d	e	f
74	85	96	70	80	90
47	58	96	87	78	98
90	70	80	90	90	70
89	98	78	89	77	87
86	67	57	48	68	57
59	47	48	67	58	69

Drill 2

a	b	c	d	e	f
470	580	690	770	707	407
999	969	888	858	474	777
777	474	888	585	999	696

Drill 3

a	b	c	d	e	f
858	969	747	770	880	990
757	858	959	857	747	678
579	849	879	697	854	796
857	967	864	749	864	795
609	507	607	889	990	448
597	847	449	457	684	599

Drill 4

a	b	c	d	e	f
85	74	96	98	78	88
957	478	857	994	677	579
657	947	479	76	94	795
887	965	789	577	649	849
90	80	70	806	709	407
407	567	494	97	80	70

Drill 5

a	b	c	d	e	f
50	790	807	90	75	968
408	97	66	480	857	57
87	479	567	947	808	970
690	85	798	587	907	89
94	754	879	67	594	847
489	880	97	907	69	579

Selecting folders/ directories and files

Only one folder/directory can be selected at a time in the left pane. Multiple files or folders can be selected in the right pane. To select multiple files or folders listed in consecutive order, click on the first object to be selected, hold down the SHIFT key, and click the last object to be selected. The entire group of folders or files is now highlighted.

To select files or folders that are scattered throughout the Contents pane/content list area, hold down the CTRL key while you click each of the desired objects.

Deleting and renaming folders

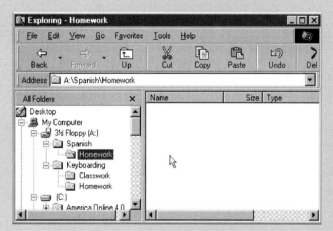

If you change your English class to a Spanish class, you could simply rename the folder. Click on the *English* folder, then click *File,* and then *Rename.* Key **Spanish**. In your Spanish class, you do not need the subfolder named *Classwork.* Click on the subfolder *Classwork,* then click *File,* and then *Delete.* Respond *Yes* to the inquiry, *Are you sure you want to remove the folder Classwork and all its contents?*

Files and folders can be moved by dragging them from one position to another. They can be copied by pressing CTRL and dragging the file to the new position.

Moving and copying files

As you create more files, you probably will need to create additional folders or directories and then rearrange existing files by moving or copying them into the new folders/directories. When a file is copied, the original file remains in place, and another copy of the file is placed at the destination. When a file is moved, the original file is removed from its original location and placed at the destination.

- Folders and files are moved by dragging the object from the Contents pane to its destination. If you drag a folder on the same disk, it will be moved. If you drag a file to another disk (from Drive A to C), it will be copied.

- To copy a file/folder, use the CTRL key while dragging the file.

- To move a file/folder, use the SHIFT key.

The file or folder that is to be copied is referred to as the **source copy;** the location where the copy is to be moved is called the **destination**. Folders and files that are moved or copied by mistake can be restored to their original location by using Undo in the Edit menu.

KEYPAD DRILLS 4, 5, 6, 0

1. Turn on NUMLOCK.
2. Strike ENTER after each number.
3. To obtain a total, strike ENTER twice after the last number in a group.
4. Key each problem until the same answer is obtained twice; you can then be reasonably sure that you have the correct answer.
   Follow these directions for each lesson.

Drill 1

a	b	c	d	e	f
46	55	56	46	55	56
45	64	45	45	64	45
66	56	64	66	56	64
56	44	65	56	44	65
54	65	45	54	65	45
65	54	44	65	54	44

Drill 2

466	445	546	654	465	665
564	654	465	545	446	645
456	464	546	545	564	456
556	544	644	466	644	646
644	455	464	654	464	554
454	546	565	554	456	656

Drill 3

400	404	505	606	500	600
404	505	606	500	600	400
500	600	400	404	505	606
650	506	404	550	440	550
506	460	605	460	604	640
406	500	640	504	460	560

Drill 4

504	640	550	440	660	406
560	450	650	450	505	550
640	504	440	640	450	660
400	600	500	500	600	400
650	505	404	606	540	560
504	404	640	404	406	606

Managing files with *Microsoft Word*

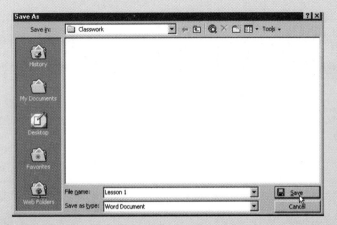

Files are most often managed with application software, such as *Microsoft Word.* To save your first document in the *Classwork* sub-folder, click *File* on the menu bar; then click *Save As* to display the Save As dialog box. In the Save in box, click *Drive A;* then click the *Keyboarding* folder; then click the *Classwork* subfolder.

In the File name box, replace the text shown with the filename **Lesson 1**. Press Save to save the file. Use the same procedure to save another new document named **Lesson 2**.

Filenaming conventions

Selecting appropriate filenames is extremely important. Files that are named in a logical, systematic manner are easier to locate than files that are named in a haphazard way. Filenames can be 255 characters long, including spaces. A period is used to separate the filename from the extension. Note the filename above, *Lesson 1.doc.* The *doc* extension indicates that the file is a *Word* document. The following symbols cannot be used in a filename: ★ + = [ ] : ; A < > ? / \ |.

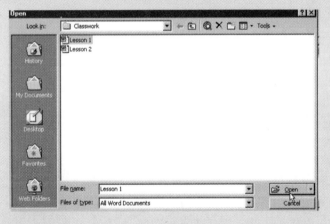

Note from the preceeding example that using a logical system of folders, subfolders, and filenames makes it easy to find files when you need them. If you needed to find the first lesson that you did as classwork in your keyboarding class, it would be logical and easy to remember to look in the Keyboarding class folder, then in the Classwork subfolder, and then for Lesson 1. Files can be opened by clicking *File* on the menu bar; then clicking *Open.*

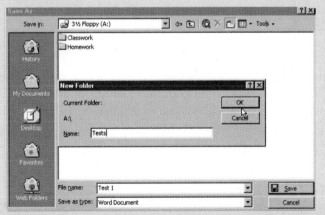

New folders can also be created from the Save As dialog box by clicking on the *Create New Folder* button. The folder can then be named in the same way that you named folders using *Windows Explorer.*

a ppendix **E**

NUMERIC KEYPAD

Keypad presentation

Keypad instruction is available in the Numeric Keypad module of *Keyboarding Pro* software. NUMLOCK must be on for you to use the software. The lessons are similar to the activities in the other keyboarding modules. Activities include Warmup, Learn New Keys, Improve Keystroking, Build Skill, and a game. The Lesson Report shows the exercises you have completed and the scores achieved.

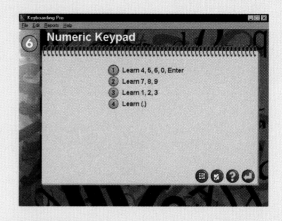

Keypad analysis

Click the **Keypad Analysis** button on the Numeric Keypad Lesson menu for additional keypad practice. You may select from nine different activities (data sets), each of which emphasizes a certain row or number type. Practice is in a timed-writing format.

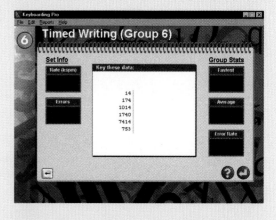

Keypad practice

Click the **Keypad Practice** button to practice the exercises on the next few pages. Strike ENTER on the keypad after each number. Strike ENTER twice to sum the amounts keyed. Click the **Print** button to print the figures.

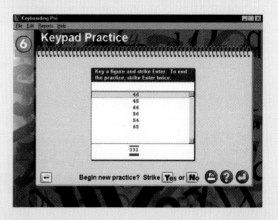

αppendix B

EDITING WORKSHOP 1

Format existing text
Document 1

1. Open *select*.
2. Save as **ew1-d1.**
3. Select the heading. Bold and center it.
4. Select "The subject" and "The predicate" and underline the text (character format).
5. Place the insertion point in the first paragraph and change to DS (paragraph format).
6. Change the top, left, and right margins to 1.5" (page format).

Proofread and edit
Document 2

1. Open *edit* from the formatting template. Save as **ew1-d2.** Print.
2. Write the proofreaders' marks shown below in ¶ 1 on your printed copy.
3. Proofread the remainder of the document marking each error you find with the proper proofreaders' mark.
4. Make the corrections.
5. Save again and print.

Did you find 16 additional errors?

Congra*t*ulations! You have already learned ~~a number of~~ *several* formatting guide lines that can enhance the appear*a*nce of a document. To reinforce these skills take every opportunity to critique the documents you produce *and* *as* ones that you receive as well. Ask these questions: What are the weaknesses? What are the strengths of this document? How can I improve this document?

Cut and paste
Document 3

1. From the formatting template, open *letter*. Save as **ew1-d3.**
2. Use Cut and Paste to move letter parts to the proper position.
3. Insert and delete lines as needed.

Writing 14

To access these writings on *MicroPace Pro* software, key **W** and the writing number. For example, key **W14** for Writing 14.

 all letters   gwam   3' | 5'

Much of the cost of hiring a new employee is clear:	3	2 40
Recruiting trips, placement fees, and advertising expenses are	8	5 43
much higher than ever before. Recruiting, even when successful	12	7 46
and free of problems, accounts for only part of the cost. The	16	10 48
lower productivity rate of a new employee while she or he is	20	12 51
being trained is a hidden cost factor. The time lag between when	25	15 53
a person is hired and when that person actually becomes produc-	29	17 56
tive may frequently extend from six to ten months.	32	19 58
As expensive as the cost of recruiting and training is,	36	22 60
the investment is very worthwhile if an employee is kept produc-	40	24 63
tive and remains with the company. A large number of poor em-	44	27 65
ployees who stay on the job become uninspired about their jobs.	49	29 68
Such people are retirees in residence. The workers who may feel	53	32 70
that their expectations have not been realized begin to do just	57	34 73
enough to get by and find the greatest challenge and fulfillment	62	37 75
in finding new ways to avoid work.	64	38 77

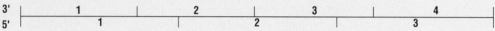

Writing 15

 all letters   gwam   3' | 5'

Telephone conference calls have been used for years. Today,	4	2 47
graphic data can also be conveyed over telephone lines to enhance	3	5 50
the calls. Two types of devices are used to send the data. The	10	8 52
first type is an electronic blackboard. The terminal, although	17	10 55
it does look like a blackboard, is really used to send written	21	13 57
material over telephone lines to a screen. The second type is a	26	15 60
digitized graphics tablet. The graphics tablet looks very much	30	18 63
like a tablet of art paper. An image is formed on a pressure-	34	20 65
sensitive surface, and the data is entered into the computer.	38	23 68
Conference calls may not be as effective as face-to-face	42	25 70
meetings, but they are far less expensive than the travel	47	28 73
required for many face-to-face meetings. The time workers spend	51	31 75
away from the office while they are traveling is also costly.	55	33 78
The key to success in using conference calls is to select	59	35 80
carefully the type of meeting to be conducted by a call. The	63	38 83
primary objectives of many types of meetings can be attained	67	40 85
through conference calls, especially if the calls are enhanced by	72	43 88
utilizing terminals to transmit graphic data.	75	45 89

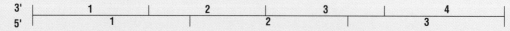

1. Open *create* from the template. Save as **ew1-d4**.
2. Edit and format the report as follows:
   - Set 1" side margins and 1.5" top margin.
   - Change line spacing to DS. Indent paragraphs.
   - Key and center the heading **CREATIVITY—A VALUED TRAIT** in bold.
   - Bold the side headings.
   - Cut and then paste the sentence marked in ¶ 2.
   - Use Cut and Paste to reverse ¶s 3 and 4.
   - Make other edits as marked.

CREATIVITY--A VALUED TRAIT

The goals of successful business executives are stated in terms of productivity, profits, and effective management of human resources. To attain these goals, executive are compelled to recruit highly qualified candidates for managerial positions. One highly valued trait is creativity.

Creativity Concepts

Creative people are usually characterized as having active imaginations and original thoughts. They avoid the limitations of traditional boundaries (Maynard, 1998, 2). Creativity is difficult to define, but it is easily recognized.

Creativity Software

Several Soft ware Packages designed to enhance creativity are available. A common trait of all the packages is that they force the learner through a structured process to generate alternative solutions to a problem. Although the software sells well, many people question the validity of using a structured process to enhance creativity. To them, creativity is the antithesis of structure. The best-selling packages are relatively inexpensive.

Creativity Development

Are people born creative or does creativity have to be nutured and developed? Many experts believe that creativity can be acquired or, at least, enhanced with effective training (Jones, 1999, 7). Other scholars doubt seriously that creativity can be learned (Albo, 1998, 34). Most people agree, though, that creativity is very difficult to measure.

Drill 2
Improve speed/accuracy on statistical copy
1' and 2' writings; figure *gwam*; circle errors

 all letters/figures   *gwam*   2'

• 4 • 8 • 12	
For the period that began January of last year, the revenue	6

For the period that began January of last year, the revenue — 6
for common stock was $197 million, a rise of 23.3% over the same — 13
interval last year. With a yield of 8.78% in average shares out- — 19
standing, revenues per share rose an extra 10.7%, from $1.61 for — 26
the period just over in January this year to $1.84 in an earlier — 32
period. The primary reason for an increment this size is due to — 39
a 5.21% increment in area quotas, many of which were met on time. — 45

2' | 1 | 2 | 3 | 4 | 5 | 6 |

Drill 3
Assess skill: statistical copy
3' or 5' writings

 all letters/figures   *gwam*   3' | 5'

The Barak & Rinezi folio for the end of the year (Memo #98) — 4 | 2
says that its last-quarter income was "26% above the historic — 8 | 5
revenues of last year." The folio also says that the increase was — 13 | 8
due to an upsurge in net sales of "just over 4 1/3%." — 16 | 10

The increase is the seventh consecutive quarter in which — 20 | 12
Barak & Rinezi have shown a profit; and the chief executive of — 24 | 15
this old firm--Paul Rinezi--has told one industrial group that he — 29 | 17
is slated to ask his board for an "increase of almost $1.50 a — 33 | 20
common share" as its dividend for this financial year. — 36 | 22

The company for the past 24 years has had its primary office — 41 | 24
at 400 Big Ruby Road; the main plant is in Abilene at 17 Autumn — 45 | 27
Avenue. The company employs about 350 area people, and yearly — 49 | 29
sales will total about $3.5 million. Paul Rinezi has acted as — 53 | 32
company CEO for 11 years; he took over the post after his uncle — 57 | 34
had been the head for over 22 years. — 60 | 36

3' | 1 | 2 | 3 | 4 |
5' | 1 | 2 | 3 |

Edit letter
Document 5

Open *ayers* from the template disk. Save as **ewl-d5**. Set a tab at center and format the letter in modified block. Use hanging indent for enumerations. Add the current date. Revise as marked.

Mr. and Mrs. Arnold Ayers
3857 Wildcat Rock Rd.
Banner Elk, NC 28604-3053

Dear Mr. and Mrs. Ayers

This letter confirms your appointment on March 24, at 9:30 a.m. On this initial visit, we will review your previous tax situation and your records. Please bring the following items with you:

current

1. Your tax records for the past ③ years. *sp*

2. Any correspondence your have recieved concerning your federal or state taxes during the past ③ years. *sp*

3. A completed copy of the income tax organiser that I have prepared for you. *enclosed*

You donot have to bring your reciepts to this meeting. However, you should maintain them for your records. I look forward to working with you. *both of*

Sincerely

Wayne C. Hoggs, CPA

Tax Consultant

xx

Enclosure

Format references

Document 6

1. Open *ewl-a16* from the template disk.
2. Format the references for a leftbound report (1.5" top and left margins).
3. Use hanging indent; change underlines to italic.

REFERENCES *no bold*

Albo, Ashley S. <u>Creativity Assessment in Institutions of Higher Learning</u>. Dallas: Lone Star Publishing Company, 1995. *8*

Jones, Marilyn. "Creativity Training for Instructors of Gifted Students." <u>Training Digest</u>, Volume 28, March 1999 5-12. *pp*

Maynard, Michael. Creativity Enhancement. Chicago: Premiere Educational Publishing Company, 1994.

SKILLBUILDING WORKSHOP 3

Drill I
Variable rhythm patterns

each line twice SS; DS between 2-line groups; rekey difficult lines

Fluency (key phrases and words, not letter by letter)

1 it is | it is he | to us | am due | by the man | an end | by the body | go with
2 cut the firm | due to the | go to the end | did pay us | form a half firm
3 they wish us to go | kept the man down | held the box down | cut the ox

4 Did the busy men dismantle the shamrock ornament for the visitor?
5 The key to the eighth problem is to spell rogue and theory right.
6 When Jane and I go to the city, we may visit the chapel and mall.

7 The auditor had problems with the theory to make a profit for us.
8 Diane did rush the lapdog to the city when it bit their neighbor.
9 If the altos are on key, they may enrich the chant in the ritual.
| 1 | 2 | 3 | 4 | 5 | 6 | 7 | 8 | 9 | 10 | 11 | 12 | 13 |

Control (key at a steady but not fast pace)

10 we saw | ad in | as my | we are | on him | ate up | we act ill | add gas to oil
11 age was | you are only | jump on art | my faded nylon | red yolk | few were
12 best care | you read | tax base | after we oil | saw data | agreed rate was

13 Water and garbage rates fell after my rebates were added in July.
14 Acres of wet grass and poppy seeds were tested for zebras to eat.
15 Jo ate the lumpy beets and sweet tarts but craved a stewed onion.

16 Jimmy saw a cab in my garage; I was awarded it in an estate case.
17 Dad feared we'd pay extra estate taxes after debts were assessed.
18 Rebates on oil, added to decreases in taxes, affect oil reserves.
| 1 | 2 | 3 | 4 | 5 | 6 | 7 | 8 | 9 | 10 | 11 | 12 | 13 |

Variable-rhythm sentences (vary pace with difficulty of words)

19 Dad attested to the fact that the barbers paid the auditor's tax.
20 Giant oaks and sassafras trees edged the east lane of the street.
21 Holly may join us by the pool to meet the eight big team members.

22 Did you get sufficient green material to make the eight sweaters?
23 All crates of cabbages were saved after I agreed to make payment.
24 Both visitors were totally enchanted as they watched the regatta.
| 1 | 2 | 3 | 4 | 5 | 6 | 7 | 8 | 9 | 10 | 11 | 12 | 13 |

*a*ppendix C

COMMUNICATION WORKSHOP 1

Drill 1
Capitalization
Key the sentences, correcting all capitalization errors. Number each item and DS between them.
Reference: RG1

1. mara will visit glacier national park and vancouver, british columbia, this fall.

2. eric and kate bought 6 notebooks. each notebook holds 350 pages.

3. mohammed is striving to earn his mba in six years at columbia university.

4. i saw the quote in section c of the *times* regarding the governor of ohio.

5. joseph lutke earned his cpa and was promoted to vice president of finance on monday, april 3.

6. the production department will meet march 3 in the wells conference room.

7. robin is enrolled in accounting 101; lee is in a marketing class.

8. complimentary closings range from informal (cordially yours, sincerely yours, sincerely) to formal (very truly yours, yours very sincerely).

9. we told them smart write is a registered trademark of holt, inc.

10. george is the leading sales representative in the western region.

Drill 2
Number expression
Key each phrase, applying correct number expression. Number each item.
Reference: RG1

1. class of about 450 students

2. prize of one thousand dollars

3. Was it three percent or five percent?

4. nine o'clock meeting that was extended beyond noon

5. 2 days to check on about one hundred fifty thousand returns

6. three two-foot strips

7. 26th of May is when

8. two boxes of letterhead and twelve reams of paper

9. building listed near $2.5 million

10. received three hundred calls the first day

11. Francis gave only $.75.

12. invited six girls and twelve boys

13. Over $2,000,000 was raised.

14. will be working until 6 o'clock for 4 days

15. only 5 of the 35 members

16. 3 of us will be here all day.

17. with a ten percent budget cut planned for the 1st of next year

18. paid fifty dollars for 8 tickets at two p.m.

19. a $50 value

20. 1 of the 12-poster sets plus a 64-page user's guide

Drill 8
Guided writing:
improve speed/accuracy
Key as 1' guided writings, working for either speed or control.

Optional: Key as a 3'
writing.

To access writings on
MicroPace Pro, key **W** and the
timing number. For example,
key **W11** for Writing 11.

Writing 11

gwam 3'

•	4	•	8	•	12

Anyone who expects some day to find an excellent job should   4 | 34

    •   16   •   20   •   24

begin now to learn the value of accuracy. To be worth anything,   8 | 38

    •   28   •   32   •   36   •

completed work must be correct, without question. Naturally, we   13 | 43

   40   •   44   •   48   •

realize that the human aspect of the work equation always raises   17 | 47

   52   •   56   •   60   •   64

the prospect of errors; but we should understand that those same   20 | 51

    •   68   •   72   •   76

errors can be found and fixed. Every completed job should carry   26 | 56

    •   80   •   84   •   88   •

at least one stamp; the stamp of pride in work that is exemplary.   30 | 60

Writing 12

•	4	•	8	•	12

No question about it: Many personal problems we face today   4 | 34

    •   16   •   20   •   24

arise from the fact that we earthlings have never been very wise   8 | 38

    •   28   •   32   •   36   •

consumers. We haven't consumed our natural resources well; as a   13 | 43

   40   •   44   •   48   •

result, we have jeopardized much of our environment. We excused   17 | 47

   52   •   56   •   60   •   64

our behavior because we thought that our stock of most resources   20 | 51

    •   68   •   72   •   76

had no limit. So, finally, we are beginning to realize just how   26 | 56

    •   80   •   84   •   88   •

indiscreet we were; and we are taking steps to rebuild our world.   30 | 60

Writing 13

•	4	•	8	•	12

When I see people in top jobs, I know I'm seeing people who   4 | 34

    •   16   •   20   •   24

sell. I'm not just referring to employees who labor in a retail   8 | 38

    •   28   •   32   •   36   •

outlet; I mean those people who put extra effort into convincing   13 | 43

   40   •   44   •   48   •

others to recognize their best qualities. They, themselves, are   17 | 47

   52   •   56   •   60   •   64

the commodity they sell; and their optimum tools are appearance,   20 | 51

    •   68   •   72   •   76

language, and personality. They look great, they talk and write   26 | 56

    •   80   •   84   •   88   •

well; and, with candid self-confidence, they meet you eye to eye.   30 | 60

3' | 1 | 2 | 3 | 4 |

Drills 3 and 4
Capitalization

Key the salutations and complimentary closings, using correct capitalization. Number each item and DS between each.

Reference: RG1

Drill 3

1. ladies and gentlemen
2. dear mr petroielli
3. dear sir or madam
4. dear service manager
5. dear reverend schmidt
6. dear mr. fong and miss landow
7. dear mr. and mrs. green
8. dear senator kukanis

Drill 4

1. very sincerely yours
2. yours truly
3. very truly yours
4. sincerely yours
5. cordially yours
6. respectfully yours
7. sincerely
8. very sincerely yours

Drill 5
Letter addresses

Apply correct capitalization, number expression, and abbreviations in the letter addresses. Assume capitalization in letter addresses in Items 7 and 8 is correct. Key each address at the left margin; return 4 times between addresses.

Reference: RG5 for correct two-letter state abbreviations.

1. mr. aaron farrell
   223 east 3 street
   ft. wright, kentucky 41001-1420

2. ms. andrea phfehler
   412 morris road
   la jolla, california 92037-3310

3. mr. hoyt warner
   vice president of operations
   elgin manufacturing co.
   364 east 42nd street
   ypsilanti, michigan 48197-2211

4. mr. carlos rodriquez
   manulife international, inc.
   491 Paseo de la Cruz
   Mexico City 06500
   MEXICO

5. mr. scott veith
   p.o. box 175976
   orem, utah 84057-2399

6. ms. carol henson
   alger inc., suite 248
   pueblo, colorado 84001-6243

7. mr adam dabdoub
   1130 confederation drive
   Quebec City PG G1J2G3
   CANADA

8. mr. d. l. foust
   foust travel inc., suite 38
   779 cascade
   Calgary AB T3E 0R5
   CANADA

Drill 6
Composition

DS the ¶, inserting a proper noun in each blank and applying correct capitalization and number expression.

last _____ , my friend _____ and I had a holiday, so we decided to make the most of our day and take a bicycle trip to _____. before leaving, we stopped at _____ to purchase some high-energy foods to sustain us on our trip. we packed our saddle bags and left about _____ o'clock, traveling _direction_ on _____ street. although we were not on a sightseeing trip, we did pass _____ and _____. by _____ p.m., we returned home exhausted from our journey of _____ miles.

Drill 7
Assess skill growth: straight copy

1. Key 1' writings on each ¶ of a timing. Note that ¶s within a timing increase by 2 words.

    Goal: to complete each ¶.
2. Key a 3' timing on the entire writing.

 To access writings on *MicroPace Pro*, key **W** and the timing number. For example, key **W8** for *Writing 8*.

Timings are also available as Diagnostic Writings in *Keyboarding Pro*.

gwam

Writing 8: 34, 36, 38 *gwam*

	1'	3'

Any of us whose target is to achieve success in our professional   13   4
lives will understand that we must learn how to work in harmony   26   8
with others whose paths may cross ours daily.   35   12

We will, unquestionably, work for, with, and beside people, just   13   16
as they will work for, with, and beside us. We will judge them,   26   20
as most certainly they are going to be judging us.   38   24

A lot of people realize the need for solid working relations and   13   28
have a rule that treats others as they, themselves, expect to be   26   33
treated. This seems to be a sound, practical idea for them.   40   37

Writing 9: 36, 38, 40 *gwam*

I spoke with one company visitor recently; and she was very much   13   4
impressed, she said, with the large amount of work she had noted   26   9
being finished by one of our front office workers.   36   12

I told her how we had just last week recognized this very person   13   16
for what he had done, for output, naturally, but also because of   26   21
its excellence. We know this person has that "magic touch."   38   25

This "magic touch" is the ability to do a fair amount of work in   13   29
a fair amount of time. It involves a desire to become ever more   26   34
efficient without losing quality--the "touch" all workers should   39   38
have.   40   38

Writing 10: 38, 40, 42 *gwam*

Isn't it great just to untangle and relax after you have keyed a   13   4
completed document? Complete, or just done? No document is   25   8
quite complete until it has left you and passed to the next step.   38   13

There are desirable things that must happen to a document before   13   17
you surrender it. It must be read carefully, first of all, for   26   22
meaning to find words that look right but aren't. Read word for   39   26
word.   40   26

Check all figures and exact data, like a date or time, with your   13   31
principal copy. Make sure format details are right. Only then,   26   35
print or remove the work and scrutinize to see how it might look   39   39
to a recipient.   42   40

1'	1	2	3	4	5	6	7	8	9	10	11	12	13
3'		1			2			3			4		

Drill 1
Review use of the apostrophe
1.5" top margin; default side margins; use bold and indent as shown; center the title

USING AN APOSTROPHE TO SHOW POSSESSION

1. Add **'s** to a singular noun not ending in **s**.

2. Add **'s** to a singular noun ending in **s** or **z** sound if the ending **s** is pronounced as a syllable; as, Sis's lunch, Russ's car, Buzz's average.

3. Add **'** only if the ending **s** or **z** is awkward to pronounce; as, series' outcome, ladies' shoes, Delibes' music, Cortez' quest.

4. Add **'s** to a plural noun that does not end in **s**; as, men's notions, children's toys, mice's tracks.

5. Add only **'** after a plural noun ending in **s**; as, horses' hoofs, lamps' shades.

6. Add **'s** after the last noun in a series to show joint possession of two or more people; as, Jack and Judy's house; Peter, Paul, and Mary's song.

7. Add **'s** to each noun to show individual possession of two or more persons; as, Li's and Ted's tools, Jill's and Ed's races.

Drill 2
Review use of quotation marks
1.5" top margin; default side margins; indent examples to the first tab

SPACING WITH QUOTATION MARKS

Use quotation marks:

after a comma or a period; as,
    "I bought," she said, "more paper."

before a semicolon; as,
    She said, "I have little money"; she had, in fact, none.

before a colon; as,
    He called these items "fresh": beans, peas, and carrots.

after a question mark if the quotation itself is a question; as,
    "Why did you do that?" he asked.

before a question mark if the quotation is not a question; as,
    Why did he say, "I will not run"?

Drill 4
Build production skill

1. Key 1' writings (18 *gwam*) on the letter parts, arranging each line in correct block format. Ignore top margin requirements.
2. Return 5 times between drills.

1 May 15, 200-|Mr. Brad Babbett|811 Wier Ave., W.|Phoenix, AZ 83018-8183|Dear Mr. Babbett

2 May 3, 200-|Miss Lois J. Bruce|913 Torch Hill Rd.|Columbus, GA 31904-4133|Dear Miss Bruce

3 Sincerely yours|George S. Murger|Assistant Manager|xx|Enclosures: Warranty Deed|Invoice

4 Very cordially yours|Marvin J. Cecchetti, Jr.|Assistant to the Comptroller|xx|Enclosures

Drill 5
Reach for new goals

1. From the second or third column at the right, choose a goal 2-3 *gwam* higher than your best rate on either straight or statistical copy.
2. Take 1' writings on that sentence; try to finish it the number of times shown at the top of the goal list.
3. If you reach your goal, take 1' writings on the next line. If you don't reach your goal, use the preceding line.

		1' timing	
	words	6 times gwam	5 times gwam
Do they blame me for the goal?	6	36	30
The 2 men may enamel 17 oboes.	6	36	30
The auditor may handle the problem.	7	42	35
Did the 4 chaps focus the #75 lens?	7	42	35
She did vow to fight for the right name.	8	48	40
He paid 10 men to fix a pen for 3 ducks.	8	48	40
The girl may cycle down to the dormant field.	9	54	45
The 27 girls paid their $9 to go to the lake.	9	54	45
The ensign works with vigor to dismantle the auto.	10	60	50
Bob may work Problems 8 and 9; Sid did Problem 40.	10	60	50
The form may entitle a visitor to pay for such a kayak.	11	66	55
They kept 7 panels and 48 ivory emblems for 29 chapels.	11	66	55

| 1 | 2 | 3 | 4 | 5 | 6 | 7 | 8 | 9 | 10 | 11 |

Drill 6
Improve concentration

Set a right tab at 5.5" for the addresses. Key the Internet addresses in Column 2 exactly as they are listed. Accuracy is critical.

The paperless guide to New York City	http://www.mediabridge.com/nyc
A trip to outer space	http://spacelink.msfc.nasa.gov
Search engine	http://webcrawler.com
Government printing office access	http://www.access.gpo.gov/index.html
MarketPlace--corporate information	http://www.mktplace.com
Touchstone's PC-cillin virus scan	http://www.antivirus.com

Drill 3
Review confusing words

1. Use 1" top margin; default side margins.
2. Indent example lines to the first tab.
3. Use bold for the confusing words and the title.

accept (v) to take or receive willingly.
except (v) to exclude, omit.
> They all can **accept** the invitation **except** Bjorn, who is ill.

addition (n) the result of adding.
edition (n) a version in which a text is published.
> This fifth **edition** is an excellent **addition** to our texts.

advice (n) opinion as to what to do; helpful counsel.
advise (v) to recommend; to give information.
> I **advise** you never to listen to bad **advice**.

already (adv) previously; prior to a specified time.
all ready (adj) completely ready.
> It was **already** too late by the time dinner was **all ready**.

any one (n) any singular person in a group.
anyone (pron) any person at all.
> **Anyone** could tell the hat did not belong to **any one** of us.

assistance (n) the act of helping; help supplied.
assistants (n) those who help.
> We hired the **assistants** to give us **assistance** at five o'clock.

further (adv) to a greater degree (time or quantity).
farther (adv) at a greater distance (space).
> Look **further** into the future; rockets will travel **farther**.

it's contraction of "it is" or "it has."
its (adj) possessive form for the pronoun "it."
> **It's** a long time since the lion had **its** last meal.

lay (v) to put down; to place.
lie (v) to rest; to be situated.
> **Lay** a blanket on the bed; I want to **lie** down for awhile.

passed (v) moved along; transferred.
past (adj, adv, prep) gone by; (n) time gone by.
> It was **past** five o'clock when the parade **passed** by.

sale (n) act of exchanging something for money.
sell (v) to exchange property for money.
> We must **sell** these lamps; plan a **sale** for next week.

setting (v) to place.
sitting (v) to rest in place.
> I am **setting** this fruit here; it was **sitting** in the sun.

your (adj) belonging to you.
you're contraction of "you are."
> If **you're** not careful, you will be late for **your** meeting.

appendix D

SKILLBUILDING WORKSHOP 2

Drill 1
Compare skill sentences

1. Take a 1' writing on line 1; determine *gwam* and use this score for your goal as you take two 1' writings each on lines 2 and 3.

2. Take a 1' writing on line 4; determine *gwam* and use this score for your goal as you take two 1' writings each on lines 5 and 6.

1 Did the visitor on the bicycle signal and turn to the right?
2 The 17 girls kept 30 bushels of kale and 29 bushels of yams.
3 *The hen and a lamb roam down the field of rocks to the corn.*
4 The penalty she had to pay for the bogus audit is a problem.
5 Handle 10 ducks, 46 fish, and 38 hams for the island ritual.
6 *We got the usual quantity of shamrocks for Pamela to handle.*
   | 1 | 2 | 3 | 4 | 5 | 6 | 7 | 8 | 9 | 10 | 11 | 12 |

Drill 2
Review number and symbol reaches

Key each line twice SS; DS between 2-line groups; repeat difficult lines.

1 The inn opened at 6789 Brentt; rooms are $45 (May 12 to July 30).
2 I paid $1.56 for 2% milk and $97 for 48 rolls of film on June 30.
3 Order #4567-0 (dated 2/18) was shipped on May 30 to Spah & Erven.
4 Send Check #3589 for $1,460--dated the 27th--to O'Neil & Company.
5 Ann's 7% note (dated May 13) was just paid with a check for $285.
6 Send to The Maxi-Tech Co., 3489 D Drive, our Bill #10 for $25.67.
7 I wrote "Serial #1830/27"; I should have written "Serial #246/9."
   | 1 | 2 | 3 | 4 | 5 | 6 | 7 | 8 | 9 | 10 | 11 | 12 | 13 |

Drill 3
Improve keying techniques

Concentrate on each word as you key it; key each group twice; DS between 3-line groups.

direct reaches

1 runny cedar carver brunt numbs humps dunce mummy arbor sects hymn
2 Irvyn jumped over a clump of green grass; he broke my brown pump.
3 My uncle Cedric carved a number of brown cedar mules in December.

adjacent reaches

4 trios where alert point buyer spore milk sands sagas treads ports
5 There were three points in Porter's talk on the ports of Denmark.
6 Has Bert Welker prepared loin of pork as her dinner on Wednesday?

double letters

7 glass sells adder offer room sleek upper errors inner pretty ebbs
8 The committee soon agreed that Bess's green wool dress looks odd.
9 Three sweet little moppets stood happily on a green grassy knoll.
   | 1 | 2 | 3 | 4 | 5 | 6 | 7 | 8 | 9 | 10 | 11 | 12 | 13 |

reference

guide

Capitalize

1. First word of a sentence and of a direct quotation.

   We were tolerating instead of managing diversity.

   The speaker said, "We must value diversity, not merely recognize it."

2. Names of proper nouns—specific persons, places, or things.

   Common nouns: continent, river, car, street
   Proper nouns: Asia, Mississippi, Buick, State St.

3. Derivatives of proper nouns and geographical names.

   American history   English accent   German food
   Ohio Valley   Tampa, Florida   Mount Rushmore

4. A personal or professional title when it precedes the name or a title of high distinction without a name.

   Lieutenant Kahn   Mayor Walsh   Doctor Welby
   Mr. Ty Brooks   Dr. Frank Collins   Miss Tate
   the President of the United States

5. Days of the week, months of the year, holidays, periods of history, and historic events.

   Monday, June 8   Labor Day   Renaissance

6. Specific parts of the country but not compass points that show direction.

   Midwest   the South   northwest of town

7. Family relationships when used with a person's name.

   Aunt Helen   my dad   Uncle John

8. Noun preceding a figure except for common nouns such as *line, page,* and *sentence*.

   Unit 1   Section 2   page 2   verse 7   line 2

9. First and main words of side headings, titles of books, and works of art. Do not capitalize words of four or fewer letters that are conjunctions, prepositions, or articles.

   Computers in the News   *Raiders of the Lost Ark*

10. Names of organizations and specific departments within the writer's organization.

    Girl Scouts   our Sales Department

Number expression

General guidelines

1. Use **words** for numbers *one* through *ten* unless the numbers are in a category with related larger numbers that are expressed as figures.

   He bought three acres of land. She took two acres.
   She wrote 12 stories and 2 plays in the last 13 years.

2. Use **words** for approximate numbers or large round numbers that can be expressed as one or two words. Use **numbers** for round numbers in millions or higher with their word modifier.

   We sent out about three hundred invitations.
   She contributed $3 million dollars.

3. Use **words** for numbers that begin a sentence.

   Six players were cut from the ten-member team.

4. Use **figures** for the larger of two adjacent numbers.

   We shipped six 24-ton engines.

Times and dates

5. Use **words** for numbers that precede *o'clock* (stated or implied).

   We shall meet from two until five o'clock.

6. Use **figures** for times with *a.m.* or *p.m.* and days when they follow the month.

   Her appointment is for 2:15 p.m. on July 26, 2000.

7. Use **ordinals** for the day when it precedes the month.

   The 10th of October is my anniversary.

Money, percentages, and fractions

8. Use **figures** for money amounts and percentages. Spell out *cents* and *percent* except in statistical copy.

   The 16% discount saved me $145; Bill, 95 cents.

9. Use **words** for fractions unless the fractions appear in combination with whole numbers.

   one-half of her lesson   5 1/2   18 3/4

   (continued)

Pronoun case

Use the nominative case

1. When the pronoun acts as the subject of a verb.

Jim and I went to the movies.
Mike and she were best friends.

2. When the pronoun is used as a **predicate pronoun.** (The verb be is a linking verb; it links the noun/pronoun to the predicate.)

It was she who answered.
It was he who left.

Use the objective case

1. When the pronoun is used as a **direct** or **indirect** object.

Jill invited us to the meeting.
The printer gave Bill and me the tickets to the game.

2. When the pronoun is an **object of the preposition.**

I am going with you and him.
This issue is between you and me.

Agreement of pronoun and antecedent

The **antecedent** is the word the pronoun refers to.

The antecedent must agree with the pronoun in **person** (first, second, third), **gender** (feminine, masculine, neuter), and in **number** (singular or plural).

1. The antecedent must agree with the pronoun in **person.**

Someone had left his or her computer on the plane.
The ash tree has lost its leaves.

2. The antecedent must agree with the pronoun in **gender.** (neuter when gender of antecedent is unknown).

Gail said that she liked her doll.
The chair sits firmly on its legs.
The dog looked for its master for days.

3. The antecedent must agree with the pronoun in **number.** If the antecedent of a pronoun is singular, use a singular pronoun. If the antecedent is plural, use a plural pronoun.

All members of the class paid their dues.
Each of the Scouts brought his sleeping bag.

Basic grammar

Use a singular verb

1. With a **singular subject.** (The singular forms of to be include: am, is, was. Common errors with to be are: you was, we was, they was.)

The man works hard. He is angry; she was late.

2. With most **indefinite pronouns:** another, anybody, anything, everything, each, either, neither, one, everyone, anyone, nobody.

Each of the candidates has been critical.
Neither of the boys is able to attend.

3. With **singular subjects** joined by or/nor, either/or, neither/nor.

Neither your grammar nor your punctuation is correct.
Either Jody or Jan has your dish.

4. With a **collective noun** (family, choir, herd, faculty, jury, committee) that acts as one unit.

The jury has reached a decision.
The council is in an emergency session.
But:
The faculty have their assignments. (Each has his/her own assignment.)

5. With words or phrases that express periods of time, weights, measurements, or amounts of money.

Fifteen dollars is what he earned.
Two-thirds of the money has been turned in.
One hundred pounds is too much.

Use a plural verb

6. With a **plural subject.**

The students are working hard.
The lights are turned off at five o'clock.

7. With **compound** (two or more) **subjects** joined by and.

Success and notoriety come with the award.
Carbohydrates and fats are important to your diet.

8. With **some, all, most, none, several, few, both, many,** and **any** when they refer to more than one of the items.

All of my friends have seen the movie.
Some of the teams have won two or more games.

Addresses

10. Use **words** for street names First through Tenth. Use **figures** or ordinals for streets above Tenth. Use **figures** for house numbers other than number **one.** (If street name is a number, separate it from house number with a dash.)

One Lytle Place   Second Ave.   142--534 St.

Proofreading procedures

Proofread documents so that they are free of errors. Error-free documents send the message that you are detail-oriented and a person capable of doing business. Apply these procedures after you key a document.

1. Use Spelling.

2. Proofread the document on screen to be sure that it makes sense. Check for these types of errors:
   - Words, headings, and/or amounts omitted.
   - Extra words or lines not deleted during the editing stage.
   - Incorrect sequence of numbers in a list.

3. Preview the document on screen using the Print Preview feature. Check the vertical placement, presence of headers or footers, page numbers, and overall appearance.

4. Save the document again and print.

5. Check the printed document by comparing it to the source copy (textbook). Check all figures, names, and addresses against the source copy. Check that the document style has been applied consistently throughout.

6. If errors exist on the printed copy, revise the document, save, and print.

7. Verify the corrections and placement of the second printed copy.

Proofreaders' marks

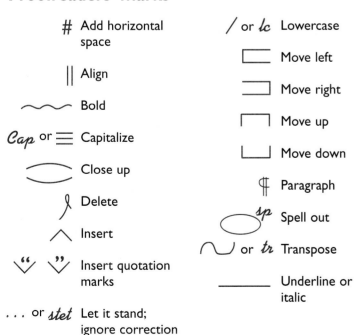

# Add horizontal space	/ or *lc* Lowercase
‖ Align	Move left
⌇ Bold	Move right
Cap or ≡ Capitalize	Move up
⌣ Close up	Move down
⟩ Delete	⧧ Paragraph
⋀ Insert	*sp* Spell out
⌄⌄ Insert quotation marks	⌣ or *tr* Transpose
. . . or *stet* Let it stand; ignore correction	Underline or italic

Word division

With the use of proportional fonts found in current word processing packages, word division is less of an issue. Occasionally, however, you will need to make decisions on dividing words, such as when using the Columns function.

The following list contains generally accepted guidelines for dividing words.

1. Divide words between syllables only; therefore, do not divide one-syllable words.

2. **Short words:** Avoid dividing short words (five letters or fewer).

   area   bonus   since   ideal

3. **Double consonants:** Divide words with double consonants between the double letters unless the root word ends with the double letters. In this case, divide after the second consonant.

   mis- sion   trim- ming   dress- ing   call- ing

4. **One-letter syllables:** Do not divide after a *one-letter* syllable at the *beginning* of a word or before a *one-* or *two-letter* syllable at the *end* of a word; divide after a *one-letter* syllable within a word.

   enough   abroad   starter   friendly
   ani- mal   sepa- rate   regu- late

5. **Two single-letter syllables:** Divide between two single-letter syllables within a word.

   gradu- ation   evalu- ation

6. **Hyphenated words:** Compound words with a hyphen may be divided only after the hyphen.

   top- secret   soft- spoken   self- respect

7. **Figures:** Avoid dividing figures presented as a unit.

   #870331   190,886   1/22/99

8. **Proper nouns:** Avoid dividing proper nouns. If necessary, include as much of the proper noun as possible before dividing it.

   Thomas R./Lewiston   *not* Thomas R. Lewis/ton
   November 15,/ 2000   *not* November/ 15, 2000

Punctuation

Use an apostrophe

1. To make most singular nouns and indefinite pronouns possessive (add **apostrophe** and **s**).

   computer + 's = computer's Jess + 's = Jess's

   anyone's one's somebody's

2. To make a plural noun that does not end in s possessive (add **apostrophe** and **s**).

   women + 's = women's men + 's = men's

   deer + 's = deer's children + 's = children's

3. To make a plural noun that ends in s possessive. Add only the **apostrophe**.

   boys + ' = boys' managers + ' = managers'

4. To make a compound noun possessive or to show joint possession. Add **apostrophe** and **s** to the last part of the hyphenated noun.

   son-in-law's Rob and Gen's game

5. To form the plural of numbers and letters, add **apostrophe** and **s**. To show omission of letters or figures, add an **apostrophe** in place of the missing items.

   7's A's It's add'l

Use a colon

1. To introduce a listing.

   The candidate's strengths were obvious: experience, community involvement, and forthrightness.

2. To introduce an explanatory statement.

   Then I knew we were in trouble: The item had not been scheduled.

Use a comma

1. After an introductory phrase or dependent clause.

   After much deliberation, the jury reached its decision.

   If you have good skills, you will find a job.

2. After words or phrases in a series.

   Mike is taking Greek, Latin III, and Chemistry II.

3. To set off nonessential or interrupting elements.

   Troy, the new man in MIS, will install the hard drive.

   He cannot get to the job, however, until next Friday.

4. To set off the date from the year and the city from the state.

   John, will you please reserve the center in Billings, Montana, for January 10, 2000.

5. To separate two or more parallel adjectives (adjectives could be separated by *and* instead of a comma).

   The loud, whining guitar could be heard above the rest.

6. Before the conjunction in a compound sentence. The comma may be omitted in a very short sentence.

   You must leave immediately, or you will miss your flight.

   We tested the software and they loved it.

7. Set off appositives and words of direct address.

   Karen, our team leader, represented us at the conference.

   Paul, have you ordered the CD-ROM drive?

Use a hyphen

1. To show end-of-line word division.

2. In many compound words—check a dictionary if unsure.

   • Two-word adjectives before a noun:

   two-car family

   • Compound numbers between twenty-one and ninety-nine.

   • Fractions and some proper nouns with prefixes/suffixes.

   two-thirds ex-Governor all-American

Use italic or underline

1. With titles of complete literary works.

   College Keyboarding *Hunt for Red October*

2. To emphasize special words or phrases.

   What does *professional* mean?

Use a semicolon

1. To separate independent clauses in a compound sentence when the conjunction is omitted.

   Please review the information; give me a report by Tuesday.

2. To separate independent clauses when they are joined by conjunctive adverbs (however, nevertheless, consequently, etc.).

   The traffic was heavy; consequently, I was late.

3. To separate a series of elements that contain commas.

   The new officers are: Fran Pena, president; Harry Wong, treasurer; and Muriel Williams, secretary.

Use a dash

1. To show an abrupt change of thought.

   Invoice 76A—which is 10 days overdue—is for $670.

2. After a series to indicate a summarizing statement.

   Noisy fuel pump, worn rods, and failing brakes—for all these reasons I'm trading the car.

Use an exclamation point

After emphatic interjections or exclamatory sentences.

   Terrific! Hold it! You bet! What a great surprise!

Addressing procedures

When generating an envelope from a letter displayed on the screen, delete the punctuation and convert the address to ALL CAPS format before printing the envelope. An envelope can also be generated when a letter is not displayed. Business letters are usually mailed in envelopes that have the return address pre-printed; return addresses are printed only for personal letters or when letterhead envelopes are not available.

When preparing an envelope using an electronic typewriter or some other technology, follow the spacing guidelines below:

Small envelope. On a No. 6 3/4 envelope, place the address near the center—about 2 inches from the top and left edges. Place a return address in the upper left corner (line 2, 3 spaces from left edge).

Large envelope. On a No. 10 envelope, place the address near the center—about line 14 and .5" left of center. A return address, if not preprinted, should be keyed in the upper left corner (see small envelope).

An address must contain at least three lines; addresses of more than six lines should be avoided. The last line of an address must contain three items of information ONLY: (1) the city, (2) the state, and (3) the ZIP Code, preferably a 9-digit code.

Place mailing notations that affect postage (e.g., REGISTERED, CERTIFIED) below the stamp position (line 8); place other special notations (e.g., CONFIDENTIAL, PERSONAL) a DS below the return address.

```
MS SANDRA BAER
1286 QUEISSER RD
NEW ORLEANS LA 70127-0967                    [33 USA]


                  MR WAYNE GREEN |2"
                  6655 PARVA AVE
                  LOS ANGELES CA 90027-2111

                                          [33 USA] [33 USA]

                                          REGISTERED

              MS AMY VREEDE         |2"
              COMMUNICATIONS LIMITED
.5" left of center  57 SANTA YNEZ ST
              SANTA ANA CA 92708-1537
```

Folding and inserting procedures
Large envelopes (No. 10, 9, 7 3/4)

Step 1	Step 2	Step 3

Step 1: With document face up, fold slightly less than 1/3 of sheet up toward top.

Step 2: Fold down top of sheet to within 1/2" of bottom fold.

Step 3: Insert document into envelope with last crease toward bottom of envelope.

Small envelopes (No. 6 3/4, 6 1/4)

Step 1	Step 2	Step 3
	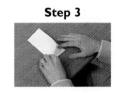	

Step 1: With document face up, fold bottom up to 1/2" from top.

Step 2: Fold right third to left.

Step 3: Fold left third to 1/2" from last crease and insert last creased edge first.

Window envelopes (full sheet)

Step 1	Step 2	Step 3

Step 1: With sheet face down, top toward you, fold upper third down.

Step 2: Fold lower third up so address is showing.

Step 3: Insert document into envelope with last crease toward bottom of envelope.

Two-letter state abbreviations

Alabama, AL	Guam, GU	Massachusetts, MA	New York, NY	Tennessee, TN
Alaska, AK	Hawaii, HI	Michigan, MI	North Carolina, NC	Texas, TX
Arizona, AZ	Idaho, ID	Minnesota, MN	North Dakota, ND	Utah, UT
Arkansas, AR	Illinois, IL	Mississippi, MS	Ohio, OH	Vermont, VT
California, CA	Indiana, IN	Missouri, MO	Oklahoma, OK	Virgin Islands, VI
Colorado, CO	Iowa, IA	Montana, MT	Oregon, OR	Virginia, VA
Connecticut, CT	Kansas, KS	Nebraska, NE	Pennsylvania, PA	Washington, WA
Delaware, DE	Kentucky, KY	Nevada, NV	Puerto Rico, PR	West Virginia, WV
District of Columbia, DC	Louisiana, LA	New Hampshire, NH	Rhode Island, RI	Wisconsin, WI
Florida, FL	Maine, ME	New Jersey, NJ	South Carolina, SC	Wyoming, WY
Georgia, GA	Maryland, MD	New Mexico, NM	South Dakota, SD	

Letter parts

Letterhead. Company name and address. May include other data.

Date. Date letter is mailed. Usually in month, day, year order. Military style is an option (day/month/year: 17/1/99).

Letter address. Address of the person who will receive the letter. Include personal title (*Mr., Ms., Dr.*), name, professional title, company, and address.

Salutation. Greeting. Corresponds to the first line of the letter. Usually includes name and courtesy title; use *Ladies and Gentlemen* if letter is addressed to a company name.

Body. Message. SS; DS between paragraphs.

Complimentary close. Farewell, such as *Sincerely.*

Writer. Name and professional title. Women may include a personal title.

Initials. Identifies person who keyed the document (for example, *tr*). May include identification of writer (*ARB:trn*).

Enclosure. Copy is enclosed with the document. May specify contents.

Copy notation. Indicates that a copy of the letter is being sent to person named.

Envelope

IMAGE MAKERS
5131 Moss Springs Rd.
Columbia, SC 29209-4768

MS MARY BERNARD PRESIDENT
BERNARD IMAGE CONSULTANTS
4927 STUART AVE
BATON ROUGE LA 70808-3519

Block letter (open punctuation)

Professional Office Consultants, Inc.
584 Castro St.
San Francisco, CA 94114-2201
415-555-8725
415-555-8775 (FAX)

Dateline — January 17, 200-
DS
Letter address — Ms. Amanda Castillo, Office Manager
TeleNet Corporation
24 Technology Dr.
Irvine, CA 92865-9845
DS
Salutation — Dear Ms. Castillo
DS
Body — Thank you for selecting Professional Office Consultants, Inc. to assist with the setup of your new corporate office. You asked us for a recommendation for formatting business letters. We highly recommend the block letter style because it is easy to read.

This letter is keyed in block format. As you can see, all lines begin at the left margin. Most letters can be keyed using default side margins and then centered vertically on the page for attractive placement. The block letter format is easy to key because tabs are not required.

We think that you will be happy using the block letter format. Over 80 percent of businesses today are using this same style.
DS
Complimentary close — Sincerely
DS
Writer's — Anderson Cline
Title — OA & CIS Consultant
DS
Reference initials — tr

Modified block letter (mixed punctuation)

IMAGE MAKERS
5131 Moss Springs Road
Columbia, SC 29209-4768
(803) 555-0127

October 27, 200-

Ms. Mary Bernard, President
Bernard Image Consultants
4927 Stuart Ave.
Baton Rouge, LA 70808-3519

Dear Ms. Bernard:

The format of this letter is called modified block. Modified block format differs from block format in that the date, complimentary close, and the signature lines are positioned at the center point.

Paragraphs may be blocked, as this letter illustrates, or they may be indented from the left margin. We suggest you block paragraphs when you use modified block style so that an additional tab setting is not needed. However, some people who use modified block format prefer indented paragraphs.

Although modified block format is very popular, we recommend that you use it only for those customers who request this letter style. Otherwise, we urge you to use block format, which is more efficient, as your standard style.

Both formats are illustrated in the enclosed *Image Makers Format Guide*. Please note that the block format is labeled "computer compatible."

Sincerely,

Patrick R. Ray
Communication Consultant

tr

Enclosure

Copy notation — c Scot Carl, Account Manager

Letter placement table

Length	Dateline position	Margins
Short: 1-2 ¶s	Center page or 3"	Default
Average: 3-4 ¶s	Center page or 2.7"*	Default
Long: 4+ ¶s	2.3" (default + 7 hard returns)	Default

Default margins or a minimum of 1".

*Raise date to 2" if several extra features are included.

Personal business letter

Janna M. Howard
587 Birch Cir.
Clinton, MS 39056-0587
(601) 555-4977

Current date ——————

> The return address may be keyed immediately above the date, or you may create a personal letterhead as shown here.

Mrs. Linda Chandler
Financial News
32 North Critz St.
Hot Springs, AR 71913-0032

Dear Mrs. Chandler

My college degree in office systems technology and my graphics design job experience in the United States and Taiwan qualify me to function well as a junior graphic designer for your newspaper.

As a result of my comprehensive four-year program, I am skilled in the most up-to-date office suite packages as well as the latest version of desktop publishing and graphics programs. In addition, I am very skilled at locating needed resources on the information highway. In fact, this skill played a very important role in the design award that I received last month.

My technical and communication skills were applied as I worked as the assistant editor and producer of the *Cother Alumni News*. I understand well the importance of meeting deadlines and also in producing a quality product that will increase newspaper sales.

After you have reviewed the enclosed resume, I would look forward to discussing my qualifications and career opportunities with you at *Financial News*.

Sincerely

Janna M. Howard

Enclosure

Personal business letter

Resume

JANNA M. HOWARD

Temporary Address (May 30, 2000)
587 Birch Cir.
Clinton, MS 39056-0587
(601) 555-4977

Permanent Address
328 Fondren St.
Orlando, FL 32801-0328
(407) 555-3834

CAREER OBJECTIVE — To obtain a graphic design position with an opportunity to advance to a management position.

EDUCATION — *B.S. Office Systems Technology*, Cother University, Mobile, Alabama. May 1998. Grade-point average: 3.8/4.0. Serve as president of Graphic Designers' Society.

SPECIAL SKILLS
- Environments: *Microsoft Windows*® and *Macintosh*®
- Application software: *Microsoft Office Professional*®/ *Windows 95*®, *PageMaker*®, *CorelDraw*®, *Harvard Graphics*®
- Internet: *Netscape*®, *Mosaic*®
- Keyboarding skill: 70 words per minute
- Foreign language: Chinese
- Travel: Taiwan (two summers working as graphic design intern)

EXPERIENCE — *Cother University Alumni Office*, Mobile, Alabama. Assistant editor and producer of the *Cother Alumni News*, 1997 to present.
- Work 25 hours per week.
- Design layout and production of six editions.
- Meet every publishing deadline.
- Received the "Cother Design Award."

Cother Library, Mobile, Alabama. Student Assistant in Audiovisual Library, 1996-1997.
- Worked 20 hours per week.
- Created *Audiovisual Catalog* on computerized database.
- Processed orders via computer.
- Prepared monthly and yearly reports using database.
- Edited and proofed various publications.

REFERENCES — Request portfolio from Cother University Placement Office.

Resume

Standard memo

1.5"

Tab (1" from left margin)

TO: Executive Committee
DS
FROM: Colleen Marshall

DATE: November 8, 200-

SUBJECT: Site Selection
DS
Please be prepared to make a final decision on the site for next year's Leadership Training Conference. Our staff reviewed the students' suggestions and have added a few of their own. The following information may be helpful as you make your decision:
DS
1. New York and San Francisco have been eliminated from consideration because of cost factors.
DS
2. New Orleans is still open for consideration even though we met there three years ago. New Orleans has tremendous appeal to students.

3. Charleston, San Antonio, and Tampa were suggested by students as very desirable locations for the conference.

Site selection will be the first item of business at our meeting next Wednesday. I'm attaching various hotel brochures for each site.
DS
xx
DS
Attachments

Standard memo

Standard memo with distribution list

1.5"

Tab (1" from left margin)

TO: Team Leaders
DS
FROM: Form Paragraph Task Force

DATE: Current

SUBJECT: Initial Meetings with Task Force
DS
The task force assigned the responsibility for developing form paragraphs to use in key departments of our company plans to work in your department beginning two weeks from today. Please assign two representatives from your department to coordinate the work with us.
DS
The procedure that the Executive Committee asked us to follow is to collect samples of typical correspondence, meet with departmental representatives to collect additional information, and then to prepare a draft of the form paragraphs for review. After we receive your feedback on the draft copy, we will schedule a meeting to finalize the paragraphs.

Matthew Redfern has been assigned as the task force coordinator for your department. Please direct all communications about the project to him.
DS
xx
DS
Distribution List:
Nestor Garcia, Claims
Roberta Layman, Underwriting
Rosa Romero, Agency Services
Diana Wang, Business Services

Standard memo with distribution list

Standard unbound report and outline format

Margins: *Top* 1.5" for first page and reference page; 1" for succeeding pages; *Side* 1" or default; *bottom* 1".

Spacing: *Educational reports:* DS, paragraphs indented .5". *Business reports:* SS, paragraphs blocked with a DS between.

Page numbers: Second and subsequent pages are numbered at top right of the page. DS follows the page number.

Main headings: Centered; ALL CAPS; 14 pts.

Side headings: Bold; main words capitalized; DS above and below.

Paragraph headings: Bold; capitalize first word, followed by a period.

NOTE: Larger fonts may also be used for headings.

Report documentation

Internal citations: Provides source of information within report. Includes the author's surname, publication date, and page number (Bruce, 2000, 129).

Endnotes: Superior figure keyed at point of reference within report. All sources placed on a separate page at the end of the report in numerical order. Endnotes precede the bibliography or references.

Bibliography or references: Lists all references, whether quoted or not, in alphabetical order by authors' names. References may be formatted on the last page of the report if they all fit on the page; if not, list on a separate, numbered page.

First page of unbound report

1.5"

BASIC STEPS IN REPORT WRITING
DS

The effective writer makes certain that reports that leave her or his desk are technically correct in style, usable in content, and attractive in format.
DS

Side heading → **The First Step**
DS

Information is gathered about the subject; the effective writer takes time to outline the data to be used in the report. This approach allows the writer to establish the organization of the report. When a topic outline is used, order of presentation, important points, and even various headings can be determined and followed easily when writing begins.

Default side margins → **The Correct Style**

The purpose of the report often determines the style. Most academic reports (term papers, for example) are double-spaced with indented paragraphs. Most business reports, however, are single-spaced; and paragraphs are blocked. When a style is not stipulated, general usage may be followed.

The Finished Product

Most capable writers will refrain from making a report deliberately impressive, especially if doing so makes it less expressive. The writer does, however, follow the outline carefully as a first draft is written. Obvious errors are ignored momentarily. Refinement comes later, after all the preliminary work is done. The finished document will then be read and reread to ensure it is clear, concise, correct, and complete.

Second page of unbound report

2
DS

and thus oxygen becomes a crucial part of any aquatic ecosystem. Dissolved oxygen is derived from the atmosphere as well as from the photosynthetic processes of aquatic plants. Oxygen, in turn, is consumed through the life activities of most aquatic animals and plants (Bruce, 2000, 129). When dissolved oxygen reaches very low levels in the aquatic environment, unfavorable conditions for fish and other aquatic life can develop.

Conclusion

The absence of dissolved oxygen may give rise to unpleasant odors produced through anaerobic (no oxygen) decomposition. On the other hand, an adequate supply of oxygen helps maintain a healthy environment for fish and other aquatic life and this supply may help prevent the development of unacceptable conditions that are caused by the decomposition of municipal and industrial waste (Ryn, 1999, 29).
DS

REFERENCES
DS

Book → Beard, Fred F. *The Fulford County Dilemma.* Niagara Falls: Dawn General Press, 1998.

Bruce, Lois L. "Hazardous Waste Management: A History." *State of Idaho Bulletin No. 7312.* Boise: State of Idaho Press, 2000.

Periodical → Ryn, Jewel Scott. "But Please Don't Drink the Water." *Journal of Environmental Science,* Winter 1999, pp. 25-38.

Outline

EFFECTIVE PRESENTATIONS
DS

I. PLANNING AND PREPARING PRESENTATIONS
DS
   A. Opening
      1. Gain attention
      2. Set the tone
   B. Body of the Presentation
      1. Focus on objective
      2. Organize information
      3. Prepare support materials
   C. Closing
DS
II. DELIVERING PRESENTATIONS
DS
   A. Delivery Techniques
      1. Engage audience
      2. Project voice effectively
      3. Control environment
   B. Visuals and Supporting Materials
      1. Ensure readability
      2. Use effectively
III. FOLLOW-UP ACTIVITIES
   A. Discussion and Questions
   B. Postpresentation Activities

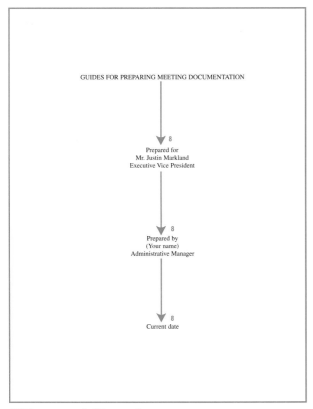

GUIDES FOR PREPARING MEETING DOCUMENTATION

↓ 8

Prepared for
Mr. Justin Markland
Executive Vice President

↓ 8

Prepared by
(Your name)
Administrative Manager

↓ 8

Current date

Title page—leftbound

TABLE OF CONTENTS
DS

iii

Table of contents—leftbound

GUIDES FOR PREPARING MEETING DOCUMENTATION
DS

The procedures used to prepare support documents for meetings in the Moss Springs Company were reviewed during the productivity analysis that was just completed.[1] The type of support documents used and the way in which they were prepared varied widely throughout the company. The primary documents used were meeting notices, agendas, handouts, visual aids, and minutes. Format was not consistent for any of the documents within or among departments. The following guides were compiled on the basis of the productivity review.
DS

1.5" left Margin

Annual Meeting
DS
The following quote from the *Moss Springs Company Policy Manual* contains the policy for documentation of the Annual Meeting:[2]

> The Annual Meeting of the Moss Springs Company shall be held within three months of the end of the fiscal year. The corporate secretary shall mail to all who are eligible to attend the meeting a notice and agenda 30 days prior to the meeting. The corporate secretary shall prepare a verbatim record of the meeting and provide each member of the board of directors with a copy of the minutes within two weeks of the meeting. The minutes shall be a part of the permanent records of the Moss Springs Company.

Other Meetings

Meetings other than the Annual Meeting will be held at the discretion of the board of directors and the appropriate company managers. Regular meetings of the board of directors are scheduled on the first Wednesday of each month. Special meetings may be called as needed. Documentation for regular and "called" meetings of the board are described in the following paragraphs.

Support Documents

The Senior Management Committee requires that an agenda be distributed prior to all formal meetings of committees and of staff at departmental level or higher. Minutes must be prepared and distributed to all participants after the meeting. Support documents for informal meetings and work units are left to the discretion of the individuals conducting the meetings.

First page of leftbound report (bold headings)

4

REFERENCES
DS

Anderson, Mary. *Effective Meetings.* Boston: Bay Publishing Co., 1998.

Moss Springs Company Policy Manual. Chicago: 1999.

Wasu, Anil. *Enhancing Productivity: The Moss Springs Company.* Chicago: Productivity Consultants, Inc., 1999.

References

Repetitive stress injury (RSI)

Repetitive stress injury (RSI) is a result of repeated movement of a particular part of the body. A familiar example is "tennis elbow." Of more concern to keyboard users is the form of RSI called **carpal tunnel syndrome (CTS)**.

CTS is an inflammatory disease that develops gradually and affects the wrist, hands, and forearms. Blood vessels, tendons, and nerves pass into the hand through the carpal tunnel (see illustration below). If any of these structures enlarge or if the walls of the tunnel narrow, the median nerve is pinched, and CTS symptoms may result.

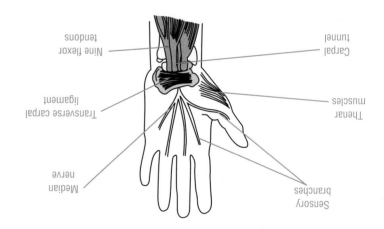

Palm view of left hand

Labels: Carpal tunnel, Thenar muscles, Sensory branches, Median nerve, Transverse carpal ligament, Nine flexor tendons

Symptoms of RSI/CTS

CTS symptoms include numbness in the hand; tingling or burning in the hand, wrist, or elbow; severe pain in the forearm, elbow, or shoulder; and difficulty in gripping objects. Symptoms usually appear during sleeping hours, probably because many people sleep with their wrists flexed.

If not properly treated, the pressure on the median nerve, which controls the thumb, forefinger, middle finger, and half the ring finger (see top right), causes severe pain. The pain can radiate into the forearm, elbow, or shoulder and can require surgery or result in permanent damage or paralysis.

Areas affected by carpal tunnel syndrome

Causes of RSI/CTS

RSI/CTS often develops in workers whose physical routine is unvaried. Common occupational factors include: (1) using awkward posture, (2) using poor techniques, (3) performing tasks with wrists bent (see below), (4) using improper equipment, (5) working at a rapid pace, (6) not taking rest breaks, and (7) not doing exercises that promote graceful motion and good techniques.

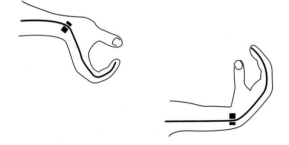

Improper wrist positions for keystroking

Other factors associated with CTS include a person's genetic makeup; the aging process; hormonal influences; obesity; chronic diseases such as rheumatoid arthritis and gout; misaligned fractures; and hobbies such as gardening, knitting, and woodworking that require the same motion over and over. CTS affects over three times more women than men, with 60 percent of the affected persons between the ages of 30 and 60.

Reducing the risk of RSI/CTS

Carpal tunnel syndrome is frequently a health concern for workers who use a computer keyboard or mouse. The risk of developing CTS is less for computer keyboard operators who use proper furniture or equipment, keyboarding techniques, posture, and/or muscle-stretching exercises than for those who do not.

Keyboard users can reduce the risk of developing RSI/CTS by taking these precautions:

1. Arrange the workstation correctly:
   a. Position the keyboard directly in front of the chair.
   b. Keep the front edge of the keyboard even with the edge of the desk or table so that the wrist movement will not be restricted while you are keying.
   c. Position the keyboard at elbow height.
   d. Position the monitor about 18 to 24 inches from your eyes with the top edge of the display screen at eye level.
   e. Position the mouse next to and at the same height as the computer keyboard and as close to the body as possible.

2. Use a proper chair and sit correctly:
   a. Use a straight-backed chair, or adjust your chair so that it will not yield when you lean back.
   b. Use a seat that allows you to keep your feet flat on the floor while you are keying. Use a footrest if your feet cannot rest flat on the floor.
   c. Sit erect and as far back in the seat as possible.

3. Use correct arm and wrist positions and movement:
   a. Keep your forearms parallel to the floor and level with the keyboard so that your wrists will be in a flat, neutral position rather than flexed upward or downward.
   b. Keep arms near the side of your body in a relaxed position.

4. Use proper keyboarding techniques:
   a. Keep your fingers curved and upright over the home keys.
   b. Keep wrists and forearms from touching or resting on any surface while keying.
   c. Strike each key lightly using the fingertip. Do not use too much pressure or hold the keys down.

5. When using a keyboard or mouse, take short breaks. A rest of one to two minutes every hour is appropriate. Natural breaks in keyboarding action of several seconds' duration also help.

6. Exercise the neck, shoulder, arm, wrist, and fingers before beginning to key each day and often during the workday (see Precaution 5). Suggested exercises for keyboard users are described below. You can do all the exercises while sitting at your workstation.

Exercises for computer keyboard users

1. **Strengthen finger muscles.** (See Drill 1 on p. RG12.) Open your hands, extend your fingers wide, and hold with muscles tense for two or three seconds; close the fingers into a tight fist with thumb on top, holding for two or three seconds; relax the fingers as you straighten them. Repeat 10 times. Additional finger drills are shown on p. RG12.

2. **Strengthen the muscles in the carpal tunnel area.** While sitting with your arms comfortably at your side and hands in a fist, rotate your hands inward from the wrist. Repeat this motion 10 to 15 times; then rotate outward from the wrist 10 to 15 times. Extend your fingers and repeat the movements for the same number of times.

3. **Loosen forearms.** With both wrists held in a neutral position (not bent) and the upper arm hanging vertically from the shoulder, rotate both forearms in 15 clockwise circles about the elbow. Repeat, making counterclockwise circles.

4. **Stretch the arms.** Interlace the fingers of both hands; with the palms facing forward, stretch your arms in front of you and hold for ten seconds. Repeat at least once. Next, with your fingers still interlaced, stretch your arms over your head and hold for ten seconds. Repeat at least once.

5. **Loosen elbows.** Place your hands on your shoulders with elbows facing forward; slowly move your arms in increasingly larger circles in front of you 10 to 15 times.

6. **Relieve shoulder tension.** Interlace the fingers of both hands behind your head and slowly move the elbows back, pressing the shoulder blades together; hold for ten seconds. Repeat at least once.

Finger gymnastics

Brief daily practice of finger gymnastics will strengthen your finger muscles and increase the ease with which you key. Begin each keying period with this conditioning exercise. Choose two or more drills for this practice.

DRILL 1. Hands open, fingers wide, muscles tense. Close the fingers into a tight "fist," with thumb on top. Relax the fingers as you straighten them; repeat 10 times.

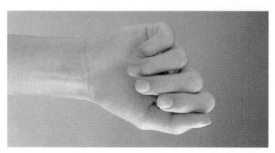

DRILL 2. Clench the fingers as shown. Hold the fingers in this position for a brief time; then extend the fingers, relaxing the muscles of fingers and hand. Repeat the movements slowly several times. Exercise both hands at the same time.

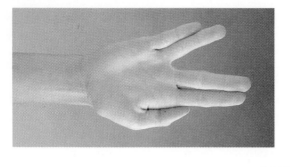

DRILL 3. Place the fingers and the thumb of one hand between two fingers of the other hand, and spread the fingers as much as possible. Spread all fingers of both hands.

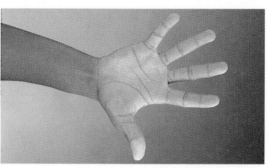

DRILL 4. Interlace the fingers of the two hands and wring the hands, rubbing the heel of the palms vigorously.

DRILL 5. Spread the fingers as much as possible, holding the position for a moment or two; then relax the fingers and lightly fold them into the palm of the hand. Repeat the movements slowly several times. Exercise both hands at the same time.

DRILL 6. Rub the hands vigorously. Let the thumb rub the palm of the hand. Rub the fingers, the back of the hand, and the wrist.

DRILL 7. Hold both hands in front of you, fingers together. Hold the last three fingers still and move the first finger as far to the side as possible. Return the first finger; then move the first and second fingers together; finally move the little finger as far to the side as possible.

index

Function	Menu or Toolbar	Lesson Introduced
Alignment	Toolbar; Format, Font	34
AutoCorrect	Tools, AutoCorrect	35
Bold	Toolbar; Format, Font	34
Borders	Toolbar; Format, Border/Shading	50
Center Page	File, Page Setup	35
Close	File, Close	31
Copy	Toolbar; Edit, Copy	46
Cut	Toolbar; Edit, Cut	46
Delete	Backspace or Delete Key	33
Exit	File, Exit	31
Font Size	Toolbar; Format, Font	34
Hyperlinks	Toolbar; Insert Hyperlink	51
Indent	Toolbar; Format, Paragraph	45
Insert Mode	Insert Key	33
Italic	Toolbar; Format, Font	34
Line and Page Breaks	Format, Paragraph	49
Line Spacing	Format, Paragraph	36
Manual Page Break	CTRL + ENTER	48
Margins	File, Page Setup	45
Merge/Split Cells	Table; Merge Cells; Split Cells	57
Open	Toolbar; File, Open	32
Page Numbers	Insert, Page Numbering	49
Paste	Toolbar; Edit, Paste	46
Print	Toolbar; File, Print	31
Print Preview	Toolbar; File, Print Preview	39
Ruler	View, Ruler	41
Save/Save As	Toolbar; File, Save	31
Selecting Text	Mouse	34
Show/Hide	Toolbar	33
Spelling	Toolbar; Tools, Spell Check	35
Tables	Table, Insert Table	53-57
Tabs	Horizontal Ruler; Format, Tabs	41
Underline	Toolbar	34
Undo/Redo	Toolbar	46
Window	Window	46